Justinian Caire
AND
Santa Cruz Island

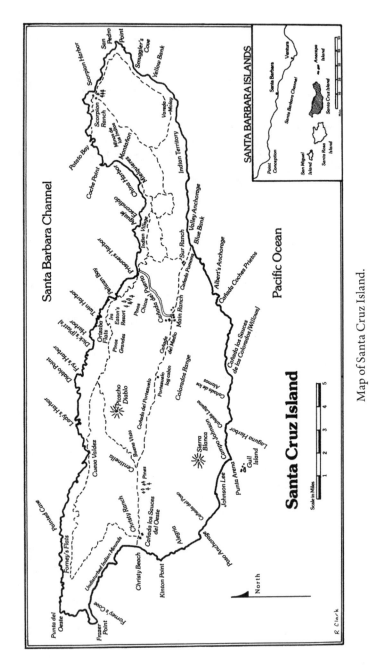

Map of Santa Cruz Island.
Reproduced by permission from Helen Caire,
Santa Cruz Island (Spokane, Wash.: Arthur H. Clark, 1933), *frontispiece.*

Justinian Caire
AND
Santa Cruz Island
The Rise and Fall
of a
California Dynasty

By
FREDERIC CAIRE CHILES
FOREWORD BY MARLA DAILY

THE ARTHUR H. CLARK COMPANY
An imprint of the University of Oklahoma Press
Norman, Oklahoma
2011

Library of Congress Cataloging-in-Publication Data

Chiles, Frederic Caire, 1947–

Justinian Caire and Santa Cruz Island : the rise and fall of a California dynasty / by Frederic Caire Chiles ; foreword by Marla Daily.

p. cm.

Includes bibliographical references and index.

ISBN 978-0-87062-400-1 (hardcover : alk. paper) 1. Caire, Justinian, 1827–1897. 2. Caire, Justinian, 1827–1897—Family. 3. Santa Cruz Island (Calif.)—History. 4. Santa Cruz Island (Calif.)—Biography. 5. Ranching—California—Santa Cruz Island—History. I. Title.

F868.S23C49 2011

979.4'91—dc22

2011009548

1 2 3 4 5 6 7 8 9 10

To my mother and her sisters,
who lived this story and gave me a love of history
and a respect for the truth

Some people put these things out of their minds and sort of forget them. . . . I don't want to forget. . . . I don't want to let them take the best of me but I want them to be there because this is what happened. This is the truth, you know—history.

César Chávez

Contents

Illustrations

Unless otherwise indicated in the caption,
all photographs are courtesy of the Caire Family Archive.

Foreword

Santa Cruz Island is the largest in a chain of eight Channel Islands located off the coast of Southern California. At ninety-six square miles, it is larger than the District of Columbia, three times larger than Hong Kong, and four times the size of Manhattan. For most of the nineteenth and twentieth centuries, it held the distinction of being the largest privately owned island off the continental United States. Two families guided the island's fate through most of its private years: the Caires for fifty-seven years (1880–1937), followed by the Stantons for another fifty (1937–1987). By the turn of the twenty-first century, however, Santa Cruz Island had passed from private ownership into the hands of the National Park Service and a private conservation organization, The Nature Conservancy. How it came to pass that Santa Cruz Island was spared from development is intertwined with this intriguing account of Justinian Caire and his fractious descendants.

Justinian Caire died at his home in Oakland, California, on December 10, 1897. Caire's widow, Albina, and two of her daughters and her two sons were pitted against her other two daughters and their relations through marriage—the Rossis and Gherinis. The escalating legal battles over power, money, and control spanned two decades (1912–1932) and ultimately ended in the partitioning of Santa Cruz Island into seven parcels, one each for Albina and her six children.

Frederic Caire Chiles's *Justinian Caire and Santa Cruz Island: The Rise and Fall of a California Dynasty* is a most compelling narrative. The author, great-grandson of Justinian Caire, exposes for the first time documents, legal correspondence, and internal family memos that have been sequestered for the better part of a century by the last surviving generation of Caires who lived through the emotionally painful family litigation. This exposure follows two other accounts of Santa Cruz Island written by family members: *Santa Cruz Island: A History and Recollection of an Old California Rancho* by Helen Caire (1993), the author's maternal aunt; and *Santa Cruz Island: A History of Conflict and Diversity* by John Gherini (1997), Justinian Caire's great-great-grandson, who is descended through the plaintiffs of the original litigation. The significant detailed materials that are revealed here for the first time broaden our understanding of the complexity of the untold story of Santa Cruz Island.

MARLA DAILY
Santa Cruz Island Foundation
2010

Preface

Mysterious and exotic, known for most of the twentieth century only to a few locals, sailors, fishermen, scientists, and wine connoisseurs, Santa Cruz Island is the largest island off the California coast. As children in the 1950s and 1960s, my sisters, brothers, and I understood that the history of our mother's family was something out of the ordinary—they had once owned "the island." It was always spoken of within those invisible quotation marks, a source of family pride, this jewel in the legacy of our great-grandfather, Justinian Caire. Yet there was a dark side to this story, intertwined with public disgrace and loss. At family gatherings, a perennial topic of conversation would be reminiscences of this island on which our mother, her four unmarried sisters, and three double cousins had spent some of the happiest days of their youth. Through these stories we were very well acquainted with the achievements of previous generations on the island and with many anecdotes of the colorful characters who had lived and worked there. We knew that Justinian Caire came to San Francisco from France during the Gold Rush, and that he built a successful business in what was then a rough-and-tumble city. We knew that he made some shrewd investments, including one in the island ranch. We were familiar with many of the smallest details about the vanished world of Santa Cruz Island that he created, the management of which he passed on to his two sons, one of whom was our grandfather and my namesake.

It was only when we came to question why this special place no longer belonged to the family that we encountered a smokescreen of hints and innuendo, but we were promised that when we were older, we would have it all explained, that it was too complicated, and that one day we would understand. The years went by and we grew up, but still a coherent explanation was not forthcoming. By this time we knew that there had been "the lawsuit," that there had been some shameful behavior on the part of relatives of the family we knew by name only, and that the details were better left until we were a bit older and more mature. Needless to say, that time never arrived, and when the most knowledgeable member of the older generation died suddenly, with her went the chance of learning firsthand the full story of the family tragedy.

Some years later, when my brothers and sisters and I had the opportunity to spend some time on the island, we came to realize that we were among the last members of the family to have really known the generation who had delighted in this island world and had suffered terribly from its loss. I began to feel that it was imperative for us to attempt to conjure up the past and create a coherent and accurate narrative for our descendants. Thus I began to consult with my siblings and relatives to find out what sort of documentation existed that would enable me to put together the story of a California dynasty—the definitive record, if such a thing was possible— for a story that had become as much encrusted in family myth and fable as by the imaginings of writers and journalists over the decades.

Happily, I discovered in various family repositories a trove of records from both the Santa Cruz Island Company and the Justinian Caire Company along with Caire correspondence, diaries, memoirs, memoranda, and a comprehensive picture archive dating back to the 1880s—most of which had never seen the light of day. It was because so much of the business was conducted via correspondence between the island and the San Francisco head office that I was able to piece together the details of the development and management of this complex operation. The correspondence, which was carefully archived by the family, helped create a daily record of the struggle to develop the enterprise and maintain its profitability, and it led to a more comprehensive understanding of what forces brought about the calamitous outcome. The Caires, with eldest son Arthur in charge, had a very hands-on management style; hence, the correspondence between the San Francisco office and the island was voluminous, providing a highly detailed account of the trials and tribulations of ranching life more than a century ago. A small amount of digging in various family archives yielded

many boxes of annual reports to shareholders, instructions to superintendents, daily logs kept at the Santa Cruz Main Ranch, annual accounts,
inventories, and copies of correspondence in French, Italian, and English.

There were also the diaries, journals, and letters carefully preserved
by the principals on the Caire side of this bitterly divided family. The rift
occurred when Justinian Caire's two married daughters challenged their
mother, brothers, and sisters in court fifteen years after the death of their
father. For a trained historian, this was an invaluable resource that would
shed some light on the murkier corners of the family history.

There were not only the details of how and why our great-grandfather
built up his legacy, but also the particulars of the family's efforts to come
to terms with the actions at law that ultimately succeeded in forcing them
to liquidate the business that he had devoted his life to building. The emergent picture elucidated the emotional and financial toll exacted by twenty
years of litigation. My grandfather and his older brother, enjoined by their
father's will to carry on his businesses and act as trustees for their sisters,
saw their fortune destroyed and their good names and that of their mother
besmirched. My mother's generation paid the price in youthful hopes
deferred and aspirations that remained tantalizingly out of reach—always
to be realized "after the lawsuit."

The legal team responsible for this family tragedy was led by an in-law
who made no secret of his desire to pry open the Justinian Caire legacy for
the monetary benefit of his family and his allies, and ultimately to "break
the Caires." Although I have relied throughout on eyewitness testimony
regarding the most contentious aspects of the intrafamily litigation, I recognize that some of the facts are open to interpretation, and the strong
feelings created by more than two decades of emotional and legal wran-
gling might have influenced some remembrances as they were set down at
the time and in later years.

The Caire control of the entire island lasted from 1880 to 1925, with a
90 percent ownership from 1925 to 1937. The first thirty-two years were
devoted to the creation and maintenance of Justinian Caire's vision of an
integrated, self-sustaining agricultural venture based on sheep, cattle, and
wine. The years 1912 to 1932 were dominated by the lawsuit, and the final
five years were spent in the search for a buyer. This was the age of the written word, and almost every activity was documented in some way. Some

records were lost in the San Francisco earthquake and fire of 1906, and some correspondence was destroyed out of rage and frustration, but the great majority of the documentation survived. These unpublished sources form the backbone of what follows. A combination of pride, loyalty, and shame made our mother's generation very reluctant to speak in any detail of the genesis and development of the intrafamily litigation that resulted in the loss of the island. At the same time, they made sure that key documents highlighting how this family tragedy unfolded were carefully preserved. And now, with all the participants and most of the eyewitnesses long gone, I am sure that they would agree with me, my siblings, and our cousins that it is time for our generation to pass on the most comprehensive account of this fascinating story of Justinian Caire and his legacy—the rise and fall of a California dynasty.

Acknowledgments

The writing of history is naturally a collaborative effort, and this work is no exception. Because the core of the research has been in family archives and involved many private family matters, I have relied to a great extent on the support of my family. The previous generation of Caires, particularly my mother and her sisters, awakened my fascination with Santa Cruz Island, and they were the careful custodians of the papers and pictures that formed the mainstay of my source materials. My sister, Mary B, and my brothers, John and Jim, have generously given their time, effort, and support in helping find the key materials and offering their valuable judgments about the interpretations I have put on them. My cousins Arthur Caire and Justinian Caire III helped with reading the manuscript and providing access to the glass plate negatives produced by their grandfather, Arthur Caire. Julian Barnes, my cousin Arthur, and my sister Mary B. Brock all helped translate various key documents from their original French. Clarence McProud and John Mahoney gave advice and interpretation to the legal questions that were central to the narrative. Chris Fitzgerald kindly advised on wine-related questions. Paul Alleway cheerfully contributed his graphics expertise. The staff of the library of the California Historical Society was obliging in supplying materials and answering questions. Professor Chuck Churchill gave a very supportive reading of an early version of the manuscript. Marla Daily of the Santa Cruz Island Foundation (with the kind cooperation of The Nature Conservancy) was instrumental in arranging for my generation and our children to experience the island at first hand and provided invaluable advice on the manuscript. Ann Huston of the National Park Service (NPS) was generous with her time in helping with translation and advice. Dewey Livingston's "Historic Resource Study of the Channel Islands," written for the NPS, was an excellent resource. Bob Clark of Arthur H. Clark Co. provided much help and encouragement. For all their assistance and advice, I am most grateful to all these individuals and groups in making this book as good as it can be. Any factual errors and misinterpretations are my own. Finally, in terms of encouragement on a daily basis, it is to my wife, Jacky Davis, that I owe the greatest debt for her good advice, careful reading, and encouragement. She knows better than anyone how important that has been to me.

Justinian Caire
AND
Santa Cruz Island

CHAPTER 1

Beginnings

In the narrow gorge at the head of the valley of the Durance River, near the present-day border between France and Italy, is the small French city of Briançon. By the early 1800s it had been home to the family of Jean Baptiste Caire for centuries.[1] Located at one end of the Mont Genevre pass, Briançon had enjoyed commercial success and relative prosperity for centuries based on its advantageous location on the trade routes between the city-states of northeastern Italy and the interiors of France, Switzerland, Austria, and southern Germany. But by the years in which this particular story begins, Briançon's best days of economic opportunity were well behind it. Decades of war, revolution, and international treaties had seen power in the region slip away from the land trade routes between the powerful city-state of Genoa and the trans-Alpine interior. These links were displaced by the political and economic power of Turin and the seaports of the Kingdom of Sardinia, which under the terms of the 1815 Congress of Vienna now controlled that part of the Mediterranean basin.

It was into this world of quiet economic decline on December 3, 1827, that Justinian Caire was born and officially presented to his uncle, the mayor and municipal magistrate of the Briançon Commune.[2] Born to middle-aged Marie Anne Adelaide Arduin Caire (forty-three) and Jean Baptiste Caire (forty-seven), Justinian was the last of their nine children

---

[1] Letters of Citizenship of J. Pierre Caire, 29 September 1756, photocopied and translated by Jeanne Caire, "Memoir," 1972, Caire Family Papers and Diaries, in the author's possession (hereafter cited as Jeanne Caire, "Memoir").

[2] Records of Births, Marriages, and Deaths of the Commune of Briancon, 3 December 1827, Jeanne Caire, "Memoir."

who grew to adulthood. It was clear to Justinian's father that for ambitious Briançonais, opportunity lay elsewhere. Among Justinian's siblings were emigrants to Egypt and California, whereas the oldest son, Adrien, had enjoyed a successful commercial career in Peru before establishing himself in Paris as an exporter of art objects and other merchandise.

Justinian Caire was raised and educated in Briançon. His school exercise books reveal an industrious student well-versed in mathematics, science, literature, and languages. In 1846, at the age of eighteen, he left school and followed his father's wishes by taking a job working for cousins in Genoa who owned a hardware business. In Genoa Justinian worked to learn the world of business and to master Italian. He also enrolled in a school of commerce, where he made friends with a fellow student named Giosue Molfino and, through him, met his sister, Maria Cristina.

After about five years of apprenticeship and study, having learned something of the theory and practice of business life, he joined in partnership with another entrepreneurial Frenchman from the Italian side of the Mont Genevre pass. In 1851 Justinian Caire and Claude Long set sail together from Le Havre bound for San Francisco—a five-month voyage. The ship they sailed on, the *Aurelie,* carried their cargo of French hardware and luxury goods with which they intended to set up shop. The two men were like thousands of other hopeful Frenchmen and other Europeans who were headed for the boomtown of San Francisco, whose mushrooming growth in the wake of the Gold Rush was the stuff of ambitious dreams in all parts of the world. Where they found the capital to buy the stock, pay for transport around Cape Horn, and set up in San Francisco is unrecorded, but a likely source was Justinian's older brother Adrien Caire, the wealthy and successful Parisian exporter. The company of Caire & Long first appeared in the 1852 San Francisco city directory at 178 Washington Street, opposite the site now occupied by the landmark Transamerica pyramid.

Three months after the business was established, Caire & Long experienced one of the raging fires that periodically swept this city of wood, canvas, oil lanterns, and open fires. The stock was destroyed, but another consignment was already on its way; like the rest of the city they were soon back in business. To avoid a repeat of this type of calamity, the canny Caire took the precaution of building a fireproof cellar lined with sheet iron where he could quickly deposit his stock in case a fire threatened. The company was not troubled by fire for another fifty-four years. The partners went their separate ways in 1856, and the name of the business was changed to Caire Brothers, reflecting Adrien's role in sourcing and supplying merchandise from France.

His commercial roots were now well-established in California, but Justinian Caire had some unfinished personal business in Genoa. In late 1854 he returned to Genoa via the Isthmus of Panama to marry Maria Candida Cristina Sarah Molfino, or Albina as she was known throughout her long life. When Justinian had been living and working in Genoa, he had courted Albina with persistence, even taking dancing lessons to make himself more socially acceptable. And although the lessons were said not to have been a great success, the Molfino girl found him attractive, as did her mother, Brigida Molfino, the stern *materfamilias* (head of the family). After her husband had died in a cholera epidemic in 1835, Brigida Molfino had raised seven children and had taken over the family's ship chandlery business. She continued to run the business even after her family had grown, keeping the family enterprise afloat and amassing a prodigious vocabulary of nautical expressions and curses in several languages.

Given the reluctance of the Catholic Church to sanction marriages in the Advent period before Christmas, the wedding on December 13 was a subdued affair. Afterward, the young newlyweds made a visit to his parents in Briançon, where they gathered up two of Justinian's nephews, Adrien Merle and Eugene Geraud, ages thirteen and fourteen, to take back to California with them. They travelled on to Paris to pay a visit to Justinian's brother and business partner, Adrien, and his wife, Aglaë, to whom Albina took a great liking. The newlyweds and nephews set sail for San Francisco shortly thereafter, traveling across the Atlantic to Nicaragua, then by rail and steamer across the Isthmus of Tehuantepec, and finally by steamer up the Pacific coast to San Francisco, arriving there early in the spring of 1855. Despite the encumbrance of Albina's trousseau trunk, Justinian preferred this route as being much shorter than the five months around Cape Horn and less disease-ridden than the faster route via Panama, where he had contracted malaria on his way back to Italy the year before.

As they entered San Francisco harbor, Albina's first response to the sight of the rambling wooden metropolis was apparently one of perplexity. Coming from a city of brick and stone, she looked across the sprawl of wood and canvas structures that made up the rough-and-tumble San Francisco of

(*left*) Justinian Caire, ca. 1855.
(*right*) Maria Candida Christina Sarah "Albina" Caire,
not long after she was married.

of 1855 and asked, "I see the barns, but where are the houses?"[3] Despite her
initial misgivings, the young couple settled into a nice wooden house on
the side of Telegraph Hill. Their house on Vallejo Street was a short walk
from the Caire brothers' business premises on Washington Street between
Montgomery and Sansome. This location was fortuitous, because Justinian's ambition to succeed had him working late most nights. It was on one
such night six years later that, hearing fire alarm bells from the direction of
Telegraph Hill, he surmised there might be an emergency in the making.
His supposition was correct. He arrived at the same time as the bucket bri-
gade to find his house in flames and his wife and four children huddled on
the sidewalk across the street. According to his eldest daughter, Delphine,
it was the enthusiasm of the firemen to quell the blaze that did as much
damage to the house and its contents as the conflagration itself. The efforts
of the firemen were largely in vain. The house was uninhabitable, and the
Caires were forced to accept the kindness of their friends and neighbors,

---

[3] Jeanne Caire, "Memoir."

the Larcos, who lived nearby on Green Street. The Caire family must have found the change appealing because they soon moved into a home of their own on the same street, at 313 Green Street, where they lived until they moved to Oakland in the mid-1870s.[4] It was a boom time for entrepreneurs in San Francisco. Bold and hopeful multitudes continued to flood in from all parts of the world. Where enterprising businessmen like Caire had begun by selling mining pans and equipment needed by individual placer miners, they now shifted their offering to equipment and supplies that would be essential to the operation of the new gold mining and refining companies that were consolidating the gold fields not only in California, but also in Nevada and other mining states throughout the West. Then, with the development of viticulture in the 1870s and 1880s, another line of merchandise was added to supply the new wineries that were springing up in all parts of California. The business prospered, and in 1880, now called Justinian Caire Company, it moved to more imposing premises in the 500 block of Market Street, between First and Second streets.

Their customers included many of the most famous mining names in the West. The North Star Mine Company, California Consolidated Mining Company, Gold Peak Mining Company, Gold Crater Mine, Mono Mining Company, New York & Grass Valley Gold Mining Company, Nevada Goldfield Reduction Works, Union Copper Mining Company, and many others went to Justinian Caire Company for their assay supplies and chemicals. Winery customers included the Ben Lomond Wine Company, California Consolidated Vineyard Company, Italian Vineyard Company, Italian Swiss Colony, Lodi Wine Company, Paul Masson Champagne Company, St. George Vineyard Company, Placer County Winery Company, To-Kalon Vineyard Company, G H Wente and Company, Western Distilleries, and the Woodbridge Vineyard Association. Justinian Caire Company also had regular customers for the chemical products that it sourced from all over the country and Europe. The California & Hawaiian Sugar Company, Denver Fire Clay Company, DuPont de Nemours, Eureka Iron and Wire Works, Pacific High Explosive Company, U.S. Navy Yard, and Benicia Arsenal were customers as were high schools and colleges in places like Oakland, Alameda, Crockett, Salinas, and Esparto. The company sold supplies to Mendocino

---

[4] Delphine Caire, "Journal," vol. 1, Caire Family Papers and Diaries, in the author's possession (hereafter cited as Delphine Caire, "Journal," vol. 1).

State Hospital, the University of California, and the University of Oregon. Other customers were among the biggest companies and institutions in the building of California and the West: the Southern Pacific Company; Miller & Lux; Spreckels Sugar; Standard Oil; Stanford University; the University of California; the U.S. mint in San Francisco and in Carson, Nevada; the U.S. Geological Survey; and the Wells Fargo Express Company.

The Justinian Caire Company catalogue at the turn of the century ran to 290 pages, containing a hugely diverse range of products for mining, wine making, general industry, and education in the hard sciences. The company stocked or could source assayer's materials, chemical apparatus, centrifuges, cement testing apparatus, gauges for gas analysis, stoves, barometers, Bunsen burners, beakers, batteries, bottles, test tubes, clamps, lab vessels of all descriptions, mariner compasses, surveyor compasses, microscopes, tape measures, surveyor levels, pumps of all types, pyrometers, radiometers, rain gauges, oil testers, test tubes, viscosity testers, acids, chemicals, and reagents. Among other products for wine makers were electric thermometers for use as frost indicators in vineyards and orchards, hydrometers, alcohol testers, and corks. There were also stills for distillers. The company had mineral collections for sale to schools and a library of textbooks on a range of subjects, including assaying, organic chemistry, geology, laboratory practice, and metallurgy. Their mining goods ranged from prospector picks to an array of portable stamp mills "to enable the miner to state whether it is profitable to erect a large mill." There were thermometers for bakers, brewers, canners, clinics, confectioners, dairymen, and householders. Other thermometers were for incubators, milk sterilizing, and winemaking and for tanks and for vulcanizing rubber. The catalogue proudly displayed the title, *Dealers in and Importers of Chemists' and Assayers' Supplies, Balances, Chemical Glassware and Clay Goods.* They imported merchandise from Paris, London, Birmingham, Reading, Hamburg, Meissen, Jena, Antwerp, and Rotterdam.

The building at 521–523 Market Street, between First and Second streets, proclaimed "Justinian Caire Company" stamped in the metal facade in letters three feet high, with the frontage of the upper floors advertising, "Vineyard and Bottling Supplies," "Assayers' and Chemists' Materials," and "Hardware."[5]

---

[5] "Justinian Caire Company Catalogue and Price List" and 1901 photograph, Caire Family Papers and Diaries, in the author's possession. Market Street was later renumbered, and the address became 571–73. It is now occupied by the headquarters of the Standard Oil Co.

Justinian Caire Co. on Market Street in San Francisco,
prior to the 1906 earthquake.

Logo of Justinian Caire Co.

Like others in his position, Caire was interested in other opportunities in which to invest his profits. He bought land in San Mateo, Menlo Park, and in southern California. In the mid-1860s he became a director of the *Societe Francaise d'Epargnes et de Prevoyance Mutuelle*, the French Savings Bank of San Francisco, one of the financial institutions that catered to specific immigrant and religious populations in the San Francisco of those days. In February 1869, along with his fellow bank directors, he made another significant investment. The nine directors, including Caire's friend and neighbor, Nicolas Larco, incorporated the Santa Cruz Island Company to acquire the 61,440 acres of Santa Cruz Island for ranching operations.[6] They paid $150,000 [$2,445,000], or approximately $2.44 [$40] an acre for the land and all goods and chattels connected with the operation.[7]

---

[6] In the chapter that follows there is an overview of the changing title to Santa Cruz Island. There is a large bibliography that treats the pre-history and early history of Santa Cruz Island, much of which is included at the end of this work.

[7] To understand the impact costs and prices had on the story of the Caires and Santa Cruz Island, I believe it is helpful to translate the historical amounts into contemporary prices using a calculator based on the Consumer Price Index (CPI), which in any year is the cost of a bundle of goods and services purchased by a typical urban consumer compared with the cost of that bundle of goods and services in a base period. The amount the French Savings Bank directors paid for Santa Cruz Island is the equivalent of approximately $2,445,000 in 2008 dollars, the latest year for which a comparison is possible. Hereafter key monetary amounts are presented with their 2008 equivalents following them in brackets. From Officer and Williamson, "Purchasing Power of Money."

CHAPTER 2

Chumash Limuw Becomes
the Island of the Holy Cross

The largest of the eight California Channel Islands had been known to western explorers since Juan Rodríguez Cabrillo's sea voyage in 1542. He was followed by various seafarers in the sixteenth, seventeenth, and eighteenth centuries who sailed along the California coast and reported on the topography and indigenous cultures that they found there.

What they discovered was the complex and sophisticated aboriginal society of the Chumash, which dated back to at least 6000 BC. At the beginning of the California Mission Period (1772–1834), an estimated 2,000–3,000 Chumash lived on the northern three Channel Islands. There were some ten villages on Santa Cruz Island—then called Limuw by the Chumash—alone. Because of the inhabitants' reliance on the sea for sustenance and trade, these villages were located in the various coves and inlets of the island.

Santa Cruz Island purportedly got its present-day name during the land and sea exploration led by Captain Gaspar de Portolá in 1769, which claimed California, including its islands, for Spain. After a visit to the island by the seagoing part of the expedition aboard the *San Antonio* and an exchange of gifts with the Chumash at the village known to them as *Kaxas* (later Prisoners' Harbor), it was discovered that a staff topped with an iron cross had been left behind. Although iron was highly prized by the Chumash, the next day they paddled out to one of the expedition's ships in their *tomols* (plank-built boats approximately canoe-shaped) to return the staff.[1] Thenceforth the island was called *La Isla de la Santa Cruz* (Island of the Holy Cross), and it was recorded with this name on a map of the exploration in 1770. The name also appeared as "Santa Cruz" on the maps George Vancouver's expedition in 1793.[2]

In the early years of the Spanish rule, the Chumash continued to live in their island communities as they had from time immemorial, but their days were numbered as diseases previously unknown to the native population took their toll. In 1803 there were still sufficient numbers of Chumash Indians on Santa Cruz Island for the establishment of a mission to be strongly considered, but by 1807 the decline in the island population, particularly from the spread of measles, was so precipitous that the idea was abandoned. By 1822 the last of the island's Chumash were said to have left voluntarily, headed for the missions at San Buenaventura and Santa Barbara.[3] Their numbers had dwindled, their trade in locally produced beads was destroyed, and they were subject to the depredations of Aleut sea otter hunters. They had neither the numbers nor the resources to resist.

It was the end of an era that had lasted some 6,000 years, and it was the beginning of a new time in the history of Santa Cruz Island. In 1821 Mexico finalized its independence from Spain and, under the leadership of Agustín Iturbide (Agustín I), laid claim to all the former Spanish possessions in Mexico and in Baja and Alta, California. The impact of these distant events was felt on Santa Cruz Island only in 1830 when the Mexican government attempted to enforce an edict deporting convicted criminals to the California presidios rather than keeping them in Mexican jails. In March of that year, the *Maria Ester* sailed into Santa Barbara with about eighty prisoners on board. Having previously been turned away from San Diego, the captain was not surprised to meet with strong resistance from the citizens of Santa Barbara. After about a month of stalemate, it was decided that thirty-one of the most hardened convicts would be removed to Santa Cruz Island and left there with enough supplies to survive while they contemplated their crimes. Not long after they were put ashore a fire destroyed their provisions, and the prisoners showed enough ingenuity to build rafts and sail back to the mainland, where some were absorbed into

---

[1] Fr. Estevan Tapis to Gov. Jose Arrillaga, 1805, cited in Livingston, "Draft Historic Resource Study," 459, 461 (hereafter cited as Livingston, "Study").

[2] Woodward, *Sea Diary of Fr. Juan Vizcaino*; and Palou, *Historical Memoirs of New California*.

[3] Tapis, "Biennial Mission Reports."

the local population and others, after a stint in the local guardhouse, were sent to the provincial capital in Monterey. They disappeared from history, but the memory of their sojourn on the island remains in the name of the main port on its northern coastline: Prisoners' Harbor.[4]

The Spanish plan for colonization of its Alta California territories[5] had been the tried and tested combination of religion and armed force, expressed through the chain of missions and their accompanying four presidios.[6] Eventually, this tactic was supplemented by the concept of land grants to local settlers, which could be made through the governor. In practice, little land if any was granted during the period of Spanish rule; however, in the era of Mexican rule, the issuing of land grants accelerated and private ownership of land increased greatly, especially after the secularization of the mission system in 1834.

The decades of the 1830s and 1840s in Alta California reflected the tumultuous conditions prevailing in Mexico at the time. The machinations of the despotic general and president Antonio Lopez de Santa Anna resulted in a group of prominent *Californios* (Mexican residents of California) declaring independence under the governorship of Juan Bautista Alvarado. But the Californios splintered into several factions; a peace of sorts occurred in 1838, brokered through the efforts of Andres Castillero, a native Spaniard and captain in the Mexican Army. As his reward, Castillero was given a land grant that permitted him to choose one of the Channel Islands. After a bit of wavering over Santa Catalina, he fixed on the choice of Santa Cruz Island, and this request was granted in 1839 by Governor Alvarado, acting on behalf of the government of Mexico. Castillero thus became the first private owner of the island.[7]

Little development took place in the era of Castillero's ownership of the island. He was largely absent, spending much of his time in Mexico and distracted by his more lucrative discovery of the New Almaden quicksilver mine near San Jose, which intertwined his business affairs with a Tepic businessman, Alexander Forbes. Forbes and Eustace Barron (1790–1859) operated a concern called Barron, Forbes & Co, with interests in various silver mines in Mexico. Barron and Forbes eventually acquired complete

---

[4] Ord, *Occurrences in Hispanic California*; and Bancroft, *History of California*, vol. 5, 47–49.

[5] That is, modern-day California.

[6] Located in San Diego, Santa Barbara, Monterey, and San Francisco.

[7] Tays, "Captain Andres Castillero."

ownership of the New Almaden mine, which resulted in the mixing of their affairs with Castillero's Santa Cruz Island.

The result of the 1846 war between Mexico and the United States changed the nationality of Californians, and the 1848 peace treaty of Guadalupe Hidalgo attempted to safeguard property rights of the former Mexican citizens now living in the new territories of the United States. But with the discovery of gold and the arrival of thousands of new immigrants, there was intense pressure on the land titles of the huge Californio holdings from the earlier era. Congress attempted to solve the problem by establishing a land commission that would examine the validity of Californio land claims.

Castillero duly filed a petition to confirm his title to Santa Cruz Island, and in spite of the maneuverings of several local citizens, his ownership was confirmed in 1857 and upheld by the U.S. Supreme Court in 1860. In the legal struggle, Castillero was helped by the nephew of Eustace Barron, William Eustace Barron (1822–1871). William was a San Francisco commission merchant in partnership with James Bolton in the firm of Bolton, Barron & Company. He lived primarily in San Francisco and acted as agent for Castillero in the face of challenges to his title. After confirmation of the title, a survey was made and a patent, signed by President Andrew Johnson, was issued, which stated that the island had as "its boundaries the water's edge," and one hundred acres was reserved for the use of the government to erect a lighthouse.[8]

A few primitive ranch facilities were constructed on Santa Cruz Island in the early 1850s, and either Castillero or Barron hired local Santa Barbara resident Dr. James Barron Shaw to manage the operation. Shaw was a relative of Eustace Barron and had moved to Santa Barbara in 1850. In 1851 he paid the Santa Barbara taxes on the island for Castillero. In May 1852 he went to Tepic and returned to Santa Barbara with instructions to manage the island. It was at this time that the first permanent ranch structure was built in the central valley of the island, and evidence suggests that this was the point at which pigs were first introduced to the island. According to testimony in a contemporary court case, the animals in question were "unmanageable and had withdrawn to the mountains where they ranged in a wild state, not being worth the catching."[9]

---

[8] Daily, *California's Channel Islands*.
[9] *Thomas Wallace More v. M.J. Box*, 9 November 1857.

In the same year that legal title to the island was confirmed, it was transferred from Castillero to William Barron, and in 1858 it was advertised for
sale.[10] The initial attempts to find a buyer failed, and William Barron, perhaps thinking that a going concern would attract more interest, instructed
Dr. Shaw to establish a sheep ranch.[11]

Shaw, born in London and trained as a physician in England and Scot-
land, set about building a ranching operation and is said to have bought
1,000 head of sheep in Los Angeles and herded them to Santa Barbara for
shipment to the island.[12] Within a couple of years, it is thought that the
number of livestock had grown substantially, and there were two hundred
acres of land under cultivation growing animal feed. Although the unsuc-
cessful sale offering of 1858 listed only fifty sheep, within a year the records
show a substantial increase in the livestock on the island, quite possibly in response to the Civil War fever sweeping the country, with wool

[10] A 25 May 1858 ad in the *Daily Alta California* that ran for several weeks listed for sale an "Island
    for sheep raising. For sale—an island containing about 60,000 acres of land, well-watered, and
    abounding in small valleys of the best pasturage for sheep. There are no wild animals on it that
    would interfere with the stock. There is a good harbor and safe anchorage. The owner is now in
    the city, and if a party should desire to place stock on it, an arrangement may be made to do so, by
    putting the island, to a certain extent, against the stock furnished. There are about fifty sheep now
    upon the island. Apply at 119 Sansome Street."

[11] It seems likely that Dr. James Barron Shaw was also a relative of William Barron, as he is noted in
    Storke's *History of Santa Barbara* as visiting relatives in Mexico.

[12] James Barron Shaw (1814–1902) was the son of a Scottish father and an English mother and graduated
    from the University of Glasgow (1836) and the Royal College of Surgeons. Shaw made three trips
    around the world, serving as ship's surgeon on a variety of sailing vessels, before arriving in Santa
    Barbara on 6 January 1850. He practiced medicine and became the first president of the Santa Bar-
    bara County Medical Society. In 1851 he began paying the taxes on Santa Cruz Island on behalf of
    island grantee, Andres Castillero. In May 1852 Shaw traveled to Tepic, Mexico, to visit friends and
    relatives. When he returned a year later, he began managing Santa Cruz Island for island grantee
    Andres Castillero. When the island sold to William E. Barron in 1857, Shaw continued as manager
    for the next twelve years, until it was sold to the Santa Cruz Island Company in 1869. He was one
    of the investors in Santa Barbara's first wharf, built at the foot of Chapala Street prior to the con-
    struction of Stearn's Wharf. He also invested in a number of ranches, including Los Alamos, La
    Laguna de San Francisco, La Patera, and the Ortega Ranch in Montecito. In Santa Barbara Shaw
    built a large mansion near the northwest corner of State and Montecito streets. On 16 May 1861 in
    San Francisco, Shaw married Helen Augusta Green. William Eustace Barron, owner of Santa Cruz
    Island, served as best man. The Shaws had four sons, only one of whom survived to adulthood,
    James Barron Shaw, Jr. (1862–1935). William E. Barron was his godfather. James B. Shaw, Jr., mar-
    ried Alice Teresa Perkins in Santa Barbara on 29 March 1886. They had three children (grandchil-
    dren to James Barron Shaw), all of whom married but none of whom had children. James Barron
    Shaw died on 6 January 1902 at eighty-eight years of age and is buried in Santa Barbara Cemetery
    along with his wife and namesake son. Daily, "California Channel Islands Encyclopedia."

suppliers anticipating a spike in demand. It seems safe to assume that war-time requirements were the motivating force behind the rapid expansion of the number of sheep on the island, with the Santa Barbara Assessor's records showing more than 24,000 there by 1864.[13]

By the end of the decade, Shaw had overseen the establishment of a well-recognized sheep ranch on Santa Cruz Island. Contemporary photographs portray several adobe buildings in the central valley, along with wooden corrals, shearing sheds, and a substantial wharf at Prisoners' Harbor. From the wharf Shaw shipped animals to Santa Barbara and to cities along the coast, as far north as San Francisco. An effusive article in the *New York Times* from the early 1870s sang the praises of the island as a "splendid property," citing revenues of $76,000 [$1.48 million], principally from the herd of 40,000 to 45,000 sheep, and profits of $48,000 [$936,000].[14] But during a drought two years later, a U.S. Geological Survey Report underscored the perils of sheep ranching in this part of California. The writer noted that "pasture had become so thin that the sheep at the time of my visit were wandering in very small bands that they might the more readily find food. Even the sage-brush was disappearing as year after year the sheep had eaten away at its leaves. . . . It is impossible to conceive a more dreary waste than was here produced as the result of over-pasturage."[15] It was said by another source that in the winter of 1876–1877, 70,000 sheep were killed for their pelts and tallow on Santa Cruz Island. This figure seems exaggerated, but the drought was certainly a disaster for the sheep raising industry on the southern California mainland. There, financial problems and population pressures led to the breakup of the huge ranches of earlier days and a shift to more mixed land and animal husbandry on smaller units. But across the Santa Barbara Channel, although the herd was decimated, Santa Cruz Island's unique geography meant that it did not feel the same pressures; hence, the ranch remained intact and was largely dedicated to traditional sheep raising practice.[16]

In early 1869 the era of William Barron's ownership came to a close when he sold Santa Cruz Island to a group of ten San Francisco investors

---

[13] *Thomas Wallace Moore v. M.J. Box*, 9 November 1857. On the wartime demand for sheep and wool, see Cleland, *Cattle on a Thousand Hills*, 139.

[14] *New York Times*, 24 January 1874, cited in Livingston, "Study," 484.

[15] Wheeler, *Report upon the United States Geographical Surveys*, cited in Livingston, "Study," 485.

[16] Cleland, *Cattle on a Thousand Hills*, 209.

headed by Gustave Mahé.[17] Mahé became president of the newly incorporated Santa Cruz Island Company. He was also the president of the
French Savings Bank of San Francisco, of which Justinian Caire was also
a director.[18] The French Savings Bank was a financial focus for immigrant
French San Franciscans, some of whom were encouraged to invest based
on the word and reputation of Caire. By 1868 the French Savings Bank had
a robust 3,800 depositors, with $3.3 million [$51.5 million] on deposit and
$3.8 million [$59 million] on loan.[19]

In July 1874 Mahé and Caire, along with fellow directors Adrien Gensoul and Camilo Martin, borrowed $41,000 [$800,000] from the bank to
buy twenty shares (20 percent) of Santa Cruz Island Company stock from
several of the other shareholders. The funds for this transaction were borrowed personally from the bank by Caire. As Mahé, Gensoul, and Martin
were officers of the bank, they were prohibited from borrowing directly

---

[17] Gustave Mahé (1831–1878) was president of the French Mutual Benefit Society in San Francisco as
well as director general of the French Savings and Loan Society, La Societe Francaise d'Espargnes
et de Prevoyance Mutuelle. He, along with fourteen other founding French and Italian shareholders, established the Buenaventura Mining Company in 1863, a venture with interests in gold and
coal mines. Justinian Caire was its president, and Nicholas Larco its secretary.

[18] On 29 March 1869 the deed to Santa Cruz Island was conveyed from William E. Barron to the Santa
Cruz Island Company and its ten stock holders: Pablo Baca, Justinian Caire, Giovanni Battista
Cerruti, Thomas J. Gallagher, Adrien Gensoul, Nicolas Larco, Gustave Mahé, Camilo Martin,
T. Lemmen Meyer, and Alexander Weill. At the time, each owned one-tenth of the capital stock of
the company (a total of 600 shares valued at $500 each for a total of $300,000). They acquired the
island as a basis for sheep and livestock operations. These men were also the directors of the French
Savings Bank in San Francisco. At the time of the company's formation, there was widespread
cooperation between the French and Italian communities of San Francisco, particularly among
powerful businessmen. In 1873 the company reorganized and changed its capital stock to a total of
100 shares valued at a total of $500,000, or $5,000 a share. Under the reorganization, the number of
stockholders decreased from ten to nine: Pablo Baca, T. J. Gallagher, and Nicolas Larco dropped
out of the company, and Henry Ohlmeyer and J. V. Delaveaga were added as stockholders. Gustave
Mahé owned two-tenths of the stock, with one-tenth each owned by the other eight stockholders.
The company had no debts or liabilities. After the suicide of Mahé and the failure of the French
Savings Bank, Justinian Caire began acquiring additional company stock, and by 1878 he owned
seventeen of the one hundred shares. Although transfer records and other corporate papers were
destroyed in the 1906 San Francisco earthquake, it is known that by about 1880 Justinian Caire had
become the majority shareholder of the Santa Cruz Island Company, though there seems to be
evidence that AP More, owner of neighboring Santa Rosa Island, held a 30 percent interest in Santa
Cruz Island at some point in the early 1880s. Before he died in December 1897, Justinian Caire
transferred the entire capital stock of the Santa Cruz Island Company to his wife, Albina Cristina
Sara Molfino Caire, who outlived Caire by twenty-seven years.

[19] Armstrong and Denny, *Financial California*, 67–69.

from their institution. Caire, because he was not an officer of the bank and was widely recognized as a good credit risk, was able to obtain a loan for all the money needed for the share purchase on an agreement with Mahé, Gensoul, and Martin that all the income from these shares would be used to pay the interest on the debt and repay the loan principal. Caire then re-loaned the portion of the proceeds needed for his partners to purchase their shares. Although this was a personal loan made to Caire, the bank held all the shares of the Santa Cruz Island Company purchased in this transaction as collateral. Later that year, there was a further stock pur-chase opportunity from another of the Santa Cruz Island Company direc-tors for the sum of $6,000 [$117,000]. Once again, Caire signed a personal note with the bank and re-loaned a portion of the proceeds to his three fellow directors. The records show that as of September 1874, Caire was personally liable to the bank for $47,700 [$930,000] in loans. In addition, he was jointly liable for $15,000 [$293,000] owed directly to another of the former Santa Cruz Island stockholders for the purchase of his shares. This brought Caire's total indebtedness up to a total of $62,700 [$1.23 million]. On March 19, 1875, the Santa Cruz Island Company declared a dividend and the bank received $2,400 [$48,500] for the thirty shares held as secu-rity to back up Caire's loan. Mahé paid the interest due to the bank as of that date. However, when the company declared a larger dividend later that year, Mahé, using his position as bank president to cover his tracks, quietly pocketed the cash for his own use instead of paying it to the bank, as he had promised Caire. This crime was one of the means that Mahé used to fund his lavish lifestyle and sustain his preeminent position in the French community. His other frauds included using new depositors' funds to pay interest on other deposits as well as dividends to himself and other share-holders of the bank, a scheme later given its name by Charles Ponzi in 1920, and more recently practiced by Bernie Madoff, among others.

There had been little or no bank supervision in California prior to 1878. In that year, the state legislature established a commission to examine the numerous San Francisco savings banks. Their suspicions about the health of the banking industry were not allayed when the first bank examined, the Masonic Savings Bank, was revealed to be holding forged securities as part of its asset base. The commissioners ordered it closed. The next bank, the Mechanics and Farmers Savings Bank had capital of $60,000 [$1.4 million] and owed depositors $373,000 [$8.3 million]. It, too, was forced to close. When the commissioners turned their attentions to the French Savings Bank, they discovered liabilities (deposits) of $5.5 million [$122 million] and insufficient assets to back them up.[20]

On September 17, 1878, Mahé realized that his financial manipulations were about to become public knowledge. Faced with financial and social ruin, he put a pistol to his head and committed suicide. With perhaps unseemly haste, he was buried the next day. At the funeral, a friend of Justinian Caire's took pity on his "sickly appearance" and draped his overcoat on the shoulders of his shattered colleague.[21] The bank suspended trading of its shares that day. Rumor and counterrumor swirled through the French community. In October Judge Dwinelle of the 15th District Court declared the bank insolvent and appointed ex-governor F. F. Low as receiver. This action was contested, and the California Supreme Court set aside the appointment two months later. On December 30, a meeting of the anxious depositors was held in Platt's Hall on Montgomery Street, near Bush, to hear the fate of the bank. In the auditorium that had witnessed the fiery orations of politicians and the witticisms of famous literary figures such as Oscar Wilde and Mark Twain, the directors faced a stormy meeting with depositors. The following day, those people who were crowded into a similarly packed meeting heard that the directors were resisting going into liquidation; however, the directors did finally have to take that step on January 22, 1879. Just before that date, a new bank with the same title was organized and the affairs of the old bank were turned over to the new one.[22]

In March of that year, Caire discovered that Mahé had paid the bank almost none of the interest or the principal it was owed. Caire's investment in the French Savings Bank was virtually worthless, and he was personally liable for both (a) the $47,700 [$930,000] in principal and interest owed on the note from the bank secured by the thirty shares (30 percent) of Santa Cruz Island stock borrowed against the island shares plus (b) the $6,000 [$114,000] owed to the former shareholder. Getting money where he could, Caire paid the reorganized French Bank a sum of $14,633 [$326,000] as an interim settlement of amounts he owed. Despite Caire's best efforts, the

---

[20] Armstrong and Denny, *Financial California*, 86.

[21] Personal note from Justinian Caire, signed and notarized, San Francisco, 30 March 1889, in the author's possession.

[22] Armstrong and Denny, *Financial California*, 67–69.

bank was ultimately forced to close its doors. The bankruptcy and liquidation of the bank did not deflect Caire's determination to see through his
investment in the Santa Cruz Island Company and to pay off all the debts
connected with it. Later that month, as a final settlement, he pledged himself to pay the full outstanding balance of $48,000 [$1.1 million] owed to
the bank's creditors for the purchase of the island shares.

For Caire, the failure of the bank was a debacle that not only threatened
his own personal finances, but also reverberated throughout the French
community, some of whom had invested in the bank on his advice. His
eldest daughter, Delphine, later recalled, "I will never forget the sadness
that, because of this disaster, weighed down on our family for years."[23]
Caire was truly devastated by the news of the disaster at the bank. At age
fifty-one, he faced ruin. Twenty-five years of work building up Justinian Caire Company looked about to be destroyed. Twenty-two-year-old
Delphine, who acted as his confidante and bookkeeper, remembered the
deeply somber mood in the Caire house on Harrison Street in Oakland
and the evident state of confusion felt by her father. She remembered long
silences from a man whom she had been accustomed to hearing humming
and singing around the house. It was only after many months that she
sensed a lightening of his dark mood as the debt burden began to be slowly
relieved and his finances got back on track.

On many levels the debacle of the French Savings Bank was a blow to
Caire's reputation and self-esteem whose scars were slow to heal. More
than ten years later, Caire successfully undertook a slander suit against a
Mr. O. Perrone for repeating an unfounded rumor that Caire had somehow
obtained $80,000 from the bank before it went under. The experience of
the bank failure seemingly turned Caire away from investments that were
based on trust in others and toward simpler investments that he felt he
could control personally. He invested in property in Los Angeles on 23rd
Avenue, a quarter-section (160 acres) of land in San Bernardino County,
and the Rough Diamond Mine in Chili Gulch, Calaveras County.[24]
Although he remained active in the San Francisco business community
and was listed among the charter shareholders of the San Francisco and

---

[23] Delphine A. Caire, "Journal," vol. 3.
[24] Listed as assets in "Justinian Caire Company Journal, 1906–1912," Caire Family Papers and Diaries,
in the author's possession.

San Joaquin Valley Railway (Claus Spreckels's challenge to the strangle-hold of the Southern Pacific), his considerable business energy was focused on the Justinian Caire Company and the Santa Cruz Island Company.

Caire struggled to pay off the outstanding debts that he had incurred on behalf of himself and the other Santa Cruz Island Company directors for the purchase of control of the island ranch. But his reward came as he slowly acquired all the capital stock of the Santa Cruz Island Company. Dividend records from 1882 show a total of thirteen stockholders, with Caire having a controlling interest because he took ownership of all the shares pledged against the loans used to purchase those shares. By 1886 he owned 100 percent of the stock in the Santa Cruz Island Company.[25] Six years earlier, notwithstanding his partial ownership, Caire's interest in the development of the island began with a vision of creating a self-sustaining, diversified sheep and cattle ranch and vineyard operation. This was the job that would take the seventeen remaining years of his lifetime and beyond. Born of the need to generate income from this once passive investment in a distant island ranch, it became an elaborate and sustained construction and development program to domesticate and cultivate the natural attributes of the island, realizing a return from its agricultural potential. Moreover, this drive and energy succeeded in creating the ultimate family retreat for this powerful and private visionary.

One can only speculate as to whether Caire's chief motivation was the determination to succeed at an investment that had nearly bankrupted him. Perhaps his bitter disappointment in the nefarious deeds of trusted associates drove him to concentrate on an investment where he could be totally self-reliant for its success. It is also conceivable that he couldn't pass up the opportunity to be the sole owner of a large island ranch whose rugged peaks suggested the mountains of his childhood. But something undoubtedly fired his imagination, because by the beginning of the decade of the 1880s he was pursuing his idea. This was just the sort of challenge that an energetic man like Caire relished in an era when California immigrants dared to dream big dreams. Examples of huge ranch holdings, virtually feudal in nature, like the Rancho Tejón at the southern end of the Central Valley, were celebrated in bestsellers like Charles Nordhoff's *California for Health, Wealth and Residence* (1882). Two years later, Helen Hunt

---

[25] Delphine A. Caire, "Journal," vol. 3.

Jackson established the central myth of Southern California in *Ramona* (1884). This historical romance, unfolding within the gracious confines of a self-sufficient hacienda, was mirrored on Santa Cruz Island—albeit with a French accent—right down to the setting of the chapel in the vineyard. In addition, it was the end of the cattle era that had dominated Southern California economic life for more than half a century and was the beginning of the era of sheep raising and diversified agriculture.[26]

The vision of Justinian Caire dovetailed perfectly with the economic and cultural spirit of the times. Fate had decreed that Santa Cruz Island become central to Caire's significant success as part of the gold rush generation of immigrants. As the years passed, Caire came to cherish this most unique holding among California real estate assets. In the waning days of his life, he made clear to his sons that it was his wish that Santa Cruz Island remain the central part of his legacy, the mainstay of his family for generations to come.

Limuw, the island of the Chumash from time immemorial, now the Island of the Holy Cross with its intermittent livestock operation, had changed little over time. Now, and for more than a century, it would bear the imprint of Caire's plan for commercial land husbandry across its hills, valleys, and coastline. Over the next seventeen years the plan took shape, integrating sheep, cattle, and viticulture. The existing buildings were expanded and developed. Two kilns were constructed, one for the manufacture of bricks, and the other for making limestone mortar. From these came the materials to build the barns, warehouses, winery buildings, and, in 1890, a small chapel. Island stone was quarried, and a resident blacksmith forged railings, balconies, fittings, and hinges. A comfortable two-story family home was built at the main ranch. Full- and part-time employees included "ranch hands, team drivers, dairymen, vintners, grape pickers, sheep shearers, a wagon maker, butcher, carpenters, painters, cobbler and captain and crew of the schooner *Santa Cruz*,"[27] many of whom—particularly those associated with the rounding up and shearing of the sheep—were drawn from the local Santa Barbara population.

The Santa Cruz Island Company became a large, complex, successful, and self-sustaining operation that in most years provided a substantial

---

[26] For a more detailed discussion of these trends, see Cleland, *Cattle on a Thousand Hills*, chap. 8; and Starr, *Inventing the Dream*, 21–30.

[27] Daily and Stanton, "Historical Highlights of Santa Cruz Island."

income for Justinian Caire and his family of six children. His story had many of the elements of a classic American success—the young immigrant who arrived in San Francisco with a modest amount of start-up capital and achieved considerable wealth and property as a result of hard work and risk-taking in equal amounts. Certainly there were setbacks and difficulties along the way, but at the end of the 1880s, Caire could doubtless look back with a sense of pride and accomplishment. He was now in his sixties and had ridden the storm to gain a large measure of financial success in both his hardware and ranching businesses. His sons and daughters, now in their twenties and thirties, were showing signs of educational and cultural accomplishment. At this point, Caire had passed the day-to-day responsibility for management of his businesses to his two sons in the confident expectation that they would build on his achievements.

Justinian Caire in the early 1890s next to
the Oakland family home.

CHAPTER 3

The Justinian Caire Family

Justinian and Albina Caire had nine children. The first son, Arthur Marius, died at ten months, and the last daughter, Marie Christina, at two years of age. Another child, Albert, died at age thirteen. The eldest of the six surviving children was Delphine, followed by Arthur J., then Amelie, Aglaë, Frederic, and Hélène.

As the eldest son living to adulthood, Arthur occupied a privileged position in a household numerically and domestically dominated by women. He also grew up significantly burdened by the expectation that he would take the lead in continuing the work begun by his father. To this end, Arthur was well educated in Genoa during the family's extended sojourn from 1872 to 1876, mastering Italian and French (but forbidden by his father from learning a word of Genoese dialect). This European education was followed by schooling with the Jesuits at St. Ignatius College in San Francisco. With his scholarly temperament, Arthur excelled in chemistry and physics and showed an aptitude for science in general. In 1879 he enrolled at the University of California, taking courses in surveying and engineering, in which he showed a similarly strong mathematical bent. Unfortunately for Arthur, his studies were curtailed after a year because of Justinian's financial reverses resulting from the failure of the French Savings Bank, and Arthur joined his father in the management of the Justinian Caire business interests.

But what he had learned at Berkeley was put to good use when he undertook the first surveys of the ranches on Santa Cruz Island, ably assisted by his older sister, Delphine.[1] Also highly useful was Arthur's mastery of the new

---

[1] Delphine Caire, "Journal," vol. 3.

The Justinian Caire Family

Justinian Caire 1827–1897
m. Maria Candida Christina Sarah (Albina) Molfino 1831–1924

Delphine A. 1856–1949	Arthur M. 1858–1858	Arthur J. 1859–1942 m. Mary Suich 1876–1961	Amelie A. 1861–1917 m. Pietro Carlo Rossi 1855–1911

Arthur J. line:

1. Justinian Caire II
   1906–1986
   m. M. Bernheim
   Yvonne (b. 1939)
   Jacqueline (b. 1941)
   Justinian III (b. 1948)
2. Olivia Lucille
   1909–1993
   m. George Swortfiguer
   Arthur (b. 1947)
   Robert (b. 1951)
3. Miriam Frances
   1912–1999

Amelie A. line:

1. Albert (1882–1887)
2. Maria (1883–1960)
   m. Ambrose Gherini
   Marie (1907–2010)
   Elena (1908–1908)
   Ilda (1910–2006)
   Pier A. (1912–1989)
   Francis (1914–1998)
3. Sophia (1885–1891)
4. Luigi (1887–1991)
5. Robert (1888–1961)
6. Edmund (1888–1974)
7. Esther (1890–1968)
8. Aimee (1892–1985)
9. A. Olga (1893–1983)
10. Beatrice (1896–1989)
11. Gioberto (1897–1899)
12. Albina (1899–1988)
13. Elenore (1901–1991)
14. Pietro Carlo (1902–1992)

Albert A.	Aglaë S.	Frederic F.	Hélène A.	Marie C.
1862–1875	1864–1943	1865–1950	1867–1929	1871–1873
	m. Goffredo Capuccio	m. Lillian Suich		
	1866–1915	1878–1960		

	Aglaë S.	Frederic F.		
	1. Goffredo (1907–1986)	1. L.A. Jeanne (1902–1978)		
	m. I. Reidenauer	2. Marie (1903–2002)		
	2. Aglae E. "Cita" (1910–1994)	3. Helen (1905–1999)		
	m. M. McDougald	4. Delphine (1906–1998)		
		5. Vivienne (1910–2004)		
		m. John Chiles		
		Mary B. (b. 1945)		
		Frederic C. (b. 1947)		
		James F. (b. 1949)		
		Catherine V. (1950–2000)		
		John G. (b. 1952)		

Arthur Caire with his photographic equipment, ca. 1890.

and complicated art of photography. In collaboration with his sister Hélène, he created an invaluable visual record of those early days in the development of the Santa Cruz Island Company.

The next son in the Caire family was the fair-haired boy Albert Alexis, who was born in 1862; he was the first of Justinian and Albina's children who had his father's fair complexion, eyes, and hair. As the fourth child of the seven to survive infancy, he was said to be easy-going, clever, and full of the common sense that would have made him the so-called balance wheel within the family dynamics, had he lived. He was thirteen when he succumbed to smallpox in Genoa in 1875, during Albina's four-year stay in her native city. Albina wept bitter tears over his grave in the *campo santo* (cemetery) of Genoa as he was laid to rest next to his baby sister, Marie Christina, who had died two years before in June 1873 at the age of two.

Arthur and Albert's younger brother, Frederic, was the fifth child of Justinian and Albina who grew to maturity. Like his older brother Arthur, Frederic began his early education in the 1870s during the family sojourn in Genoa, where he mastered French and Italian. Frederic then followed in his brother's footsteps with the Jesuits in San Francisco, where his teacher of rhetoric and composition suggested that he might think about a literary vocation. But it was his singing teacher who judged Frederic to be his outstanding pupil and urged him to consider a professional operatic career as a tenor. Yet with his father getting on in years, and the businesses needing capable, trustworthy managers, he bowed to parental wishes and joined his brother in taking charge of the family firms. Athletic and popular, he was active in the Reliance Athletic Club in Oakland, cycling over the roads and trails of Alameda, Marin, and San Mateo counties. Quick-witted and wiry, he did not suffer fools gladly, and his prodigious memory enabled him to declaim great quantities of poetry and Shakespearean drama from memory. There was one memorable occasion on Santa Cruz Island when he succeeded in astonishing the famous Shakespearean actor John Barrymore with a recitation of the Bard's poetry. Frederic's operatic singing voice left an abiding memory for his children. "The *bel canto* of his golden tenor . . . filled the house with the great operatic airs of Bellini, Donizetti, Rossini, Verdi, Puccini, Bizet and many others," remembered his eldest daughter Jeanne.[2]

---

[2] Jeanne Caire, "Memoirs, 1972," Caire Family Papers and Diaries.

Delphine, the eldest sister of Arthur, Albert, and Frederic, played the role of her father's confidante in business matters, and in the early years of financial difficulties she helped with the Justinian Caire Company books. In a decision that would have been highly unusual for the time, at age twelve she was sent to France to study with her aunt Sophie, the mother superior of the Trinitarian convent near Paris. In 1868, accompanied by family friends, she embarked from San Francisco via Panama to France. The warmth and concern expressed in the correspondence that ensued between father and daughter speaks volumes about the strong bond that existed between them, as he alternately praised and cajoled her about her studies. Delphine was described by her eldest niece as a born teacher. At her father's urging, when she was reunited with her family, she acted as a tutor for her younger brothers and sisters. She and her siblings helped their mother create a haven of hospitality for friends and relatives, in particular for the children of Amelie.

Amelie was the first of the siblings to marry. In 1880, at the age of nineteen, she married the Italian immigrant pharmacist Pietro Carlo (PC) Rossi. She and PC Rossi had fourteen children. It was for the sake of many of these children that Amelie would stay at her mother and father's house on Harrison Street in Oakland for weeks at a time to partake of the perceived healthier climate of the East Bay and to make use of the extra help provided by her sisters and mother. Two of Amelie's children were born in the house of her parents, and three died there of the then-common childhood diseases meningitis, diphtheria, and scarlet fever.

The next sister was Aglaë, who was a year older than Frederic and was remembered as sociable and fun-loving. She remained in her parents' house well into her thirties, developing her skill with the piano and mandolin and cultivating her mezzo-soprano voice with a musical group in Oakland. While carrying one of Amelie's children down the stairs of the house on Harrison Street, she fell and suffered an ankle injury that proved so resistant to any local cure that the recommendation of a healer in her mother's native Italy was considered. Thus, in 1888, Aglaë traveled to Europe with her mother. Whether it was the healer, the passage of time, or a change of scene, Aglaë returned from Europe with the full use of her ankle. When she visited Italy again it was more than a decade later, this time with her niece Maria and brother-in-law PC Rossi. It was on this trip

Fred Caire in the door of Arthur's studio, ca. 1890.
Photograph courtesy of Justinian Caire III.

that she became reacquainted with Goffredo Capuccio, who had worked briefly in San Francisco for Justinian Caire Company and on Santa Cruz Island in several capacities, including superintendent. By now she was in her late thirties, two years older than Capuccio. The vivacious Aglaë and suave Capuccio got on well. They were married at the end of that year, setting up home in La Spezia, on the Ligurian coast near Genoa.

The youngest daughter living to adulthood was Hélène, who shared a love of music with Aglaë and Fred. Hélène was gifted with a fine contralto voice, often accompanying herself on the guitar. She and Aglaë shared the same music teachers. The two sisters excelled in the domestic arts—embroidery and the then-fashionable china painting—and were remembered years later by a former *mayordomo* (majordomo) of the island ranch as formidable side-saddle horsewomen. Hélène joined her brother Arthur in his enthusiasm for the new art of photography, working with him both in the field with the bulky apparatus and heavy glass plates and in the darkroom that they rigged up at home in Oakland. She never married, remaining in the family home until her mother's death in 1924. She died in her Piedmont home in 1929 at the age of sixty-two.

It was in 1871 after the difficult birth of Justinian and Albina's ninth and last child, Marie Christina, that Justinian moved his family from San Francisco down the peninsula to the countryside near Palo Alto for four months. He hoped that the country air would be good for all of them, but especially for his wife. Albina recovered somewhat, but they were concerned enough to consider reviving her health with the more ambitious plan of a lengthy visit to her native Genoa. She, Justinian, and the seven children set off the next year, going via Paris to visit Delphine at her convent school then moving on to Italy, where their eldest daughter eventually joined them. Justinian stayed with them until they were settled and then returned to San Francisco in November, moving in with the family of his nephew Adrien Merle in Medau Place on the side of Telegraph Hill. Albina recovered her health in Italy, but the visit was fatal for Albert and little Marie. The two children buried in the *campo santo* of Genoa were a lifelong regret for Albina, who, it was said, blamed herself for exposing her children to endemic European diseases so that she could have an extended visit with her mother and family.[3]

---

[3] Jeanne Caire, memorandum, unpublished Caire family papers, 1972, Caire Family Papers and Diaries, in the author's possession.

In May 1874, with his family still in Europe, Justinian moved with his nephew to Chester Street in West Oakland. It would appear that sometime during this period Justinian decided, in consultation with Albina, to move the family to Oakland, buying a house at the corner of Eighth and Harrison streets in a fashionable neighborhood near the newly developed Lake Merritt. Perhaps this decision to relocate to the East Bay was made so that his wife would not be confronted with the house on Green Street in San Francisco that held so many memories of Albert and Marie. Their thinking might also have been influenced by the "healthier" climate of Oakland that was believed to be superior to the fogs and pollution of San Francisco. Justinian's first choice would have been Menlo Park, where he also owned property, but it was deemed impractical to move that far out into the country. As it was, his commuting day had him leaving his big white home on Harrison Street at seven in the morning and not returning until nine in the evening.

On the whole, the Justinian Caire family of Oakland was a picture of genteel middle class respectability. In the accepted practice of the time, the father ran the business empire and groomed his sons to succeed him. The daughters and their mother played their roles in the domestic arts and made a gracious home that welcomed their fast-growing group of relatives.

By the turn of the century, Amelie and her husband, PC Rossi, were on the way to producing a very large family. In 1900 Fred Caire married Lillian Suich, a San Francisco beauty of Irish and Croatian background, beginning a family that would grow to five daughters in the next decade. In 1901 Arthur married Lillian's older sister, Mary. They had a son who bore the name Justinian after his grandfather and two daughters, Lucille and Miriam. All three, along with their five double cousins (and next-door neighbors) in the Fred Caire family, had a strong affectionate bond with Santa Cruz Island. This was particularly true of Justinian II, who worked at the island when it was in the Caire family and with the succeeding owners, the Stantons, to help ease the transition after the sale in the late 1930s. He remained a friend of the Stanton's son Carey and a frequent visitor to the island through the ensuing decades.

CHAPTER 4

The Caire Years on Santa Cruz Island Begin

In 1869, as Delphine was completing her education under the direction of her aunt Sophie in the convent on the outskirts of Paris, a letter arrived with the news that her father had bought a part interest in Santa Cruz Island. With California's burgeoning growth, a ranch with good access to sea transportation that could support tens of thousands of sheep and cattle to respond to the growing demand for meat, hides, and wool seemed like a sound investment.

In the following years, Delphine's role as her father's confidante meant that she closely shared the trials, tribulations, and eventual triumphs of his business dealings, especially relating to the early troubled years of the investment in the Santa Cruz Island Company. Although Caire had achieved a controlling interest in the company by 1880, he had never seen this investment for which he had fought so hard.

After their acquisition of the property in 1869, the directors of the French Savings Bank had received periodic reports on their island investment from Jean Baptiste Jouyaux, the superintendent in charge of running day-to-day operations, and from the company secretary, but none of the directors had visited the island. In the spring of 1880, now that the investment represented such a large part of his net worth, Caire decided to travel south to Santa Cruz Island and have a look for himself. He wanted to see firsthand what improvements could be made to increase the profitability of his asset. He asked his daughter Delphine and son Arthur to accompany him. Arthur's study of surveying and chemistry at the University of California would prove useful. He could contribute his scientific and drafting background and his mastery of the new art of photography to assess the present and future prospects of the island. Delphine's descriptive ability and eye for detail were probably what recommended her to her father for this trip. Caire enjoyed her company, and over the years he often confided in her.

Delphine was twenty-four and Arthur twenty-one when they boarded the steamship *Constantine* at the Pacific Mail dock in San Francisco for the trip to Santa Barbara. Half a century later, Delphine set down her thoughts and memories of that first trip to Santa Cruz Island.[1] Their father had traveled ahead, and after the overnight trip down the coast, Delphine and Arthur were met in Santa Barbara by the superintendent of the ranch, Mr. Joyaux. He ushered them on to the company's schooner, the *Star of Freedom,* and they set a course for the island.

Thus began the Caire family's direct involvement in the operation and development of Santa Cruz Island, a relationship that would last fifty-seven years and see the island change from an isolated, modest cattle operation to a largely self-supporting integrated agricultural complex, producing sheep meat, wool, beef, hides, and wine and providing both seasonal and continuous employment to scores of skilled and semi-skilled laborers from Santa Barbara County and beyond. When the Caires sailed into Prisoners' Harbor for the first time, the *Star of Freedom* tied up at the wharf that had been constructed in the late 1860s. It had been designed and built with the import and export of cattle and sheep in mind; hence, the entire length was fenced and the wharf ran perpendicular to the beach. It was connected to corrals into which livestock were driven and then held until they were moved along the wharf to the *Star of Freedom* or any other waiting vessel, such as one of the many steamers that plied the coast in those decades. In these early days, until Santa Barbara's Stearns Wharf was built in 1871, cattle for Santa Barbara were offloaded by pushing them over the side of the schooner and forcing them to swim to the shore. The sheep were herded on to lighters and landed on the beach.

The island superintendent would have had some transport ready when the schooner arrived to conduct the two young people up to the aptly named Main Ranch, perhaps using the British-built charabanc, or possibly the two-wheeled Petaluma cart that Justinian himself was later fond of driving. Proceeding up the Cañon del Puerto, as they followed the twists and turns of the creek that flowed from the mountainous country bordering the central valley of the island, Delphine remembered a natural beauty of

---

[1] Delphine Caire, "Journal," vol. 3.

heavily wooded precipitous slopes. She lamented their gradual degradation by livestock and thoughtless cutting of ancient trees for firewood and brush to use as temporary fences in sheep and cattle roundups. "Many a patriarchal tree fell to the axe of untrained woodcutters," she noted.[2]

The road, shaded for much of the three miles from the harbor to the Main Ranch, finally reached a cluster of buildings and corrals left by the previous owners. Delphine recalled two whitewashed single-story adobe houses, one for the superintendent who was in charge of the entire operation and one for the mayordomo who was in charge of the casual labor that was hired for roundups and sheep shearing. In front of the superintendent's house, with its covered veranda and shade tree, was a small garden enclosed with a simple wooden picket fence. Behind the house was a wooden building that later became the family dining room. In line with these buildings to the west were the kitchen, the men's dining room, and bunkhouses. Beyond these were corrals, wagon sheds, stables, and shearing sheds that were pressed into service during the twice yearly *corridas,* as the sheep roundups were called. All these building were located on the south bank of the creek, which ran down from the heights of the western end of the main valley. On the north bank of the creek were two buildings, one of which soon disappeared. The other was known as the bee house as it was occupied by a man who kept bees and who seemed to distinguish himself by mystifying Delphine or anyone who would listen by repeating, "My nose is my compass."[3] The building he occupied, later raised up and placed on foundation walls of masonry, became known as the *cantina vieja* (the old cellar), and according to Clifford McElrath, superintendent in the early 1920s, it was used for storing wine, particularly the watered-down wine (*piquette*) consumed by the ranch hands.[4]

At the time of this first visit to Santa Cruz Island by Justinian Caire, there were only six permanent hands, including two who were mostly employed to crew the *Star of Freedom.* There were two brothers, one of whom was in charge of the kitchen garden and orchard, while the other's duties included fetching water from the stream in a barrel on wheels to supply each of the buildings—kitchen, men's bunkhouse, and the houses of the superintendent and mayordomo. There was also a general handyman and wagon driver and a Chinese cook, whose meals were praised by Delphine and who tolerated no one else in the kitchen, neither permanent

---

[2] Delphine Caire, "Journal," vol. 3.

[3] Delphine Caire, "Journal," vol. 3.

[4] McElrath, *On Santa Cruz Island,* 7.

staff nor hired hands. The captain of the *Star of Freedom* lived with his wife and their child in a house at Prisoners' Harbor, and his second in command doubled as a carpenter when the occasion demanded.

When it came to sleeping arrangements, it was decided by Justinian that he and Arthur would sleep on folding beds at either end of the small building that later became the family dining room, whereas Delphine would sleep in the bedroom on the west side of the mayordomo's house. Every evening she would be accompanied to her room by her father, who would bid her good night and enjoin her to lock herself in securely.

The days passed quickly in extensive tours of inspection, with Delphine helping her brother in his surveying duties by holding the surveying rod and responding to his commands as he peered at his surveyor's compass. Once they had a complete measure of the principal features of the Main Ranch, they moved on to the Scorpion Ranch at the east end of the island. Because she was riding in the charabanc, Delphine could only go a little beyond the Rancho del Sur, less than halfway. At the time, there was no continuous wagon road to the east end, and only a horse trail traversed the entire distance. The wagon did not attempt the roughest part of the journey. Such was the steepness of the road that they took the precaution of strapping an outriding horse to the uphill side of the wagon to ensure that it did not roll over. Delphine recalled,

> We got out at the Campo de Melquiero, in a field strewn with myriad wild flowers of every hue. The mayordomo, Ramon Ayala, who remained with us, lit a fire . . . and using a long stick with a pointed tip as a spit, cooked a cut of lamb brought along for just such an improvised meal. This carne asada was for us a treat, and having had our fill, we were content to await the return of our riders with whom we went back to the Main Ranch.[5]

The next ranch to be visited was the West Ranch, later called the Christy Ranch, on the west end of the island. After some repairs to the road, it was judged fit to accommodate the charabanc, and Justinian, Delphine, and Arthur set off, driven by handyman John Griffin. At times the road was too steep and slippery and the passengers had to dismount and walk alongside the wagon. At the Christy Ranch, there was the *casa vieja* (old house) to be inspected. This two-story adobe structure, with its covered veranda similar to the superintendent's house at the Main Ranch, had been built by the previous regime, probably in the early 1860s. One of the interior walls had

---

[5] Delphine Caire, "Journal," vol. 3.

been decorated with an elaborate cross dated 1864. Delphine registered her disgust at the way the nearby Indian burial grounds had been desecrated, principally by the anthropologist from the Ethnographic Museum in Paris, Leon de Cessac. She lamented, "Having gathered the various specimens intended for exhibit at the Ethnographic Museum of the Trocadero Palace in Paris, instead of consigning again to the earth the bones he was not taking with him; our scientist . . . left them strewn on the ground as though they were the remains of the lowest animals."[6]

Justinian and his two children returned to the Main Ranch and remained there for several more weeks. Justinian used the time to draw up detailed maps and formulate his plans for the development of the Main Ranch, Prisoners' Harbor, Scorpion Ranch, Smugglers Cove, and Christy Ranch. The carefully drawn maps would allow him to pinpoint the exact location of a proposed improvement or new development in his correspondence with his superintendents. It was a strategy to create a complex agricultural operation that would build on what was there and turn it into a fully integrated profitable enterprise.

Justinian Caire threw himself into land husbandry. This domineering relationship to the land, prevalent in the nineteenth century, is often eclipsed nowadays by the passion for conservation of the natural world. But land husbandry, with its roots in the early pastoral vision of colonial America, was based on an older fervor for subduing nature and creating a controlled, fruitful environment in the face of an untamed howling wilderness. For religious Americans, it had the resonance of a new Garden of Eden where nature would be dominated, nurtured, and improved, and what better place to try and achieve this dream than on a relatively untouched island? Caire was completely entranced by this opportunity and resolved to make its development his life's work and to pass it on to his family so that generations to come might benefit from the fruits of his labor.

---

[6] Delphine Caire, "Journal," Vol. 3; Delphine Caire, "Memoirs, 1933," Caire Family Papers and Diaries. The French expedition under the Ministere de l'Instruction Publique was commissioned in 1877 to do research on the Channel Islands. The one member of the expedition to make it to San Francisco, M. Cessac, found that his partner had squandered the funds. "Alone in San Francisco, he made contact with the Santa Cruz Island Company, perhaps with fellow Frenchman Justinian Caire himself, and received an invitation to do research on the Island. Cessac excavated sites on Santa Cruz over a four-month period in 1877, making a series of important discoveries such as flint tools. He made a collection of four thousand artifacts which was sent to Paris, and also carried out an ethnographic study on the islands based on interviews at San Buenaventura Mission with the supposed last surviving natives of Santa Cruz and Santa Rosa Islands" (cited in Livingston, "Study," 771).

CHAPTER 5

Developing the Island I: Buildings and Water Systems

When the Caires took over Santa Cruz Island in 1880, it was already a working ranch, albeit one that was basic in its infrastructure and simple in its functioning. The sheep grazed in their herds except during the twice-yearly roundups, or corridas, which are described in detail later. The corridas were organized from the Main Ranch and the two out-ranches at either end of the island. After the sheep were collected, they were clipped and their wool sacked and shipped to the mainland, along with a number of the herd to be sold as meat. Aside from these periods of activity, the island remained quiet and tranquil, its physical aspect little changed from the time of Andres Castillero.

The earliest known illustration of the settlement in the island's central valley that would grow into what was named the Main Ranch is an 1855 watercolor that depicts a modest one-story adobe house with a veranda and another small adobe structure behind it. This painting by James Madison Alden also shows small cultivated fields between the buildings and the creek that flowed eastward down the valley. A photograph of the main ranch in 1869, the year the French Savings Bank directors purchased the island, shows the same single-story house, with a shade tree in front and a garden enclosed by a white picket fence. Most of the permanent island population gathered for the picture: three ranch hands in their overalls and one man in a suit, presumably the superintendent. As evidence of the working operation, there were also the necessary sheds and corrals for the ranching operation as it then existed. In the 1860s an adobe house was built at Prisoners' Harbor, along with a substantial wharf. At the westernmost ranch, Christy, there was a small square house with four rooms on the ground floor and a loft reached by an outside stairway. And at the eastern end of the island, at Scorpion Harbor, there were "a ranch house, corrals, shearing shed, two small fields under cultivation, and a well of brackish water."[1]

After the Caires' initial survey of the island, plans were made for the improvement of virtually every aspect of the existing operation. One of the first steps was creating a reliable and convenient water supply at the Main Ranch. Within a year or two of the Caires' first visit, a well had been sunk and wind power harnessed to fill a water tank on a raised platform that in turn supplied piped water to all the buildings. The former water carrier, his role now filled by pump, tank, and pipes, quit in disgust, noted Delphine. It was a new regime, and the pace of change on the island would quicken over the ensuing seventeen years.

Blueprints were drawn up for enlarging and remodeling the houses at the Main Ranch and at Prisoners' Harbor (also referred to as La Playa) in a French Mediterranean style that Caire found congenial. In the early 1880s, the two gables of the upper floor of the Prisoners' Harbor house were removed and the roof raised to allow for full-height bedrooms, which would open to a balcony running the length of the front of the house. The walls were strengthened by the addition of stone quoins in the four corners, shaped by skilled stonemasons whose work is still in evidence in the stonework of the chapel built early in the next decade. The green shuttered French doors of the bedrooms opened onto the balcony, with its iron railings wrought on the island by the newly hired resident blacksmith. In front of both this house and the one that would become the family residence at the Main Ranch were square gardens, surrounded on three sides by the same wrought iron fencing, this time fashioned in five-foot pickets. The gardens were a California version of the formal French garden, with paths setting off beds of old Paul Neyron roses, which supplied fragrant flower arrangements for the houses during the family visits of spring and late summer. Also included in the gardens were some of the Castilian roses that had flourished on Santa Cruz Island from time immemorial.

---

[1] "Annual Report, Santa Cruz Island, November 1, 1874–June 30, 1875," RG 23, Superintendent's File, 1866–1910, Santa Cruz Island Foundation, cited in Livingston, "Study," 525.

By the middle of the 1880s, the Main Ranch buildings included the two-story family residence, a superintendent's house (by this time with two stories), a bunk house, and a dining room for the hands. The number of workers swelled to several dozen to keep the development projects going; even more were added during the roundup, grape harvest, and winemaking seasons. The wood frame kitchen that sat behind the two main residences was remodeled into an office. Behind it, against the south bank of the valley and cut into the slope, Caire had a long building constructed from rubble rock and cement in 1887 to serve as a dining room and kitchen, later to be called the *comedor*. To the north of the houses, across the road, a small laundry building, garden house, and lath-covered seed house were constructed as well as an elaborate windmill that pumped water for the ranch from a well at that site. To the west of this complex of residences and their outbuildings, Caire had an adobe bunk house of three rooms built near the site of a former ranch shed. Further to the west, where a shearing shed (*trasquila*) and corrals had long stood, a complex of utilitarian ranch buildings rose. Closest to the residences and facing the main road toward the west, a large brick-faced horse barn was built in or before 1888, with wings stretching in either direction for saddle shop and tack room, blacksmith and carpenter shops, and tool storage. This barn sheltered dozens of horses for use on the ranch and had a living area for the stableman upstairs. Farther down the avenue a brick dairy barn accommodated a milking parlor for cows and a room for stallions on the west side. South of the dairy barn a covered sheep corral was added to the trasquila. On a south slope of the foothills near the trasquila, Caire had a two-story *matanza* (slaughterhouse) constructed in 1890; the upper floor was reached by an exterior stairway with wrought iron work typical of the finer island buildings. Corrals for sheep and cattle filled the area between the horse barn, dairy barn, and matanza.[2]

The expansion of the former superintendent's house added an upper story with three bedrooms at a cost of approximately $5,000 [$116,000] for labor and materials. This was now the house where Caire family members stayed when they visited the island, and there was a separate building for the family dining room. Enclosed by hedges and fencing, the house had a total of five bedrooms. According to Justinian and Albina's granddaughter and frequent guest, Maria Rossi Gherini, there were,

---

[2] Livingston, "Study," 504–505. Livingston amalgamates descriptions that are found in various sources, including Daily and Stanton, "Santa Cruz Island."

three upstairs rooms, all with French doors opening on the balcony. Downstairs at the center of the house was a sitting room and in each corner of the house was a bedroom opening into it, as well as on the outer porch. In the lower rear near the foot of the stairway was a small bathroom with running cold water. As occasion required, hot water from the kitchen could be brought in to take off the chill. . . . The family dining room, also separate from the main house was not far from the cook house. The important part of the houses was the front gardens—my grandparents' pride and joy. The house at Prisoners' Harbor was built for the use of anyone wanting to remain overnight, either before leaving the island or on arrival. Actually, I don't think it was much occupied at the time.[3]

That seems likely, as the more comfortable accommodations, and the company of other family members at the Main Ranch, were only three miles away up the Cañada del Puerto road. The residences, ranch buildings, and associated corrals formed the eastern and southern sides of the semi-enclosed great barnyard, approximately the size of a football field, bisected by the road that traversed most of the length of the island, leading toward its east and west ends. This was the Main Ranch, center of a world unto itself. A visitor in the 1890s described it as "a gem in the very heart of the island, surrounded by high mountains, invisible and unsuspected from the not far distant sea."[4]

---

[3] Maria Rossi Gherini, "Santa Cruz Island" (interview). Reproduced in Daily, *Santa Cruz Island Anthology*, 68.
[4] Holder, *Channel Islands*, 260–61, cited in Livingston, "Study," 509.

CHAPTER 6

Developing the Island II: Out Ranches

To organize the expansion of the business, Caire divided Santa Cruz Island into ten separate ranches, or centers of activity, that worked together to form an integrated operation. In addition to developing the Main Ranch and Prisoners' Harbor, Caire oversaw the founding or development of Christy Ranch, Scorpion Ranch, Smugglers Ranch, Forney's Cove/Rancho Nuevo, Poso Ranch, Buena Vista, Portezuela Ranch, and Sur Ranch.

The major out-ranch to exploit the agricultural potential of the eastern end of the island was at Scorpion Harbor, with a subsidiary ranch at Smugglers Cove to control ranching operations in the immediate area of the cove and its canyon. The men there spent months hauling stones out of the fields and piling them in stacks at scattered locations. By the end of 1885, the Scorpion Ranch had evolved into a busy and well-equipped colony. A road led from the harbor past a cave used for storing dairy products to a gate through which one entered the residential and shop area of the ranch. The old residence remained, with its garden and chicken yards. Across the road was a long line of small buildings, more or less one long building with ten rooms in a row, including a carpenter shop, blacksmith shop, bake oven, tool shed, bakery, granary, provision room, general store, matanza, and butcher shop. The corrals were divided into numerous large and smaller pens with gates, all carefully laid out for efficient operation during shearing and slaughter periods.

Main Ranch, ca. 1886.
Center left, first family house; the superintendent's house is to the right of it.
Photograph from glass plate negative by Arthur Caire.

A two-story adobe house was built at Scorpion Ranch in 1887 to replace earlier residence buildings from the Barron, Forbes and Company era. The Scorpion house had three rooms downstairs and two upstairs, which were reached by an exterior stairway located on the east end of the house. Its thick walls were constructed of a combination of low-fire brick, local stone, and mortar. The shed roof was raised at the south elevation to enlarge the upstairs rooms. The lifting of the roof in this manner required the framing and shingling of a wedge of wall space, which decreased the roof's slope and created a curious look to the building.[1]

At nearby Smugglers Ranch, a house and outbuildings were constructed around 1885, but it was not until a masonry building was built in 1889–1890 that the ranch became a permanent settlement; even then the place did not remain settled full-time for long. In these development years, Smugglers Ranch acted as a site of orchards and grape vines. Justinian Caire noticed the

---

[1] Livingston, "Study," 526, 531.

Scorpion Ranch: preparing for the corrida, ca. 1900.

temperate climate at Smugglers Cove and encouraged experimentation with various vines and trees. In December 1884 he imported 2,000 cuttings of *Vitis rupestris* grapes from the mainland with the plan that they would be grafted the following year with cuttings of Sicilian origin. The objective was to eventually produce a Marsala-type fortified wine, and there was much talk in the correspondence of 1887 about planting, pruning, and nurturing the vines.

Smugglers Ranch acted as an adjunct to Scorpion Ranch, which was in turn an outpost of the Main Ranch. After a great deal of expenditure in developing Smugglers Ranch, the company evidently found its operation to be unnecessary or inefficient. At the height of its development, Smugglers Ranch had three residences, a bakery, a barn of fair size, a blacksmith shop, a water system, a vineyard, a vegetable garden, and orchards of walnuts, olives, and other fruit. A good road led to the ranch from Scorpion Valley. Yet at some time around the turn of the century, the ranch was deemed a failure. Most likely neither the olive orchard nor the other fruits and nuts growing in the valley were plentiful enough to make a profit. The vineyard was not enlarged. Some have suggested that the ranch was built as an experiment and did not pass the test.[2]

---

[2] Livingston, "Study," 549–55.

Smugglers Ranch, 1880s.
Photograph from glass plate negative by Arthur Caire.

The other out-ranches were situated to the west of the Main Ranch. A map from 1890 shows a small ranch complex fronting the beach at Forney's Cove, the westernmost extent of the island. It had a ranch house, foreman's quarters, storeroom, sheep corrals, hog pen, pump reservoir, stable, and two hay barns (*zacaterias*). Some years later the Rancho Nuevo was developed two miles east of the older ranch with wood scavenged from Punta West Ranch. It boasted a two-story ranch house, stable, chicken house, and barn, all laid out in a rectangular fenced enclosure with the buildings acting as corners.

The Christy Ranch at the west end of the island was enlarged early on to take advantage of the miles of wide *potreros* (pastures), which end in bluffs facing the Santa Rosa Channel. At first called the West Ranch, it eventually took the name Christy in the early years of development. Caire had the fields expanded wherever possible and zacaterias built to protect the cut clover, alfalfa, and other forage crops from the weather. At this ranch, Caire found at least one house and some corrals. He had the ranch developed into one of the two major out-ranches of the company. The old house,

Shearing in the trasquila at Christy Ranch, 1929.

built in or before 1864 and known later as the Casa Vieja or Casa la Cruz, acted as the centerpiece of the ranch, although a larger residence was built south of the creek before 1890. When it was fully developed, Christy Ranch boasted a second residence and a store house across the creek, blacksmith shop, carpenter shop, stables, saddle and harness room, storage shed, hay barns, a well and a windmill with storage tank, and a complement of sheep corrals, hog pens, and horse corrals. Ranch workers developed vegetable gardens, corn and hay fields, and a wagon road that passed through on the way to Punta West. The new residence on the south side of the creek was of a similar design to the two-story residences constructed at Scorpion and Smugglers ranches at about the same time. In the early years of the twentieth century, the Caires occasionally travelled to Christy to stay the night in the two-story house. As late as the 1920s, there was a full-time crew of men and a cook there, occupying the old house that was used as a bunk house.

Other developments were on a simpler scale. On the southwest shore of the island there was the so-called the Poso Ranch, named for the canyon in which it stood—a complex including corrals and a shearing shed was drawn on the map. No actual ranch was ever built, though perhaps in anticipation, a grove of Italian Cypresses was planted there.

Located near the top of the pass, or Centinela, leading from the central valley to the western ranches, was Buena Vista. It was not a true out-ranch; rather, it consisted of a cabin built in the 1880s or 1890s while the road to the West Ranch was being constructed. It later housed *vaqueros* (cowboys) who found it a convenient stopping place between the Main Ranch and Christy Ranch.

Portezuela Ranch was located at the southern edge of a picturesque and productive upper extension of the central valley west of the Main Ranch. Developed in 1885, it consisted of a house, kitchen, stables, and a well, with corrals, holding pens, and newly cleared fields in the vicinity. By 1890 the ranch had grown and featured a new house, stables, three hay barns, a wood shed, and a hog or sheep pen. A vegetable garden and a vineyard appeared on the map of 1890 as well, watered by a pump near the creek. Pruning the Portezuela vines was mentioned in a letter to the superintendent in December 1897.

At the Main Ranch the adobe and rubble main house resembled those at Scorpion, Smugglers, and Christy ranches and was built at about the same time. The long comedor building, partially built into the hillside, acted as a dining room, kitchen, and carpenter shop and consisted of an adobe walled section and a log cabin.

Beyond the Main Ranch to the east about two miles was Rancho Sur. This small out-ranch comprised a wood frame dormitory moved from the Main Ranch; a building constructed in 1891 that housed a kitchen, dining room, and storeroom; a stable; and lavatories with a bell next to them. The exact use of Rancho Sur is unknown, but in the Teens and 1920s, the Caire family enjoyed riding horses to the ranch, where a barbecue had been built and a trail provided access to the beach.[3]

Many of the ranch buildings were constructed of adobe bricks that were made in the traditional way: they were fashioned of island clay and then set out in forms to bake in the sun. But Caire also had more permanent, taller structures in mind, and for these he required kiln-fired bricks and lime mortar. The two kilns—one at the Main Ranch for supplying bricks and the other at Prisoners' Harbor for making lime for mortar—operated through the 1880s and 1890s to provide building materials for the stables, the chapel, and the winery buildings at the Main Ranch as well as for the

---

[3] Livingston, "Study," 559–62. He cites an interview conducted with my mother, Vivienne Caire Chiles.

warehouses at Prisoners' Harbor. The number of bricks made in 1887 alone was 185,000—at a cost of $1,284 [$29,000].[4]

The sheep on Santa Cruz Island were already well established, but Justinian Caire improved the stock. Spanish merinos had been introduced earlier, and Caire added pure-bred Rambouillet merinos from France and other breeds from England. It is likely that the Barron, Forbes Company had introduced Mexican cattle to the island during their ownership but that Caire had those cattle eradicated and replaced by imported Durham cattle. In years of good or average rainfall, pasturage for the livestock could be found in all parts of the island, particularly in the lush Cañada de los Sauces del Oeste near the Christy Ranch, along the rolling Potrero Norte stretching eastward from Prisoners' Harbor, and on the flats westward between the foothills that made up the northern range and its natural edge on the channel coast. There were also great fields flanking the road to the Sur Ranch east of the central valley that later became acres of vineyard land. It was said that the salt-laden winds from the surrounding sea seasoned the forage so that the meat from the sheep and cattle had a particular flavor similar to that of French livestock that fed in the salty meadows of Brittany and the coasts of the Bay of Biscay. Over the years it was noted that the livestock had no interest in salt licks, having it naturally available from the salt-tinged grasses and, where there was access, from the rocks that lined the shore.[5]

In these early days, Scorpion and Smugglers ranches also played their part as sources of forage and experiments in growing olives, vines, and other Mediterranean crops. Because of the difficulties of land communication between the east end and the Main Ranch, which were cut off from each other by the transverse range called the Montañon, much of the animal feed and wheat was transported by sea to Prisoners' Harbor and then moved by wagon to where it was needed.

Horses were central to the island enterprise. They had been imported by previous regimes, including at least one pair of carriage horses that was used to pull the English-made charabanc. This vehicle, which was left by the Barron, Forbes Company, was a main source of transportation for family outings in the early days. There are many photographs of the charabanc

[4] Santa Cruz Island Company records, 1887, Caire Family Papers, in the author's possession.
[5] Helen Caire, *Santa Cruz Island*, 72.

loaded with half a dozen Caire adults and children setting off for a day at Prisoners' Harbor or some other picnic destination, the women in their voluminous skirts and picture hats, the children in knickerbockers, white blouses, and lace-up boots. Horses also had more serious purposes on a working ranch. Heavy draft horses were used for plowing and to pull the wagons needed for moving materials around the island. Saddle horses were essential for roundups and corridas as well as for maintaining contact with various parts of the island. In 1915, even though tractors and trucks had begun to appear, an inventory showed 129 horses on Santa Cruz Island, though by 1926 this number had shrunk to 83.

Communication across such geographically complicated terrain was a perennial problem. The ride from the Main Ranch to Scorpion or Christy could take half a day, but the newly invented telephone technology promised a solution. Beginning in 1885, Justinian Caire had men at work stringing the wires for what was said to be the largest known private telephone communication system in the United States, with hand-cranked telephones powered by 1.5-volt batteries. There was a line run three miles north to the caretaker's house at Prisoners' Harbor, ten miles west to the office at Christy Ranch, and ten miles east following the old trail over the Montañon to Scorpion Ranch. The lines were light, rust-resistant galvanized wire manufactured in England. They were magnetically charged, primed by a crank operated at the transmitting end, which provided a medium in which to send voice signals through the solid wire. "Each ranch was assigned a number of rings to identify it," remembered Helen Caire, "so if [their] number sounded the foreman at that place would pick up."[6] Although voice quality was variable and dependent on the vagaries of weather and maintenance, the phone system provided a workable solution for almost a century, lasting well into the Stanton era.

As important as the telephone system may have been, most communication on the island was via the network of roads and trails. Given the need to import anything that could not be manufactured on the island and to export island products from the only harbor with a significant wharf, the most heavily traveled road was the one that ran up the Cañada del Puerto from Prisoners' Harbor to the Main Ranch. About three miles long, it was laid out in the early ranching era under Barron, Forbes Company; like the

---

[6] Helen Caire, *Santa Cruz Island*, 68.

other roads on the island, it was improved in the early Caire period. The Cañada del Puerto road ended at a T-junction facing the family residence at the Main Ranch. From this junction, the main road stretched east and west toward the two ends of the island. Beyond the western end of the expanse of the barnyard, the Camino del Carro followed the ridgeline of the Colorados to Christy Ranch, eleven miles as the crow flies, adding several miles more for the necessary curves demanded by the rugged topography.

Where erosion in the canyons caused regular washouts of the road, Caire directed dry stone walls to be built. Reflecting the building skills the craftsmen had learned in the European countries of their birth, these nicely fitted walls have stood for more than 130 years. The eastward direction from the T-junction of the Main Ranch, the Camino del Este ran about two miles to the Sur Ranch at the waist of the island and then turned into a horse trail leading to Scorpion and Smugglers ranches.

Communication with the mainland was by boat. In recognition of the scale of the Santa Cruz Island operation, a post office was established at Prisoners' Harbor in 1895, with Arthur Caire as postmaster. Mail franked with the designation "La Playa" was received and dispatched from this post office for eight years until it was discontinued in 1903.

Throughout the American West of the nineteenth century, water was the great determinant of development. As the best watered of the Channel Islands, Santa Cruz Island showed great potential with its five streams that flowed throughout the year in the central valley. But the Barron, Forbes Company regime had lacked a water system to deliver it to the places where it was needed. With his customary energy and ingenuity, Caire set about remedying this situation, tapping into springs near the Main Ranch and storing this water in a 26,000-gallon concrete reservoir covered by a pitched wooden roof.

An extensive water system evolved to serve the Main Ranch complex. Caire had numerous springs developed with reservoirs and pipelines for domestic use and irrigation. The Pato system was located east of the ranch complex in the Matanza Potrero; it included a reservoir that fed the kitchen residence, garden faucets, and winery. The Gallina system crossed the creek with suspension cables and supplied garden faucets and a storage tank. The Cistern system supplied the vegetable garden and was eliminated in 1911. The Dindo system provided water for the stable, trasquila, matanza, and other ranch faucets. The old windmill pumped from a well to the main house, superintendent's house, kitchen and dining room, and dormitory. The system was modified in 1911 and 1914 when the new frame residence was constructed. A hot water system served the kitchen, superintendent's dining room and bathroom, and a washstand at the barracks. Numerous reservoirs provided water for irrigation in the vineyards and fields of the central valley.[7]

The main supply was from a spring in the canyon to the west of the Main Ranch called *El Pato* (the duck), which flowed into the central valley from the northern range. There were collecting tanks and rock dams at three other springs—the Gallina, the Dindos, and the Peacock—from where the water flowed by gravity through pipes to the Main Ranch or, later, to the winery and to some of the fields. At the east end of the island, and in other places where the water supply was less predictable, wells were sunk. At Scorpion Ranch the well was hand dug and lined with rock to a depth of around thirty-five feet, its water raised by windmill to a concrete reservoir.

---

[7] Livingston, "Study," 505.

CHAPTER 7

Diversification into Wine

Four years into his initial development plan, Caire began diversifying away from a strict ranching operation when he had the first Santa Cruz Island vineyard planted. The "president," as Caire was called by his superintendents, judged that the climate and soil of the central valley and parts of Scorpion Ranch were favorable for the cultivation of wine grapes and hence saw the original 4,000 vine cuttings set out in December 1884.[1]

It was a difficult time to contemplate entering the wine business. In the 1870s the deadly phylloxera parasite destroyed 75 percent of France's vineyards and attacked all the other wine-growing countries of Europe. At first it seemed that the California vineyards would be spared, and the winemakers of the Napa and Sonoma valleys imagined that they would profit from the misfortune of the Europeans. But the French market for California wines never developed, and by the 1880s the vineyards of Northern California were themselves in the grip of the parasite.[2] Seventy-five thousand acres of Northern California vineyards were ravaged and many fortunes destroyed. To make matters worse, the boom in wine production was never matched by the same rise in consumption levels, and prices plunged. But Caire was not dismayed. By the time he was planting his vineyards, the vine *vitis rupestris*, a phylloxera-resistant American root stock, had been identified. European varietals could be grafted on to this stock to achieve

---

[1] Santa Cruz Island Company to the Superintendent, 4 December 1884, Correspondence to and from Superintendents, 1880–1904, Santa Cruz Island Company Records, in the author's possession (hereafter cited as Correspondence, 1880–1904, Santa Cruz Island Co.).

[2] The parasite infects the roots of the vines, creating nodes inhabited by lice, starving the roots below the node of nutrients and killing the plant in the process.

the high-quality product he was aiming for. In addition, the planting he was doing in 1884 and 1885 would not come to full production until the beginning of the following decade, by which time it was expected that the market would have recovered. By 1895 there were more than 86,000 gallons of wine maturing at the winery. And as luck would have it, the infestation did not cross the Santa Barbara Channel, so the Santa Cruz Island vineyard, which would grow to almost two hundred acres, was spared.

Though the new vineyards on the island escaped the phylloxera infestation, there were other pests that attacked them, notably the wild hogs. When it came to fencing, Justinian Caire, for reasons best known to him, resisted the near-universal western fashion for barbed wire and opted for smooth wire instead. For a 250-pound boar, this was an open invitation to charge between the wires into the vineyards. Guards were posted at night, particularly at the time of the fall harvest, and they roamed between the vines with a gun or a long lance and a dog following the scent; nevertheless, with so many acres to protect the damage was sometimes prodigious.

Company records list vine stocks selected from France: the reds included Cabernet Sauvignon, Pinot Noir, Petite Sirah, Malbec, Cantal Mataro, and Hock; the whites were Muscat Frontignan, Chablis (Chardonnay), and Riesling.[3] The whites were sold with their varietal names, but the reds were often sold as generic "Burgundy" following the custom of the time for nonspecific varietals. Some of the cuttings were said to have come from Justinian Caire's old acquaintance Charles Lefranc, who owned a vineyard in Saratoga for which he imported vine cuttings from France. Caire reportedly also purchased some of the original vines planted on the island from Charles Krug.[4] In all probability, the island's white wines kept their varietal names because of their high quality. Referring to the island whites, one expert asserted, "few people in California at the time were growing anything better than Caire's Burger and Riesling."[5]

As the years went on, certain varietals were given vineyard designate status, like the Riesling called "Vuelta Dorada," which referred to the bend in the road through a part of the vineyard where the setting sun made it glow with a golden light. Other parts of the vineyard were given exotic or descriptive names, such as "Asiatic," "Africano," "Mission," and "Church." For more

---

[3] The subject of the island's wine is discussed in detail in Pinney, *Wine of Santa Cruz Island.*

[4] Livingston, "Study," 563, citing a memo from Jeanne Caire.

[5] Pinney, *Wine of Santa Cruz Island,* 33.

than twenty years the wine was sold in bulk to distributors in Santa Barbara, San Francisco, and Los Angeles. Labels designed by Arthur Caire for the time when the company would sell directly into the lucrative bottled wine market pictorially told the story of the Santa Cruz Island Company. A circle of vines surmounted by a rustic cross enclosed a view of the schooner in Prisoners' Harbor with a ewe, a lamb, and a woolsack in the foreground. A banner below proclaimed Santa Cruz Island and Santa Barbara County California. Based on company records, the yearly production averaged 42,000 gallons, though there was more in the better years, such as 1910 when 95,000 gallons were produced. An inventory of the wine cellar on the island by the San Francisco distributor in 1912 calculated almost 160,000 gallons on hand, about 90 percent of it red wine. The varietals mentioned in the report were Zinfandel, Mataro, Grenache, Burgundy, Carignan, Trousseau, Muscat, Riesling, Bordele, Burger, and Sauvignon, giving a snapshot of a changing pattern of the vineyards on Santa Cruz Island.[6]

Soon, along the foothills of the Colorados bordering the Main Ranch and extending east more than halfway to the Sur, the bright green symmetry of the rows of growing vines provided a pleasing contrast to the wildness of the red-gold peaks above. In the district where the Burgundy vines grew high above the bank of the Cañada del Medio creek, a thick hedge of wild roses bloomed through the summer. In the time of the harvest, as the vineyard workers cut bunches of grapes and threw them into the stacked boxes, the pale pink flowers of the roses were replaced by the red of thick clusters of rose hips. A small building on the north side of the valley facing the residence compound, called the bee house and dating from the time of the earlier regime, was pressed into service as the first winery and cellar, or *cantina,* before its replacement by the new winery buildings and their water supply, which were completed in 1893.

It would appear that generally the wines were held in oak casks for two years before release to the market, and the cellar contained stocks of wine from many different years, sometimes blended at the specific request of either Arthur or Frederic Caire. As for the quality of the Santa Cruz Island wines, the general conditions for viticulture were good to excellent, the vine stock was of the finest, and the winemakers and cellar men were the

---

[6] Ciocca-Lombardi Wine Co. to Santa Cruz Island Company management, 18 January 1912, Correspondence of the Santa Cruz Island Company, 1912, Santa Cruz Island Company Records, in the author's possession; and Pinney, *Wine of Santa Cruz Island,* 66.

Vineyard and workers, Main Ranch, ca. 1910.
Photograph from glass plate negative by Arthur Caire,
courtesy of Justinian Caire III.

Winery as part of Main Ranch, ca. 1900.
Photograph from glass plate negative by Arthur Caire.

Santa Cruz Island wine label.

best that could be found in order to produce wines of superior quality. For example, the Zinfandel was noted for being a full-bodied wine, fermented to dryness, with a higher alcohol content—qualities sought after in many of today's top Zinfandels. From family lore, as well as company records, one can assume that the market enthusiastically accepted Santa Cruz Island wines. In San Francisco, the St. Hubert Vineyard Company was the agent for Santa Cruz Island wines, and from 1912 to 1918, the Ciocca-Lombardi Wine Company was the primary northern California customer. Records show that in 1912 they bought 224,000 gallons of red wine—Zinfandel, Burgundy, Carignan, Bordelaise, Mataro, and others—from a variety of years; in 1913 they bought 111,000 gallons of the same mix of wines. Their buying was reduced to 27,000 gallons in 1914, and Arthur noted the competitive advantage of mainland producers who shipped their wine in tank cars rather than in the puncheons and barrels of an earlier era.[7] In Los

---

[7] Correspondence and Receipts for the Account of Ciocca Lombardi Wine Co., Correspondence to and from Superintendents and Other Clerical Personnel, 1906–1924, Santa Cruz Island Company Records, in the author's possession (hereafter cited as Correspondence, 1906–1924, Santa Cruz Island Co.).

Angeles, the West Glendale Winery was an early buyer, along with Italian Vineyard Company of Cucamonga and the Los Angeles Wine Company. Closer to home was L. Cerf and Company of Ventura. A local direct customer was the Raffour House Hotel on City Hall Plaza in Santa Barbara, to whom the island also sold turkeys at Christmas time. The Raffour purchases in the first decade of the twentieth century averaged 275 gallons a year. Larger deliveries took place in 84-gallon (318-liters) puncheons, and the smaller in barrels of 31.5 gallons (119 liters). The correspondence with these companies and customers was carried on in the native language of the proprietor—French, English, or Italian.

A distinctive feature of the early days of the vineyards was the positioning and building of a small chapel in a part of the vineyard on the north side of the central valley opposite the main family residence. Building the Chapel of the Holy Cross was a project that Justinian Caire had nurtured for several years, and Delphine was convinced that he wanted to create it as a memento of the chapels that dotted the slopes of his native French Alps. The chapel was truly a Santa Cruz Island project: local materials were lovingly worked by craftsmen whose constructions spoke for the scores of immigrant workers who called the island home for some period in their lives. As had been the case with the warehouses at Prisoners' Harbor and the stables at the Main Ranch, an expert French mason made the red bricks from island clay fired nearby and the mortar from lime found on the island and fired at Prisoners' Harbor. The island stone for the entrance archway, arched window frames, and carved stone quoins for the corners was worked by a highly able Italian stonemason. The windows on the north side of the chapel began halfway up the wall because of concern that this was the weather side facing the hill above, and in a storm there might be a landslip that would damage that side of the chapel. On the less vulnerable south side of the chapel, facing the family residence, the windows attained the full height of the side wall. The wrought iron railing in the interior that separates the nave from the sanctuary was the work of a master Sicilian ironworker.

At 27 feet by 18 feet, with side walls 13 feet high and end walls rising to 23 feet, this was a triumph of rustic ecclesiastical architecture in miniature. Caire had the initials DOM carved above the door as they are on many Italian churches. Above these a cross was carved in the stone, the same symbol that was chiseled on every alternate quoin. The little belfry with its bell and cross above completed the structure. The white plastered internal walls rose to a gently vaulted ceiling, painted blue and adorned with the stars that decorate so many Italian chapels. A plain raised wooden altar with a tabernacle surmounted by a simple dark wood cross faced the congregation. This was a family chapel, with an absolute capacity of worshippers of twenty-five to thirty, but a large open area just outside the double doors allowed for expansion of the chapel's congregation. Having overcome the ecclesiastical objections of the diocese of Los Angeles based on a misunderstanding of ownership and access, it was at last completed. The sixty-four-year-old Caire gazed contentedly from his house across the valley at the chapel set amongst the new vines, and he framed a question to Delphine that spoke volumes about how his mind worked. In the Franco-Italian patois of the Caire family, he asked her, "*Ne dirait-on pas un prese-pio?*" (Wouldn't you say that it was like a little Nativity setting?).[8]

The consecration of the chapel and its first services were conducted in 1891 by Father Genna, a San Francisco–based Sicilian Jesuit from Arthur's alma mater, St. Ignatius College. Justinian's sister-in-law Aglaë had sent hand-embroidered altar cloths from Paris in response to hearing her brother-in-law speak about the construction of the chapel. For her part, Albina wanted to ensure a warm welcome and good attendance at the mission that Father Genna was to run for the men. Coming from European countries where the Catholic Church was strongly associated by the peasantry with the forces of reaction and repression, many of the men had been raised in the countervailing tradition of anticlericalism and mistrust of the Catholic Church. Albina went to their dining room while they were eating and urged them to attend this mission, which was being given as much for them as the family. She was listened to respectfully, and over the days that the Jesuit was on the island the family attended services in the morning, but after the day's work was over, the chapel was strictly for the men's mission; the sermons and prayers were intended only for them. Genna took his pastoral duties seriously and pressed a sleepy Fred Caire into service as an altar boy for the early morning masses, despite the fact that the young Caire had been up a good bit of the previous nights supervising the loading of sheep onto one of the coastal steamers.

---

[8] Delphine A. Caire to Fr. Charles Philipps, 23 November 1936, cited by Helen Caire, *Santa Cruz Island*, 178, and by Daily, *Chapel of the Holy Cross*.

During the days Genna busied himself visiting the men at their work in the vineyard and elsewhere to speak with them about returning to the faith of their childhoods. At the conclusion of the mission, there was the ceremony of benediction with the Ave Maria sung in a fine contralto voice by Justinian Caire's youngest daughter, Hélène. A large mission cross, fashioned by one of the island carpenters, was carried by the men in procession through the vineyard, with hymns and prayers, and set up as a memorial. A glass plate photograph by Arthur commemorates the event. Father Genna stands in the decorated doorway of the chapel, flanked by thirty-nine ranch hands in their dark "city" clothes, gazing somberly at the camera from under their broad-brimmed hats. The sun shines down on the little chapel set among the rows of six-year-old, head-pruned vines. Standing about three feet high, the vines march away toward the horizon under a cloudless sky.

CHAPTER 8

The Vision Completed

As part of his long-range plan, Justinian Caire recognized that the Santa Cruz Island Company had to diversify from sheep and cattle if it wanted to survive and prosper. As with all Caire's investments in the agriculture and infrastructure of Santa Cruz Island, the investments were for the long run, with Caire confident that his various markets would return to a positive cycle, and he and his descendants would reap the benefits.

The development work continued under the watchful eyes of Justinian and his two sons. Two years before the chapel was built, Justinian and Delphine went to Europe, spending time in France, Italy, and Switzerland; mixing business and pleasure; seeing friends and relatives; and concluding some affairs that he had been unsuccessfully trying to resolve from a distance. Once these issues had been dealt with, Justinian and Delphine found themselves back in Paris, where the 1889 World Exposition was taking place. Held to celebrate the 100th anniversary of the beginning of the French Revolution, the exposition covered almost a square kilometer, including its most famous symbol, the Eiffel Tower. The various parts of the exposition were linked by a narrow-gauge railway with open cars named after the town where it was manufactured, Decazeville. Caire was much taken with the system, which was designed to be used in industrial and manufacturing sites, such as coal mines, where space was at a premium. With an eye to the future development of Santa Cruz Island, Caire ordered a system to be installed at Prisoners' Harbor connecting the pier with the double warehouse that had been built two years before to store wool during a period of low prices.[1] For years afterward, the flatbed cars were used to transport the bales of wool and barrels of wine from the warehouse out to the end of the pier, where they could be loaded onto the company schooner or one of the passing steamers that called regularly at the island.

There was another errand that Caire wanted to accomplish in Paris: he wanted to acquire a grand table service of twenty-four settings for the island. He and Delphine visited the Paris headquarters of the firm Baccarat, and failing to find anything that he liked, Caire decided to have a service made to order. A man of simple tastes, he favored fine white china without any of the gilding fashionable at the time, but all the same he wanted a table service and glassware that was strongly identified with the island. He commissioned one of the Baccarat designers to create a decoration of a rustic cross flanked by two Chumash Indians. Delphine recalled that although her father was satisfied with the result, the rest of the family reacted skeptically to the design, which they referred to behind his back as the "service of the cross." Rendered in gray and black, the two Chumash figures of the French designer's imagination rather resembled two mourning women huddled by a rough cross. The same representation was etched into the glassware, and the total impression was not calculated to instill much *joie de vivre* around the dinner table. Consequently, it was used very infrequently at island dinners over the years.

After a stay of a few days in Paris, father and daughter set off for Germany, where they called on a business colleague in Hamburg, then traveled back to Le Havre by way of Cologne and Coblenz before catching their ship back to New York. After a trip across the continent that took in Niagara Falls, Canada, and Michigan, they arrived back home in time for Christmas 1889.

The development of the island continued. One of the early vintages was maturing in the vats, and the price of wool was recovering from the slump of the mid-1880s. It was at about this time that the Caires began a program of flood and erosion control. This system consisted of creek diversions and rock wall construction as a way to stem damage to fields and structures and to make more efficient use of bottom lands. Beginning in the early 1880s and continuing for about twenty-five years, the company expended a tremendous number of man-hours reshaping the creek beds, building rock retaining walls, and installing check dams in smaller creeks and drainages all over the island.

---

[1] Helen Caire, *Santa Cruz Island*, 65.

The labor force expanded to a size never seen before or since. As of September 1889, there were 110 workers on Santa Cruz Island. Seventy were working at the Main Ranch, and ten were at Smugglers Ranch. There were fourteen at Scorpion Ranch, eight at West Ranch, and eight at Portezuela. With this size workforce there was a substantial turnover of personnel. In all, approximately 1,300 workers spent time on the island between 1884 and 1906. Predictably, the highest turnover was among general laborers, many of them immigrants who applied at the San Francisco office and were sent down to Santa Barbara without ever having seen the ranch or island and with no idea of what they were getting into. The payroll book for the years 1884–1889 reveals that with a few exceptions, all the permanent ranch workers' names at this time were Italian. By way of contrast, all of the more seasonal specialized vaquero and shearer names were of Spanish/Californio derivation.

Over this period there were thirty-four job titles listed in the company records, ranging from superintendent and majordomo to driver and laborer. But perhaps underscoring the exceptional nature of the island and the expanse of Justinian Caire's ambitions, there were masons, cellar men, farriers, dairymen, charcutier, stonecutters, warehousemen, and sailors. Not only were there numerous job titles on the island to be filled, there was an elaborate system of noting on what grounds employees were terminated. They were "thanked," "left voluntarily and honorably," were "dismissed," or "discharged." All these designations had different implications about whether the employee would ever be considered for employment again. The superintendents were expected to report on the men's conduct to the head office in San Francisco. To be discharged or dismissed meant that the person in question should never be taken back.[2] Discipline was strict and the overall setup paternalistic, but on the whole it was not much different from comparable ranches of the time, considering the isolated nature of the setting. It was a world that would suit a certain type of worker, and those who found it congenial stayed for years, or returned seasonally year after year, passing the jobs from father to son.

The tree planting program initiated by Caire continued apace. Overseen by Delphine, seedlings were nurtured in the large lath house at the Main Ranch. Groves of blue gum eucalyptus were planted as windbreaks

[2] Santa Cruz Island Company Payroll Book 1889–1893, cited in Livingston, "Study," 616–20.

Vegetable garden, Main Ranch, ca. 1900.
Photograph from a glass plate negative by Arthur Caire.

to the west and east of the Main Ranch and at the other ranches, growing quickly in the favorable island climate. Monterey pines and cypresses
were also planted in the central valley and around the out-ranches. A nut
grove of almost 500 walnut and almond trees was laid out as part of the
Main Ranch, along with a fruit orchard of peach, apricot, pear, apple, fig,
orange, and lemon trees. A largely experimental olive grove and vineyard
were planted at Smugglers Ranch. Around the family compound were ole-
anders, pepper trees, acacias, locusts, and Italian stone pines. The first of
these pines was planted at the edge of the compound from a seed Albina
brought from Italy. It grew to a tremendous height, and the bench built
around its trunk had to be periodically enlarged over the years. This bench
served as a focus for outdoor socializing and singing, particularly after dinner on fine summer evenings. Often the concluding song at the time, and at
family gatherings for decades afterward, was "Bon Soir, Mes Amis."

The expanded scale of the operation now required a larger vessel that
could reliably carry a number of livestock or other island produce, such

The schooner *Santa Cruz* in Prisoners' Harbor, ca. 1920.

as wool and wine. The *Star of Freedom*, which had been part of the purchase of the island, might take all day to cross the channel if the wind was against her. To develop the business it was imperative to acquire a larger, faster vessel with auxiliary power to deal with adverse wind conditions. Caire turned to the master shipwright of the west coast, Matthew Turner, commissioning him to build the schooner *Santa Cruz*. Launched in May 1893 at Turner's Benicia yards, she was 64 feet in length and 18.6 feet in the beam. With her gasoline-powered engine, she could be relied on to cross the channel in less than four hours, the captain setting his course due south from Santa Barbara Harbor, aiming at the V-shaped dip in the ridge line of the northern range behind Prisoners' Harbor. Fully loaded, the *Santa Cruz* could carry 200 to 250 head of sheep—enough to fill a rail car—or fifteen to twenty head of cattle, which was sufficient for the local market. And following Caire's injunction to Turner to "build her strong," she was easily capable of managing the channel in all weathers and of making the run down the coast with island wine or other produce for Los Angeles.

The main outlines of the development plan envisioned by Justinian Caire the businessman and investor were now in place. The Santa Cruz Island Company was a going concern with income streams from sheep, cattle, wool, and wine. For 1880, an estimate of the gross income from the wool clip was $40,000 [$837,000].[3] Even in 1881, a dry year in which adverse weather conditions forced a reduction in the sheep herd, the island shipped 14,500 sheep and showed a profit of $6,567 [$137,000] on revenues of $21,000 [$439,000].[4] In 1882, 12,000 sheep were shipped to meat packers in San Francisco. Between 1885 and 1896, the average yearly clip yielded approximately 800 sacks of wool. In spring 1894, livestock shipments brought income of $1,641 [$42,000]. Near Christmas the same year, there were shipments of ducks, geese, turkeys, and chickens.[5] Justinian Caire's investment was paying off. Delphine spoke of the family's relief in May 1886 on hearing that her father, with the help of the island income, had cleared all his lingering debts from the French Savings Bank debacle of the previous decade. The listing of dividends for 1887 showed the president being awarded over $49,000 [$1.1 million]; for 1890, $34,000 [$830,000]; and for 1891, over $30,000 [$732,000].

Just as important for Justinian Caire, the family man, he and his wife, their six children, and their many grandchildren had a unique paradise in which to enjoy themselves. As Justinian expressed it to a local newspaper, "I have bought the property with my money as a heritage to my children. I have spent a great deal in the way of improvements and love to go there myself and enjoy the quiet [of the] place."[6] Here was a man who was looking forward to his family continuing to get pleasure and economic benefit from his legacy. Unfortunately, his wife would live to see that ambition completely thwarted.

---

[3] Superintendent Joyaux to Justinian Caire, 20 January 1880, Correspondence, 1880–1904, Santa Cruz Island Co.

[4] Memorandum by Superintendent Joyaux, February 1882, Correspondence, 1880–1904, Santa Cruz Island Co.

[5] Wool Clip Records, Shearing Records, Santa Cruz Island Co. Records. The ledger records break down the different types of sheep sheared and where they were rounded up on the Island (cited in Livingston, "Study," 581).

[6] *Santa Barbara (Calif.) Daily Independent*, 30 August 1893, cited in Livingston, "Study," 659.

CHAPTER 9

The Enterprise Continues

A photograph from the early 1890s shows Caire next to his family house in Oakland—a prosperous upright man in his mid-sixties, with a white beard, whose bowler hat, waistcoat, frock coat, bow tie, and cane speak of an earlier era.[1] He is not leaning on the cane—at this stage of his life it would appear that it was still more of a prop than a necessity. But within a couple of years, he would suffer a slight stroke during one of his many visits to Santa Cruz Island, and no empire, of whatever size, lasts forever. It was perhaps with this in mind that Caire began to require his superintendents to keep a complete daily record for his benefit and for his sons, who had been assuming the lion's share of the management duties of the Santa Cruz Island Company and the Justinian Caire Company. The injunction on the cover of the superintendent's diaries from 1896–1898 provides insight into Justinian Caire's mind: "Put <u>only facts</u>, not reports, and write them down <u>when</u> they <u>occur</u>" (underlines in the original).[2]

These daily reports give the most complete picture of life and work on the island from the point of view of the superintendent, who generally directed operations from the Main Ranch. Every aspect was noted, measured, and

---

[1] In researching this chapter, I used the following sources for background information: Delphine Caire, "Journal," vol. 3; Arthur Caire, "Diaries, 1911–1940," Caire Family Papers and Diaries, in the possession of Justinian Caire III (hereafter cited as Arthur Caire diaries); Helen Caire, *Santa Cruz Island*; Caire Family Photograph Archive, in the author's possession; "Superintendent's Daily Diary 1896–1898," Santa Cruz Island Co. Records (hereafter cited as Superintendent's diary 1896–1898); Correspondence, 1880–1904, Santa Cruz Island Co.; Financial records, Santa Cruz Island Co. Records; Eaton, *Diary of a Sea Captain's Wife*; Daily, *California's Channel Islands*; Maria Rossi Gherini, "Santa Cruz Island" (interview); John Gherini, *Santa Cruz Island*; and Weber, *Old Napa Valley*.

[2] Superintendent's diary 1896–1898.

passed on to the head office, including an accounting of the number of sheep sheared, according to the nine districts; a record of the sowing of more than thirteen fields; a yearly inventory of the company store; a yearly wine inventory by type; and a ranch-by-ranch livestock inventory, divided into sheep, cattle, hogs, poultry (turkeys, chickens, pigeons), goats, dogs, and cats. The reports were sent to San Francisco, where the early ones were destroyed in the fire of 1906. Fortunately, copies of the reports remained on the island, made in a letterpress that was still in use almost three decades later when Clifford McElrath was superintendent in the early 1920s.

> There was no such thing as a typewriter: all correspondence was in longhand. We wrote with copying ink, using an ordinary pen. One then put the letter on a second sheet with a dry blotter . . . under it and a damp blotter on top. . . . The whole works was then put into the copying press, a machine with two flat iron faces and a large screw and handle like a wine press. You then screwed down to get pressure on the paper, left the letter in the press for a few minutes and out came a fairly good copy on very thin paper that had to be read from the back side of the sheet.[3]

The first entry for April 14, 1896, recalls a mild but windy day with temperatures in the sixties (Fahrenheit). Although it was a Tuesday, it was a rest day for most of the men as they had worked the previous Sunday. For the men working the northern range, there was a corrida at Cueva Valdez. The schooner arrived that day with mail and got ready to fulfill orders for 1,844 gallons of wine—ten barrels of fifty gallons each and sixteen puncheons of 174 gallons, for local customers and distributors in Santa Barbara and Los Angeles. This month there were forty-two men at work at the Main Ranch, in the kitchen, wine cellar, garden, stable, forge, and carpenter shop. Others were busy hauling sheep to Prisoners' Harbor from Potrero Norte in anticipation of the arrival of a coastal steamer. There was also work at the Main Ranch shearing and castrating sheep and sacking the wool from another corrida. There was late pruning in the vineyard. The headcount included the crew of three on the schooner and the team (*squadra*) at Scorpion Ranch. Later that week a number of vaqueros left for Christy Ranch for a corrida at the west end of the island. There was also repair work under way on the road to La Playa, from where the *Santa Cruz* left with eight

---

[3] McElrath, *On Santa Cruz Island*, 5. McElrath's description is largely accurate, though there is a significant amount of the correspondence that was typed as well, with copies made using carbon paper.

barrels of Zinfandel for further shipment on from Santa Barbara, including one barrel for the Raffour House restaurant in Santa Barbara and another barrel for a private Santa Barbara customer. A sick laborer was on board, returning to mainland to get treatment for his unnamed malady. On April 18, the coastal steamer *Bonita* arrived at noon and left the next day with 1,000 sheep. Later that day, the schooner returned from Santa Barbara with Justinian, Albina, and a party of friends.

The entries in the superintendent's diary trace the daily round of activities of the Santa Cruz Island Company at one of its most dynamic periods. This was the high point of its development phase, when the last and biggest of the brick structures—the winery and its accompanying fermentation house—were being built. They sat one above the other on the hillside just to the east of the residence complex. The full panoply of skilled and unskilled workers was at work on the island, from brick makers and bricklayers to blacksmiths, carpenters, and laborers. Then there were large numbers of regular and temporary ranch hands involved in the cattle and sheep operations.

The diary entries also show the pattern of the spring and fall corridas as they proceeded in a circuit around the island, starting at the central isthmus—Potrero del Norte and Potrero Sur near Prisoners' Harbor and the Main Ranch—and moving to Pinos Chicos in the range to the west of Prisoners' Harbor.[4] From there the vaqueros moved on to Pinos Grandes in the northern range, then further west to Punta del Diablo. Working their way westward, the vaqueros moved on to Punta West and Christy Ranch then headed south of Christy to Cañada Posa. Then they turned east through the Colorados, eventually sweeping up the potreros of the isthmus to catch any sheep that might have evaded them the first time. Last came the corrida at the east end of the island. Statistics kept by the superintendents indicated that the corridas at the east end's Potrero Llano and Potrero Nord on the isthmus were the most productive in terms of sheep rounded up.[5]

The vaqueros driving the sheep were for the most part local itinerant workers from the Santa Barbara area, many of them returning regularly to work on Santa Cruz Island and for other sheep operations, including those on San Miguel, San Clemente, and San Nicolas islands as well as the Rancho

---

[4] *Potrero* was the word used on the island to denote a field or area that was used for grazing livestock. This distinguished it from a *campo*, a field that was devoted to raising crops, such as wheat or alfalfa.

[5] Ledger of the Santa Cruz Island Co., as cited in Livingston, "Study," 580. The fall shearing for 1909 showed that the Scorpion district produced more wool than the Main Ranch.

San Julian near Lompoc. The vaqueros worked with cattle on the mainland as well. Though the majority of the vaqueros were itinerants, more than a few stayed on after the roundups to help with general maintenance and ranching duties, like repairing the many miles of fencing. They were famous horsemen, able to roll a cigarette at a canter. When they arrived at the island with their homely baggage of canvas valises and bundles, they were clean-shaven except for their soup-strainer moustaches, but within a couple of weeks their faces would be largely hidden by whiskers and thick shocks of coarse hair.

The pattern of the corridas was set before the arrival of the Caires and continued almost unchanged well into the twentieth century. As a general rule, the days of the corrida started before first light at the Main Ranch. It was often pitch dark when the breakfast bell rang, long before the dawn chorus of the island jays and other birds in the pepper trees of the family enclosure. After breakfast the riders caught their horses in the gray light of dawn and saddled up to form a circle around the mayordomo in charge of the roundup, who assigned them their posts. He pointed in the directions they were to go, but the old hands who took the same posts every corrida—some for more than fifty years—needed little instruction. The roundup in the west was only one of the sections being covered. The vaqueros might round up sheep on the northwestern coast, at Pinos Chicos or Pinos Grandes; on the rolling hills of Potrero Norte; at Christy Ranch; or at any of a dozen other places. The riders set off down one of the roads leading out of the barnyard, eastward or westward according to the decreed destination. Then they would leave the road to follow the trails into the southern or northern ranges. Here and there one of the vaqueros dropped off to reach his appointed place. When the last man reached his position at the farthest outpost of the territory being covered, the roundup began.

It started with a shout and a crack of the short braided leather quirt, the *chirrion*, and the vaqueros in the near vicinity closed in gradually. The canyons and hills resounded with the whoops and shouts of the men and the snapping of chirrions. Under the watchful eye of the mayordomo, the men pursued the sheep, responding to their every move. The tough island horses could follow the sheep almost anywhere, responding to their breaking movements. Here and there a temporary wing fence helped guide the sheep in the right direction.

The vaqueros pursued the sheep for hours, driving them up one ridge and down another as the sun rose higher in the sky. The numbers of sheep in the band increased as did the semicircle of vaqueros behind them, closing them in and urging them forward. The normally silent hills came alive with the voices of the men, the thudding of the sheep's trotters, the cracks of the *chirrions,* and the bleating of the animals. The sheep were driven toward temporary fences to guide them in the direction of the Main Ranch, Christy Ranch, Scorpion Ranch, or Prisoners' Harbor, where roundups and shearing also took place. The end of the drive might be almost in sight, but having been in the saddle for perhaps six or eight hours, it was time for a break.

If the men were in the vicinity of the Main Ranch, the cook would drive out with a wagon of provisions—bread, onions, beans, and coffee. The men would build a fire, rope and slaughter a lamb or two, and sharpen long sticks on which they roasted their chunks of meat. Perhaps the menu would be enhanced if one of the men happened across a wild pig. If there was a gourmet in the group, he might take the lamb head and place it in the coals. When he considered it cooked, he would lift it out, split the skull, and share the well-roasted brains with his fellow connoisseurs. The scent of coffee and hand-rolled cigarettes mixed with the aroma of roasted meat as the men settled down for a short siesta before returning to the saddle for the final few miles to the Main Ranch. As they approached, two or three men rode ahead to open gates and close other ones behind the last riders.

Trailing clouds of dust, the corridas would arrive at the great barnyard of the Main Ranch with the usual pandemonium of bleating, shouting, barking, and whistling. As the final sheep were driven across the barnyard, the riders appeared behind them, urging the laggards on. The last of the gates would close on the herd in their pens and the cloud of dust would begin to settle. Then the men unsaddled their horses, washed up, and got ready for dinner. The first bell rang on the hill behind the men's dining room. They strolled in its direction to line up along the railing outside, exchanging banter among themselves and with the cook, until the second dinner bell rang. After dinner the skilled shearers among them prepared their equipment for the shearing that would begin the following morning.

Just as with the days of the corrida, the shearing days began early. The sheep could not stay too long in their pens or they would begin to suffer. If the shearing was at the Main Ranch, the large shed on the north side of the great barnyard, normally silent, hummed with activity. From the corrida,

End of the corrida at the Main Ranch, ca. 1915.

the sheep were driven into the large roofed corral directly in front of the shearing shed. Then they were herded into a long runway along the length of the shearing area. When it was filled to the end, heavy gates on rollers were closed, separating the runway into small pens. A narrow gate from each pen opened into the shearing area. In place of the habitual silence, the cacophony of sound included the snipping of the shears, the tapping of sheep's trotters as they were pulled out of a pen, the thud as 90–200 pounds of sheep landed on its back, and the shuffling of feet as the shearers brought each fleece to the mayordomo to get their token (*ficha*) for each pelt. Snatches of songs, whistling, and joking small talk punctuated the continuous bleating of the penned sheep. During the shearing the mayordomo sat on a high seat built in the narrow space joining the two sections of the shearing shed. Across his knees sat a wooden shelf with slits in its surface into which he put the small metal fichas. The fichas were about the size of a penny and were stamped with a cross mounted on a hill, signifying the island ranch, with the company initials, SCICo, curved above. When a shearer finished with a sheep, he wrapped the fleece into a bundle, tossed

Sheep shearing on the wharf at Prisoners' Harbor, ca. 1895.

Game of bocce, Main Ranch, early 1890s.
*Photograph from glass plate negative by Arthur Caire,
courtesy of Justinian Caire III.*

it on to one of the broad shelves flanking the mayordomo's seat and took a ficha. After re-sharpening his shears on the whetting stones, he would choose another sheep and pull it out from its pen by a hind leg, bending once more to his task.

The other section of the shearing shed was the packing area, where the wool was stuffed into ten-foot sacks, weighed, marked, and stored until it was taken down to the warehouse at Prisoners' Harbor to wait for its shipment to the mainland. At the top of a ten-foot-high scaffold was a large metal hoop that held open the large burlap sack. Dressed in bib overalls, wide leather cuffs and belt, and green eyeshade, the packer sat on the planks surrounding the metal hoop, dropping in fleeces tossed up by his work partner. When there were enough fleeces in the sack to start packing them down, he lowered himself into the sack from a rope hanging from a beam above. Once the sack was completely full, it was loosened from the hoop and eased down to lie lengthwise. With a large curved needle and heavy thread, the sack was sewn up, leaving ears at each corner for handling. The packer and his partner then rolled the sack to the scale and weighed it. The weight, usually 300–400 pounds, was recorded and the sack rolled over to join the others. The sack was then stenciled with the company initials and was now ready for transfer by wagon to the Prisoners' Harbor warehouse. As each day of shearing drew to a close, the shearers would form a queue at the superintendent's office, where they handed over their fichas to be recorded and added to their daily pay.

After the shearing, the flock was divided into those to be shipped to market, those to be castrated, and those to be released back on to the range, the numbers dependent on the state of the market, the available feed, and the condition of the terrain and how many numbers it could sustain. At the end of April 1896, when the shearing was finished, the shearers and vaqueros returned to Santa Barbara. There was general satisfaction with how the shearing had gone under the direction of the mayordomo, Jose Jesus Ruis, and on the part of Justinian Caire, who sailed on the schooner the next day to Santa Barbara on business. From there Caire caught the train for Los Angeles.

So the pattern of the corrida and trasquila was set and changed little over the ensuing decades, despite the changes that were taking place on comparable ranches on the mainland. As one observer noted,

The Santa Cruz Island Company operated its sheep ranch quite differently from most mainland ranches: no herding occurred, instead the sheep roamed freely in the vast mountainous pastures of the Island.... On Santa Cruz Island, the large flocks roamed miles into the hardly accessible canyons and mountainsides, with hundreds becoming wild and rarely seen. This posed a problem to those rounding them up, forcing the continued use of the traditions dating from early California, where no fences held the livestock and hardy men and horses scoured the rugged mountains and valleys in lively *corridas* or roundups.[6]

In this sense, Santa Cruz Island was a ranch much more in the model of the great ranches of the Mexican period, a fact commented on by many visitors who found this central to its charm. This quaint view overlooked the efforts of Justinian Caire and his sons to control the herds of sheep by fencing (in order to minimize erosion and build up pastures with good feed) and by restricting grazing when the range became poor. Overstocking combined with drought was already having an adverse effect when Caire took over ownership of the island, and he invested much to reverse these trends, though the wildness of much of the terrain meant it was literally an uphill battle.

The Santa Cruz Island Company financial returns continued to show that Caire's investment was paying off. The superintendent's diary notes the business totals for the second quarter of 1896: almost 5,000 sheep and more than 17,000 gallons of wine shipped from the island. At an estimated price of $2 per head for the sheep and 25¢ a gallon for the wine, this would have represented a quarterly gross income of $14,250 [$363,000] for the Santa Cruz Island Company.

The superintendent's diary also has more than a few entries relating to fishermen. The fishing on the island was lightly regulated by the Caires early in the century. Beginning in 1906, Margaret Eaton, who spent months at a time on the island as the wife of an island fisherman, described a life so removed from the doings at the Main Ranch that it might well have been on a different planet. These were halcyon days for harvesting the rich and abundant marine life and paying little if anything for the privilege. It was the fishermen's contention that the land was public domain up to fifty feet above high tide, claiming that it was their right to squat on pieces of the shore for their own use. But under the original terms of the patent that confirmed Castillero's land grant, the legal reality was that the boundaries of

---

[6] Livingston, "Study," 570.

the island ranch ran to the water's edge, increasing and decreasing with the daily tides. Nonetheless, in these largely uncontrolled days, the fishermen formed a small rough-and-tumble community of characters who made the most of their temporary fishing camps. They helped each other out in times of trouble but were equally jealous of their own prerogatives and not averse to raiding each other's traps or fishing lines if the occasion arose. It was in 1906 that the Santa Cruz Island Company management, after years of feeling their generosity abused by the fishermen, attempted to begin profiting from their activities, signing an exclusive contract with Ira Eaton on the understanding that he warn off other fishermen and pay a fee of $10 a month.

During the spring of 1896, the activities at the Main Ranch carried on in good order, particularly as the so-called president was in residence, having returned from a short business excursion to Los Angeles; however, the diary notes that he was "not in very good health." Some days later the diary notes ominously, "Our President always very sick." On June 11, Justinian and Albina embarked from Prisoners' Harbor for San Francisco on the steamer St. Paul. It was to be the last time he would see his beloved island.

But his presence was far from necessary for the continued operation of the island enterprise. Stepping into his shoes, as he had been gradually doing for almost two decades, was Arthur, riding the trails to the out-ranches, taking the schooner down to Scorpion, inspecting the various ranches and their activities, and keeping a watchful eye on the superintendent and foremen. He was back and forth between San Francisco and Santa Cruz Island on a regular basis, spending a total of more than six months on the island in 1896 and 1897. He also served as the escort of his nephews, Robert and Edmund Rossi, who came down for the summer in 1896 to spend several weeks on the island. Arthur also kept in touch with the Caire business interests in Los Angeles, making trips down there on the schooner and the train. Of course, Arthur was not the only Caire offspring on the island. His sisters Hélène, Aglaë, and Amelie Caire Rossi, with her large and growing family, vacationed on the island for five weeks that summer and a similar amount of time the following summer.

A July 31, 1896, diary entry highlights the work and personality of one of the island notables, Jose Espinosa, who spent many years of his working life on the island. The Scorpion foreman, Perini, called to say that he had found a beautiful three-year-old horse dying. He asked for some medicine and the well-known horse doctoring skills of Espinosa. The superintendent used the recently installed telephone to call the vaquero where he was working at Christy Ranch. The indefatigable Espinosa rode the twenty-five-mile distance between the two ranches to nurse the horse, returning the next day with the news that it had a good chance for recovery. Hawk-faced, with shrewd piercing eyes, Jose Espinosa was one of the many characters who loom large in the history of these days. A famous horseman, he was still going strong in the 1920s, when the younger Caire generation got to know him as the *Viejo* (respected old man) and admired his skills in the saddle and with a lariat. By that time he had known three generations of Caires and his reputation as a healer of horses and a fierce mayordomo with a frightening temper was legendary. But this ferocity was reserved for the men under his command. For the Caire ladies, there was the excessive gallantry of an earlier day, as he swept off his sombrero in greeting them. There was no one who could match Espinosa at roping anything that moved—steer, sheep, or pig. The last of these three required exquisite skill, and he was widely reputed to have lassoed twenty-one in a single day. He was making his living in the saddle in the last year of his life, dying on February 10, 1926, at the age of eighty-two.

His younger brother, Cuate Espinosa, was another of the island fixtures for decades—less fierce and commanding than Jose but just as memorable because of his extensive knowledge of the island and his skill at breaking horses, a method he called "gen'ling." A great family favorite, he was often sent to act as a guide for the younger generation of Caires on their long rides out to Christy, Cueva Valdez, or Cañada Laguna, filling the hours on the trail or around a lunchtime meal of carne asada with tales of the old days when "Don Justiniano" directed the operation. Cuate knew the location of every sweet cactus tuna and every gooseberry patch on the island, a knowledge that he was happy to share with the young Caires and their friends. When he praised one of them for her horsemanship, the compliment was never forgotten.

In mid-September 1896, the grape harvest began with fifty-seven boxes of Muscat, and Cuate worked all day to teach some of the newly broken horses to provide the power for the grape crusher. The next day they crushed sixty-two boxes of Muscat but had a great deal of trouble with the crusher and had to finish the crushing by hand. On closer examination, the shaft of the crusher was found to be bent, and the machine was disassembled so that it might be repaired. The Zinfandel and Burgundy were tested for sugar content and found not yet ripe enough. There was also a little corrida at the Matanza potrero near the Main Ranch that started before daylight and finished at 9:00 A.M. Cuate acted as mayordomo in his brother's absence, though he lacked Jose's ferocity and it was noted that the vaqueros did not respond as well to his leadership.

On October 19, 1896, the *Santa Cruz* left for Santa Barbara with Arthur, who was to catch a coastal steamer for San Francisco. At the same time, Jose, Cuate, and their crew of horse breakers, their work done, were leaving the island. The payment as agreed for several weeks work and the breaking of the horses was $1,740.70 [$44,000].[7] The younger Espinosa was identified by his rate of pay as skilled labor and was rewarded accordingly for the breaking and shoeing of horses. He also had other skills, such as trapping the island foxes that preyed on the henhouses. As skilled labor, he received almost $5 a day, whereas his unskilled companions got $4.[8]

On January 31, 1897, the precarious nature of the weather was brought home when a tremendous winter storm hit the island, dumping more than six and a half inches of rain in twelve hours. The creeks came roaring out of the hills, bursting their banks and wreaking terrible damage as they went. The levee intended to protect the fields of the Main Ranch was swept away, except a section protected by a stone wall, and the fields were inundated. The barley field was partially covered with drift sand and gullied here and there. The road to the west end was cut completely for eighty-eight feet, breaking the piping from El Pato spring and causing some damage in the Burgundy vineyard. There was also damage at Scorpion, but as elsewhere, once the storm passed the men were quickly on to the task of making repairs.

The spring 1897 *corrida* brought the work force at the Main Ranch up to fifty-six. With so many men working on the island, friction and misunderstandings were bound to arise between the various levels of management. On April 25 the superintendent gave orders for all men to work that Sunday, normally a rest day, presumably with so many sheep waiting to be sheared in the trasquila. The foreman Benedetto undermined the superintendent's authority by telling some of the men that they could take the day off. The result was that all the workmen except the ten occupied in the trasquila

---

[7] Superintendent's diary 1896–1898.

[8] Ibid. This works out to $129 per week and $103 per week, respectively, in 2007 dollars.

refused to work, though every man questioned by the superintendent after the fact swore he was willing to work, but without any workmates he couldn't do anything. This was the kind of confusion and mismanagement that the Caires could not abide. A furious Arthur wrote in the margin of the diary, "Where did the superintendent have his eyes all day long? Benedetto claims to have worked that day. Why was this not reported to San Francisco? Men's false report??"

The San Francisco office was clearly dissatisfied with the performance of the superintendent. A note was pasted into the diary on the following page: "NOTICE—From this day, May 1st 1897, no entry must be made which does not state facts. Facts must be related only when they occur, if learned only after the occurrence when there is . . . enough for entry."

Having spent much of February and March on the island inspecting all the out-ranches, Arthur returned to the island again in early April. On his next visit, May 12, Arthur arrived on the schooner from Santa Barbara at 10:00 P.M. Given the lateness of the hour and his intentions for the next day, he spent the night in the house at the harbor. In the morning he rode up to the Main Ranch to demand the resignation of the superintendent. The next day a terse note pasted in the diary explained, "Mr. A. Clement presented, at the request of the General Manager [Arthur Caire], his resignation from the office of Superintendent of Santa Cruz Island, a step which he had already deemed advisable in view of correspondence exchanged between the Island and the office."

Having accomplished his mission, Arthur returned to San Francisco but was back on the island the next month, moving from ranch to ranch on an inspection tour, noting the work of the new Italian blacksmith who had been hired in San Francisco. At the end of June, the steamer *Eureka* from San Francisco called at Prisoners' Harbor with Aglaë, Amelie, her children, and two maids. Amelie had seven children by this time and was expecting another. On July 29 the schooner *Lizzie Belle W* arrived in the evening with Arthur and his brother-in-law PC Rossi. A few days later the two men left the ladies and children to set off on an overnight visit to Scorpion. The next week they were off again, this time to the west end of Santa Cruz Island, to Poso and Christy ranches, with Arthur leaving orders to replace one of the hands there who was found to be drunk. At the end of the first week of August, he returned to San Francisco via Santa Barbara, leaving Aglaë and the Rossis to enjoy themselves for another five days until they boarded the *Eureka* once again to go directly to San Francisco. In the middle of the month, Fred Caire and a friend came down to the island for a visit, touring around and joining in with a hunting party to track wild boar in the hill country around Buena Vista and Portezuela.

On September 18 Fred Caire crossed the channel to Santa Barbara on the schooner along with three of the workers. Two days later the grape harvest began in the Burgundy district of the vineyard. Fred returned to the island briefly but left it the next week for San Francisco, ending his month of business and pleasure. A couple of weeks later, Arthur arrived at Prisoners' Harbor on the schooner for a stay that would last almost two months.

On November 14 Arthur, accompanied by the foreman and the squad boss of Scorpion, went to Potrero Nord to inspect the water supply for this important pasture. A couple of days later, word came to the Main Ranch of a fight at Christy between Jose Espinosa and one of the other men. Espinosa's famous temper had gotten the better of him, and his opponent had come out on the losing end, "receiving blows on the face and side." There was no rush to judgment in the diary: "We could not arrive at the truth in the matter, and must wait for further developments." Arthur left the island on December 9. He had been there almost two months and would be traveling northward when his father played out the final drama of his eventful life, passing away at home in Oakland the following day, December 10, 1897. Justinian Caire was seventy years old. His death was given front-page coverage in the Bay Area and Santa Barbara newspapers, in which he was extolled as a business pioneer and entrepreneur, "one of the best known merchants of San Francisco."[9]

It was more than a week before the schooner arrived at the Prisoners' Harbor from Santa Barbara with the news of Justinian Caire's death. Arthur Caire wrote a personal note to assistant superintendent and winemaker Leon Valadie on December 14: "I did not arrive in time to shut the eyes of my father. He died on 10 December at 2 in the morning and I did not arrive at the house until towards 7 in the evening. He lost consciousness for 24 hours and his final hours were quite painful. We buried him on Sunday. My mother is holding up well and being brave. I think that she will endure this great unhappiness with resignation."[10] The man who had

---

[9] Obituary of Justinian Caire, *San Francisco Call*, 10 December 1897.
[10] Arthur Caire to Leon Valadie, 14 December 1897, Caire Family Papers and Diaries.

devoted the last quarter of his life, and a considerable portion of his fortune, to the building of the Santa Cruz Island enterprise was gone. Christmas 1897 would have been a somber affair at the island, at the Caire home in Oakland, and at the offices in San Francisco, though after a respectful pause for the funeral arrangements, business continued as usual.

Justinian Caire's intentions for the line of succession in the running of his companies were made clear in his will dated 1892. Indeed, his sons had been actively involved in the management of both enterprises for almost two decades. Nevertheless, it must have been a time of uncertainty with the founder having departed the scene after so many years of struggle and achievement. Justinian Caire had put the island on its course, but the end of the year 1897 also signaled the end of an era in ways that his family could not foresee. The vision of land husbandry, building an integrated, self-sufficient agricultural enterprise, would be carried on by his sons, but the development phase was largely complete. Others who did not share or care for Justinian Caire's vision had already entered or would shortly enter the family circle.

For the time being, in spite of the absence of the founder, all was as before. The business of the Justinian Caire Company and Santa Cruz Island Company carried on as usual. There were the typical ups and downs of the business cycle and the characteristic combination of good and bad years for agriculture, but nothing appeared on the surface of family life to indicate the pressures and resentments that were starting to build. And as subterranean pressure builds between tectonic plates, so it was growing within familial relations. Others who married into the Caire family came to regard the legacy of Justinian Caire as something that should involve them more fully and enable them to share more profitably in its potential liquidation. This was an attitude that would be strenuously resisted by other factions of the family determined to follow Caire's wishes that his legacy remain intact. By a curious conjunction of human and natural causes, the rupture of tectonic plates that was about to occur in the San Francisco Bay region would have reverberations that set off a clash of warring temperaments and a fundamental disagreement about land husbandry and the management of family finances. It would result in the dissolution of all that Justinian Caire had created.

Prisoners' Harbor, ca. 1897.
Center left, adobe house and brick warehouse.
Photograph from glass plate negative by Hélène Caire.

CHAPTER 10

New Blood in the Family

Shortly after Delphine and Arthur's return from Santa Cruz Island in 1880, their younger sister Amelie became engaged to the young Italian from Turin, PC Rossi. A partner in a San Francisco pharmacy near the corner of Columbus and Broadway, Rossi had come to the city five years before.[1] In the ensuing years he became acquainted with Justinian Caire and then his family, and nineteen-year-old Amelie caught his eye. Amelie's wedding to PC Rossi took place the day after Christmas 1880 at St. Mary's Church, San Francisco, with the wedding dinner at the Caires' house on Harrison Street in Oakland. The Rossi's early married life exemplifies a history replete with the typical domestic trials and tragedies that beset families in this era and which were overcome through family solidarity and personal generosity to each other.

Although he was still strained financially from clearing up the financial wreckage of the French Savings Bank left by Gustav Mahé, Justinian took it upon himself to help the newlyweds as much as possible. Rossi had his eye on a house on Powell Street near his pharmacy that he wanted for himself and his new bride. Caire bought out the lease of the sitting tenant and furnished the house with everything they might need, down to china, glassware, and kitchen utensils.

The newlyweds moved into their new home, and it was there that they had the first three of fourteen children, Albert, Maria, and Sofia. The birth of young Albert in 1882, the first of a new generation, was a cause for celebration for the entire family. Unfortunately, he suffered badly from

---

[1] All family details included in this section are from Delphine Caire, "Journal," vol. 3.

eczema, which plagued him for the whole of his short life. To complicate matters, when Albert was barely a year old, his father was struck by some grave but undiagnosed illness. Pietro seemed to recover but then suffered a relapse that sent him back to bed.

It was Delphine's opinion that this ordeal contributed to the premature arrival of the couple's second child, Maria. Although small at birth, Maria slowly gained weight. Her father, on the other hand, continued to languish. Such was the family concern about Pietro that they sent him to take the hot alkaline and cold soda and iron waters at Skaggs Springs in Sonoma County, accompanied by his teenage brother-in-law Fred as reluctant company. In the meantime Amelie took her two children to stay with her parents in Oakland. Not long after their arrival, young Maria came down with pneumonia, which was often lethal in those days, particularly among children. The infant was subjected to some highly traumatic treatments by a German doctor, from which she emerged, not surprisingly, "sullen and grouchy" and was very slow to say her first words. It was these treatments that Delphine suggested might have contributed to her tendency to bronchitis and asthma in later life. For these reasons, young Maria spent much of the winter months of her childhood in her grandparents' house in Oakland, as the milder climate of San Francisco Bay's eastern side was judged to be more salubrious and better for her constitution.

Little Albert was also a fixture at the Harrison Street house of his grandparents. All manner of treatments for his eczema were tried, including a trip to a Lake County mineral springs, which required Amelie and baby Albert, accompanied by Delphine and Fred, to take the train as far as Cloverdale, then complete their journey by stagecoach to their final destination. The spa's regime of cold baths only resulted in making Albert water phobic, and after a few days the group returned to Oakland. Once they foresaw that Albert would be with them indefinitely, Justinian and Albina took on the expense of hiring a young woman specifically to look after the infant.

Having tried the air and waters of Lake County without success, it was thought that the warmer climate and sea air of Santa Cruz Island might have some effect on Albert's condition. Amelie and her helpers traveled down to the island and set themselves up in the house at Prisoners' Harbor. Sadly, Albert's eczema showed no signs of improvement, tormenting him day and night, and they returned to Oakland for whatever other

Fred Caire (*right*) and a friend, Main Ranch, ca. 1895.
Photograph by Arthur Caire.

primitive treatments were available. He was approaching his fifth birthday at his grandparents' house when his short life was ended abruptly in 1887 by diphtheria, then a common childhood killer.

The next two Rossi children—Maria and Sofia—enjoyed good health early in their lives and were able to live in San Francisco with their parents. Amelie gave birth to child number four, Luigi "Freddy" in 1887. The following year, she became pregnant for the fifth time when Freddy was barely twelve months old, and her father advised her to come live in his house to finish her pregnancy and give birth in a place where there were plenty of adults to deal with the demands of her other children. She stayed for the last month of her pregnancy, and in August 1888 she gave birth to twin boys, Robert and Edmund. Amelie, her brood of five children, and her nursemaid continued their stay in Oakland for several more months, as Justinian in his role of paterfamilias would not consent to their return to San Francisco until Pietro succeeded in renting a home "more suited to the needs of family than the one they were living in."

All went well for the Rossi family for a couple of years, then tragedy struck again when Freddy developed a "spinal deviation" for which the doctors prescribed a body cast to straighten the curvature. He needed intensive care, and with four other small children, Amelie was once again struggling. Once more, the grandparents came to the rescue as Freddy moved to Oakland for the last ten months of his life. His spinal condition continued to deteriorate in spite of the painful cast, and he finally succumbed to meningitis in 1891.

In an age when childhood diseases were sadly much more common, the misfortunes of the Rossi children were unrelenting. Shortly after the death of Freddy, Maria and Robert came down with scarlet fever. The doctor quickly advised that the two other children, Sofia and Edmund, be removed to the grandparents' house, but it was not enough to save Sofia, who had already contracted this childhood killer and was overwhelmed by it in less than three weeks. While Sofia was struggling for her life in Oakland, the family said nothing about the child's condition to Amelie, who was pregnant again and suffering from a painful throat infection. When she learned of the death of this third child, she went into a severe depression, lashing out at her family, making harsh and completely unfounded accusations toward them that she would later disavow. The four remaining Rossi children (Amelie had given birth to another girl, named Esther, in 1890) regained their health and went on to live long lives along with six of the subsequent seven children who were born in the next decade.[2]

In spite of these private tragedies, the business career of PC Rossi (discussed in more detail below) was prospering. He joined the Italian Swiss Agricultural Colony as winemaker in 1888, and with the timely assistance of his father-in-law, Justinian Caire, he helped make the Italian Swiss Colony Wine Corporation a success. In 1901 he capped this stage of his career with the profitable sale of 50 percent of his Italian Swiss Colony stock to the California Wine Association (CWA), who were aggressively creating a monopoly position in wine from California. He acquired a seat on the board of directors of the CWA and continued as president of the Italian Swiss Colony Company as well as vice-president of Andrea Sbarboro's Italian–American Bank.[3] As befitted a man of his financial standing, he began

---

[2] Edmund Rossi, "Italian Swiss Colony" (interview), 33, mentions how much time as children they spent with their grandparents.

[3] Edmund Rossi, "Italian Swiss Colony" (interview), 20–21.

spending the summer with his large family at the vineyard and winery of Italian Swiss Colony at Asti in Sonoma County, where in 1905 he built a substantial twelve-bedroom family home, the Villa Maria. All on one floor, the U-shaped house enclosed a huge patio and had a fifteen-foot-wide porch that wrapped around the exterior. Set in eleven acres surrounded by the vineyards of the Italian Swiss Colony, with tennis, croquet, and bocce courts and a 4,000-square-foot garden, it was an impressive demonstration of PC Rossi's financial success. As their guest, Delphine related a strangely prophetic episode that occurred one Sunday. After mass, Pietro decided to take a tour of one of the vineyards and invited Amelie to go with him in a light two-wheeled sulky. Delphine was resting in the garden when Amelie and Pietro suddenly appeared. Their clothes and hair were in disarray, and Pietro had a bloody wound to the side of his face. The exact details of their accident were never fully divulged, but it emerged that they had been thrown from the sulky when the horse bolted. What struck Delphine as strange at the time was that Amelie, who was clearly suffering from shock, would not explain what had happened but, rather, kept demanding to see all her children. And even when they were presented and accounted for, she continued to insist that they were in danger. A doctor who was vacationing nearby examined Amelie and reassured the family that there was no physical damage, but he said that she had suffered a psychological trauma from which she would take time to recover.

Amelie, Pietro, Maria, the doctor, and their cook returned hurriedly on the train from Cloverdale to San Francisco the next day. They left Delphine, the nanny, and the remaining nine children, including the infant Elenore, to fend for themselves and organize their own departure for the city. All of this was accomplished with the emergency help of Aglaë, who rushed up from Oakland to lend a hand to her sister. Together they were able to close up the house and take the Rossi children back to their parents. Amelie, Delphine noted, "slowly came back to herself little by little," and Pietro was left with a slight scar on his face but showed no other signs of physical trauma. Ironically, when he died ten years later at age fifty-six, it was a result of being thrown by another runaway horse, leaving Amelie a widow with ten children, five of them still in their teens.[4]

But this unhappy accident still lay some years in the future. The Caire dynasty greeted the first decade of the new century with the addition of

[4] Edmund Rossi, "Italian Swiss Colony" (interview).

two more male relatives by marriage. The first of these new arrivals onto the family stage was Goffredo Capuccio in 1903. He had initially appeared on the scene in 1890 as an employee of the Justinian Caire Company, recommended by PC Rossi. Capuccio was one of the many immigrants hired in the 1890s as the company sought both skilled and unskilled workers wherever they could find them. He must have shown some promise, and he responded positively to the offer of being the clerk for the superintendent on Santa Cruz Island. In November 1892, the twenty-seven-year-old Capuccio took over the superintendent position from the previous incumbent. He served in that capacity for only twenty months before he was "discharged." In island parlance, this meant Capuccio was fired and was never to be considered for re-employment. It was not an amicable parting in June 1894. The reasons given by Arthur were Capuccio's "bad temper and ill advised conduct." Perhaps Capuccio's bad temper was a response to the high level of supervision to which the Caires subjected all their superintendents, but the immediate cause was the Caires' insistence on the disciplinary discharge of a protégé of Capuccio for drunkenness and disorderly behavior on the island. The result of Capuccio's blustering attempts to protect a fellow *Torinese* was that they were both dismissed from the island. Whatever the rights and wrongs of the case, it is certain that Justinian Caire took a strong dislike to his former employee, referring to Capuccio in the ensuing years—both verbally and in writing—as "a dirty little toad" (*un sale petit crapaud*).[5]

After the island fiasco, Capuccio returned to Italy and disappeared from the story for a number of years. Yet it would appear that PC Rossi maintained contact with him, because in early 1903 when Rossi and his twenty-year-old daughter Maria were traveling in Italy with Aglaë, they reconnected with Capuccio, who was now employed as an office clerk in the Cantiere Navale di Muggiano shipyard in the port of La Spezia near Genoa. Although Aglaë was a couple of years his senior, Capuccio got on well with her. Now in her late thirties, Aglaë was still considered pretty and vivacious. It was something of a whirlwind romance as Aglaë responded favorably to Capuccio's attentions. When she returned to her mother's home a few weeks later, in the autumn of 1903, she announced her intention

---

[5] Details regarding the early career of G. Capuccio and his relations with the Caire family and the circumstances surrounding the interception of Albina Caire's will are found in Arthur Caire's diaries, pp. 19 ff.

to marry the Italian clerk. Her decision did not meet with the strong-willed Albina's approval, as she remembered all too well her husband's antipathy to Capuccio. Confronted by her mother's displeasure, Aglaë offered to break off the match and return the ring the Italian had given her, but Albina relented and resigned herself to accepting her daughter's decision.

The dapper Capuccio, whose sartorial taste ran to boldly striped trousers and matching cummerbunds, arrived from Italy soon thereafter. He seemed to demonstrate a suitable level of affluence to support a family, and he and Aglaë were married in November. She and her new husband took up residence in La Spezia at the end of 1903. For a time all seemed well, but the chances of healing the previous rift between the Caires and their new son-in-law received a severe blow the following year. A letter arrived from Capuccio demanding $2,000 [$50,000] to cover the expenses of his trip to California and the furnishing of the marital home in Italy. Apparently, his putative financial wherewithal had been borrowed, with interest paid in advance, from friends and associates, notably Giuseppe Ollino, a mutual friend and business associate of PC Rossi.[6] When Arthur Caire queried Capuccio about the demand for money, Capuccio responded that because he had married into the Caire family they were obligated to take financial responsibility for him and his wife; furthermore, he said that he also had relatives depending on him for support. This viewpoint might have made sense from Capuccio's Italian standpoint, but it left the Caires feeling exasperated and resentful. Aglaë added to her mother's irritation by sending a letter saying that she intended to "assert her rights" to her share of the family fortune. Although greatly irritated with her daughter's attitude, Albina ultimately relented and sent her various sums of money to help her make ends meet and to repay the loans that Capuccio had contracted before the marriage.[7] Finally, in 1905, Arthur made a no-interest loan of $2,000 [$50,500] to his sister and her husband, though when Albina and Hélène began a long visit to Italy later that year, Capuccio further annoyed them by complaining that the Santa Cruz Island Company

---

[6] Edmund Rossi, "Italian Swiss Colony" (interview), 2. Ollino was also one of the early shareholders in Italian Swiss Colony. Edmund commented on the connection between Rossi and the founder of the colony, Sbarboro. See Arthur Caire diary, 79.

[7] Arthur Caire diary, 60, lists specific payments to his sister Aglaë and her husband, Goffredo Capuccio, from 1907 to 1910. Records of payments sent between 1904 and 1906 were destroyed in the 1906 fire.

was not producing enough income. The financial gifts from Albina to the Capuccios in these years totaled more than $1,500 [$38,000], and there is no record of the $2,000 being repaid. These amounts were in addition to the $7,000 [$177,000] in Santa Cruz Island Company dividends Aglaë received after she left the family home.

The arrival of Goffredo, Jr., into the Capuccio family in 1907 was a welcome addition to the next generation of the extended Caire family, and the Capuccios enjoyed a visit from PC Rossi and his twin sons after the twins' post-graduate year at the University of California, Berkeley, oenology program in 1909.[8] However, as that year drew to a close, Aglaë and her husband began writing letters to Albina telling of hard times at the shipyard and the likelihood of him being laid off. Interestingly, the historical record of the Cantiere Navale di Muggiano shows that, in fact, the shipyard was enjoying a high level of activity (and, indeed is still in business a century later), but in far-away San Francisco Aglaë's family was concerned. The family did not want Aglaë and her family to suffer economic hardship, so after a great deal of correspondence between the Caires, the Capuccios, and the Rossis, an assurance was given to Capuccio that a job would be found for him in San Francisco, either at the Italian American Bank, of which Rossi was vice-president, or at the Justinian Caire Company.[9]

The job at the bank never materialized, and with the encouragement of PC Rossi, in the early part of 1910 Goffredo Capuccio was again taken into the employ of his in-laws, this time as cashier and secretary of the Justinian Caire Company. As Arthur noted later, Rossi's urgings were done in the knowledge of a shared feeling that neither son-in-law of Albina Caire was receiving appropriate respect or remuneration from the Caire estate. This favor to Aglaë placed Capuccio in a position to report on the activities of the Caire brothers to PC Rossi and his son-in-law, the lawyer Ambrose Gherini.[10] Once more, Capuccio's bumptious personality caused friction between himself and his in-laws. He now saw himself as an equal partner in the management of Caire family financial affairs, but the Caires saw his position as a distinctly subordinate one. This essential difference in perspective appears to have alienated Capuccio from his wife's family, and he

---

[8] Edmund Rossi, "Italian Swiss Colony" (interview), 17.

[9] Centro per la Cultura dell'Impresa, Milano, "Il Cantiere Navale del Muggiano."

[10] Arthur Caire, memorandum, ca. 1931 (from earlier notes), 12, 19–20, Caire Family Papers and Diaries.

began to foster a close relationship with his other relatives by marriage: PC Rossi and Ambrose Gherini. Capuccio and Gherini could share PC Rossi's long-standing resentments over the way in which the Caires pointedly ignored his advice on the family's financial matters, an attitude that closely mirrored their own.

Ambrose Gherini, the second new in-law entering the extended Caire–Rossi family, married Justinian Caire's granddaughter Maria, the oldest daughter of PC and Amelie Caire Rossi, who had spent much of her childhood in the house of her grandparents. Born in 1878 to San Francisco immigrants from the Piedmont region of Italy, Gherini was an ambitious young lawyer of saturnine good looks. He had attended Lowell High School in the city and then spent a year at Stanford before moving on to a Benedictine seminary in Oregon for two years, from where he transferred to Yale. He resurfaced in San Francisco in 1902, newly graduated from Yale University and Law School, and began his legal practice in the city in 1904. Two years later, on October 30, 1906, he and Maria Rossi were married. In 1907, with his legal work prospering, they were able to move from their first house in a modest Mission District neighborhood to an altogether more respectable address on Green Street in Cow Hollow. Not long thereafter, in 1914, Gherini listed his address as 2070 Vallejo Street in Pacific Heights, four blocks west of his father-in-law's family home. It would appear he had arrived.[11]

Gherini initially made a name for himself in the Italian immigrant community as legal counsel for the Italian consulate in San Francisco, though this aspect of his career seems to have ended under a cloud. His success in pursuing work-related insurance settlements for Italian immigrants injured on the job was limited to two cases out of the eighty-five he was assigned by the consulate between 1909 and 1911, although he was apparently paid rather well by the Italian government. It was suggested at the time that his simultaneous professional relationships with the Italian consul general and with the insurance companies that would have had to reimburse the injured workers created a double conflict of interest. Gherini, the consul general, and the Italian government were reported by a Caire family relation in Turin to have severed relations on less than cordial terms.[12] But

---

[11] *Crocker Langley San Francisco Directory, 1904–1914.*

[12] Correspondence between Delphine Caire and her cousin Giustiniano Molfino, 1914–1917, in the possession of the author; and Marie Gherini Ringrose interview, 24 June 1983, cited in Livingston, "Study," 671.

for the well-connected Gherini, this was of little importance. His father-in-law and his wife's family promised good opportunities in the business and financial circles of San Francisco, including a directorship of the Italian-American bank where his father-in-law was vice-president. When his relationship with the Italian government was terminated, Gherini took on the role of vice consul for Imperial Russia in 1911, a post from which he resigned following the Bolshevik revolution in 1917.[13] It also seems likely that Gherini was encouraged by his father-in-law and by the Capuccios—by 1910 they were finally direct shareholders in the Santa Cruz Island Company—to anticipate sharing in the Caire fortune if its great property asset, Santa Cruz Island, could be pried open.

---

[13] Gherini, *Santa Cruz Island*, 126; and *San Francisco Examiner*, 3 December 1917.

CHAPTER 11

The Life and Times of Pietro Carlo Rossi

Thirty years earlier, when Pietro Carlo Rossi entered the Caire family, he had, in the expression of the time, made a good catch. For the handsome, ambitious, and impecunious twenty-five-year-old pharmacist, the established connections and generosity of the Caires presented a golden opportunity. Rossi arrived in San Francisco five years before his marriage and had worked hard to achieve a partnership in a pharmacy on the corner of Grant and Columbus.[1] Shortly after his marriage, his first step toward a stellar business career was cemented by his father-in-law's endorsement of a loan enabling him to buy out his partner in the pharmacy.[2]

Justinian Caire's reputation and the status of the Justinian Caire Company in San Francisco proved useful in other ways as well. In 1888, Rossi accepted a position as chief winemaker for the Italian Swiss Agricultural Colony, later to become the Italian Swiss Colony Wine Corporation. It was probably his expertise as a chemist that enabled him to bring a level of professionalism and rigor to the colony's products that had been lacking under the previous incumbent, but his new family connections proved even more useful to the fledgling organization in terms of development capital for the business.

The colony was established in 1881 by Andrea Sbarboro, a Genoese immigrant who parlayed his North Beach grocery store into a community center and ultimately the Italian-American Bank. A great enthusiast for

---

[1] At that time, Dupont and Columbus.
[2] Arthur Caire diary, notes (ca. 1932), p. 5.

the cooperative experiments of the nineteenth-century, Sbarboro acquired a 1,500-acre tract of land in Sonoma County with the vision of a quasi-uto-pian experiment in communal ownership.[3] He got various Italian Ameri-can capitalists to make cash investments in the venture, but at the same time Sbarboro also "sold" shares to Italian immigrants who paid for them through sweat equity, the labor that they contributed in building the vine-yard, as well as monthly cash contributions that would in time give them a genuine equity share in the project. The communitarian–utopian aspect of the project soon disappeared as the cash-strapped workers chose to be paid immediately rather than in promises of future equity in the new enter-prise. It was at about this time that Sbarboro and some of his wealthier associates, like Dr. Giusieppe Ollino,[4] brought in Rossi as chief winemaker and issued shares of stock to raise capital. Because Sbarboro had declared bankruptcy in a previous business, they had difficulty obtaining credit.

Rossi and Sbarboro were largely unknown in the small world of the San Francisco business community, and without an established business repu-tation, Sbarboro's history exacerbated the difficulties they faced in obtain-ing working capital. The solution to this credit problem presented itself through the influence of Justinian Caire's nephew, Adrien Merle, who was both business manager for Caire and a director with Rossi and Sbarboro at the Italian Swiss Colony Wine Corporation.[5] Through Merle, Justinian Caire was persuaded to have his company provide surety for a line of credit with relevant supplier firms in San Francisco. Arthur Caire noted that this had the result of "leaving the public under the impression that Justinian Caire was in back of that institution and thereby solving the credit prob-lems of the new organization."[6]

Later, when the colony began to achieve a measure of success, Rossi ques-tioned the propriety of Justinian Caire Company being the preferred sup-plier of wine making supplies, but Merle insisted that preference be given to Justinian Caire Company in recognition of their contribution to getting the

---

[3] National Italian American Federation, "Andrea Sbarboro" (biography).

[4] Edmund Rossi, "Italian Swiss Colony" (interview), 20. According to Rossi's son, Edmund, Ollino was the vice president of the colony and was a mutual friend of Rossi and Sbarboro. The other directors were Mark J. Fontana, Henry Casanova, Dr. Paolo de Vecchi, Stephan Campodonico, M. Perata, and L. Vasconi.

[5] Edmund Rossi, "Italian Swiss Colony" (interview), 29.

[6] Arthur Caire diary, notes (ca. 1932), p. 6.

colony on its feet. When Italian Swiss Colony began to enjoy greater national success in the wine market, this quid pro quo situation did not continue. As Arthur Caire noted, Justinian Caire Company was forced to compete on the open market for the Italian Swiss Colony's wine supplies business. [7]

Rossi was welcomed into the Caire family, and for a while he enjoyed a trusting relationship with Justinian Caire. In 1883 Rossi and Arthur Caire toured Santa Cruz Island together and compared notes on its development.[8] But business relations between the Caires and Rossi gradually deteriorated throughout the last years of Justinian Caire's life. They further soured in October 1891 as a result of a mutual venture in which Rossi persuaded his father-in-law to buy a large inventory of wine "at a good price of $60,000" [$1.47 million] that would be resold later, with Caire getting two-thirds of the profits. It was a time of turmoil in the wine industry, precipitated by the rapacious pricing practices of the California Wine Association as they attempted to create a monopoly. Wine prices did not rebound as Rossi predicted, and Caire's money was tied up for three years. Aware of growing competition and falling prices, Caire insisted that the wine be sold in a less-saturated market, such as the East Coast or southern states. PC Rossi decided to enter the New Orleans market and prepared the first shipment. There was a further clash that developed over the wording on the bills of lading, with Arthur Caire insisting that the shipment include the name of Justinian Caire or at least PC Rossi and not merely Italian Swiss Colony, who had no actual interest in the transaction. Rossi left for New Orleans, and after many months a portion of the wine was sold. At the Caires' insistence, the Italian Swiss Colony Wine Corporation bought the remaining wine, though the net result of the transactions showed no profit for the Caires. Justinian Caire was not amused. At a meeting called to discuss the outcome of the business venture, Rossi airily summed up, saying, "You lost the interest on your money for 3 years. I have lost my time." In fact, Italian Swiss Colony established a valuable presence in the New Orleans market, which became one of their three major markets outside of California. Justinian (whose loss in interest amounted to approximately $13,500 [$330,000])[9] muttered angrily to his son Arthur, in the French that

---

[7] Ibid., p. 7.

[8] 1 December 1884, Correspondence, 1880–1904, Santa Cruz Island Co.

[9] Benmelech and Moskowitz, "Political Economy of Financial Regulation."

was often used within the family, *"c'est nous qui sommes les dindons de la farce"* (we have been made fools of).[10]

The strained relationship between Rossi and the Caires continued through 1894, when there was a mysterious offer of stock in Italian Swiss Colony by PC Rossi. It emerged that this offer was disputed by other directors of the colony, and it was rejected by Justinian Caire. In spite of this friction, Rossi often went to his in-laws for unsecured loans throughout the 1890s, until a final loan of $11,000 [$291,000] was made in the late 1890s. This time Arthur Caire insisted on some security, which was grudgingly offered in the form of 110 shares of Italian Swiss Colony stock—the value of which, Arthur noted, was nowhere near the value of the loan.[11] Although borrowing arrangements appear to have ceased from that time, PC Rossi continued giving advice and providing contacts for wine sales of Santa Cruz Island wines and acting as a trustee of the Santa Cruz Island Company as late as 1906.[12]

Overall, as early as the late 1890s the stage was set for conflict between PC Rossi and Arthur Caire. These were two headstrong individuals: Rossi, with his drive for success, would use whatever resources were available; and Arthur Caire, equally headstrong, was determined to safeguard the survival and growth of his father's legacy. Arthur also wanted public recognition of the important financial role played by his father and his company in helping build the successful career of Rossi.[13]

---

[10] Arthur Caire diary, notes (ca. 1932), pp. 10–11.

[11] These incidents are noted in Arthur Caire's diary, notes (ca. 1932), pp. 5–12.

[12] PC Rossi to Arthur Caire, 27 February 1906 and 27 August 1906, "Santa Cruz Island Co. Journal, 1906," Santa Cruz Island Co. Records.

[13] An example of what irritated Arthur was a glaring omission of any mention of the Caires' assistance in a volume of contemporary San Francisco biography, which opened with the statement, "PIETRO C. ROSSI ... is the sole architect of his fortunes." Lewis Publishing Company, *Bay of San Francisco*, 540–41.

CHAPTER 12

The Legacy of Justinian Caire

W ith two of the family's strongest personalities at loggerheads, the undercurrents of family resentments and financial ambitions would all collide in the legal battles over the fate of Justinian Caire's legacy. These struggles of daughters against mother were based on an interpretation of the intentions of his will, which was written in the late 1880s at a time of difficult business dealings with his son-in-law. A construal of his intentions to divide his estate six ways was pursued by Caire's married daughters, Amelie and Aglaë, represented by Amelie's son, Edmund Rossi, and Amelie's son-in-law, Ambrose Gherini. The crux of these battles centered on Justinian Caire's aims when he set out his will in 1889.

The initial will was very clear. He left his entire estate to his wife for her disposition. This initial will was followed by a codicil, or second part of the will, that was written four days after the first. In the codicil, which was to come into force only if Caire was predeceased by his wife, there was a declaration that his fortune be shared equally by all his six children.[1] This codicil was presented as the moral basis for the strict legal technicalities on which a number of legal actions were based.

Clearly, the courts at the time concurred with the legal arguments put forward by the plaintiffs in both *Rossi v. Caire* and *Capuccio v. Caire*, but these questions of minority shareholder rights were quite unrelated to the issue of Justinian Caire's intentions to have his legacy preserved intact for the benefit of all his heirs. Now that the dust has more than settled on twenty years of litigation, and the courts have delivered their verdicts to

---

[1] John Gherini, *Santa Cruz Island*, 117 ff.

litigants long since dead, one might more dispassionately interpret that will in its larger context to discover its true intentions.

To do so, one first needs to recall the rough-and-tumble world of nine-teenth-century California, the environment in which Justinian Caire acquired his fortune. For better or worse, there is no denying that this was a male-dominated society. In the 1880s, the days of equal rights and recog-nition for women were far into the future—indeed, women would not even gain the vote in the United States for another three decades. Hence, the mind-set of Justinian Caire was that of a person born and raised in a world where women were revered and respected—and undoubtedly wielded a great deal of power within the family circle—but, at the same time, the place of a genteel upper-middle-class woman was definitely in the home.

Justinian Caire had spent a lifetime creating a business and ranching empire, on which he had expended huge amounts of time, energy, and money, occasionally to the detriment of his health and well-being. He had fulfilled a young French immigrant's wildest dreams of creating a domain in miniature. It is only common sense that his first wish was that his most highly prized accomplishments, the Justinian Caire Company and Santa Cruz Island Company, carry on intact after his death. Much as he loved his children, it is manifestly unlikely that he intended that his empire, so painstakingly assembled and developed over decades, be dismantled and turned into a cash pile to be divided up by his heirs.

To this end, in November 1895, Caire ordered that his commercial inter-ests be consolidated into a corporation called the Justinian Caire Com-pany. With the shares created, he placed a certain number in the name of each of his children but had all the shares endorsed back to himself as sole owner of the corporation. In early 1896, the year before he died, Caire called Arthur into his private office on Market Street and asked him to pro-duce all the stock certificates of both Justinian Caire Company and Santa Cruz Island Company from the safe. He then carefully endorsed each one to his wife Albina, remarking to Arthur, "If anything happens to me, your mother will have no annoyance."[2] Mrs. Caire was now the sole owner of all the stock in both corporations.

Although the codicil to his 1889 will gave his six children—in the event that Albina died first—equal shares in his estate, he specifically stated two

---

[2] Arthur Caire, memorandum ca. 1932, 1–3, Caire Family Papers and Diaries, notebook in the posses-sion of Justinian Caire III.

things. First, his sons were to be his executors of the will and act as "guardians of their sisters."[3] Second, his businesses were to be continued by his two sons, "with as little change and alteration as possible."[4] Today, guardianship refers to an action for a minor or a mentally incompetent adult. But in the world of the 1880s, it was much more likely that Justinian Caire, as a man of his times, meant the guardianship literally. His daughters were to receive an equal share of profits, but they would not take any part in any management of the business interests. The business interests were to be managed by his sons for the benefit of their sisters and the entire family.

By today's standards, this designation of the sons for an active role and the daughters for a passive one might seem manifestly unfair, and whether Justinian's wishes were attributable to a perceived lack of business acumen on his daughters' part is a matter one can only speculate on. However, it is important to remember that the year was 1889, and three of Caire's four daughters were still living at home in Oakland—aged twenty-two, twenty-five, and thirty-four—enjoying the genteel life befitting the comfortable economic circumstances created by their father. The one married daughter, Amelie, was heavily burdened with the first six of her fourteen children and was profoundly reliant on her parents and siblings for material and emotional support. Three of her children died in the Caire home and two were born there. For her, this was a deeply stressful time as childhood diseases took their toll and her husband focused on developing his career, working in the pharmacy all week and, in time, at Asti every weekend. In addition, her mercurial temperament, marked by significant mood swings, was well documented within the family.[5]

To Amelie's increasingly successful husband, the notion of guardianship by his brothers-in-law, Arthur and Frederic, as stipulated in Justinian Caire's will, must have seemed like a rank insult to both his wife and himself. PC Rossi was by now the president of the Italian Swiss Colony Wine Company, director of the CWA, and vice president of the Italian-American bank. He undoubtedly saw himself as an accomplished businessman whose advice and views should be respected. At the same time, it could be argued that his business activities would have alarmed the punctiliously

---

[3] Justinian Caire, will dated 24 January 1889 and codicil to will dated 28 January 1889, Alameda County Superior Court, Case No. 5540.

[4] Ibid.

[5] Edmund Rossi, "Italian Swiss Colony" (interview), 33–34; and Delphine Caire, "Journal," vol. 3.

honest, highly principled Justinian. Some of Rossi's associates in the wine business, like Percy Morgan of the California Wine Association, with its monopolistic strategy for the entire California wine industry, were associated with unscrupulous practices. And it was perhaps with this thought in mind that before his death in 1897, Justinian Caire, whose business ventures with his son-in-law were often less than satisfactory, confided to his sons that he had become uneasy about Rossi trading on the Caire name.[6]

In Justinian Caire's mind, PC Rossi, with his history of falling out with his own relatives[7] and his very high opinion of his own business acumen, represented a threat to Caire's desire to see that "the business now conducted by me in this City, should after my death be continued by my two sons ... with as little change and alteration as possible."[8] For Rossi, his father-in-law's fortune was apparently a bundle of assets to be dismantled and sold off, with the proceeds shared among his heirs, one of whom was his wife. By the early twentieth century, having built a career and a family retreat centered on Asti in Sonoma, the attitude of Rossi and his wife toward Santa Cruz Island was bound to be cooler and more calculating than that of Amelie's siblings. The island was unlikely to be a source of much income for the Rossis and was not a family retreat for them, so its only real value was economic. Rossi's attitude about selling the island, verbalized after the death of his father-in-law, was presumably shared with his new son-in-law, Ambrose Gherini, and his new brother-in-law, Goffredo Capuccio.[9] This desire to sell the island put Rossi on a collision course with Justinian Caire's two sons, who, in the manner of the times, had been designated to maintain their father's legacy and were convinced that it was their filial and familial duty to do so.

The will's intention and the long-standing practice of both of Justinian Caire's firms was that the strategic decision making and the day-to-day operations were to be overseen by the two sons, who received salaries for

---

[6] Delphine Caire, "Journal," vol. 3.

[7] Delphine Caire, "Journal," vol. 3; and Edmund Rossi, "Italian Swiss Colony" (interview), 30 ff. Rossi had fallen out violently with his father in Turin, then with his uncle Alexander Zabaldano, who had facilitated his immigration to California in 1875 and with whom he worked when he first arrived in San Francisco. Rossi was also estranged from his brother, Dominic, with whom he emigrated from Italy.

[8] Justinian Caire, codicil of will dated 28 January 1889.

[9] Arthur Caire, memorandum, ca. 1931 (based on earlier notes), 13, 27, Caire Family Papers and Diaries, in the possession of Justinian Caire III.

their activities. Each child was given title to seven shares of the Santa Cruz Island Company (a 7 percent interest), but the title was recorded in Justinian's name. During the ill health that marked the last year of his life, he assigned the title to Albina, demonstrating that he had no intention of distributing all the shares equally to his children but, rather, intended to leave the distribution ultimately to his wife. Justinian further instructed Arthur to distribute cash payments, when possible, based on each child's nominal share holding, while leaving ownership of all the shares with Albina.[10] The profits, as they arose, were to be shared among the family members, based on their nominal share holdings, with the largest share given to the mother as the head of the family and majority stockholder. In any case, running the companies was something that Arthur had been doing for almost twenty years and Frederic for more than a decade, with their mother and sisters sharing in the profits, to the benefit of all.[11]

The immigrant Justinian Caire and his wife Albina had taught their children the value of family solidarity. This was the time-honored way that émigré families prospered in a land that owed them nothing. For the sons of Justinian and Albina, who had forsaken their personal ambitions for the greater good of the family enterprises, it was unthinkable that the family would divide his legacy.

In spite of these differing opinions about managing Justinian Caire's empire, for the time being everyone more or less got along. These tremors on the surface of family life were visible throughout the first decade of the twentieth century, but the bedrock of family harmony and unity seemed as solid as the building that housed the four-story offices and showroom on Market Street in San Francisco.

---

[10] Arthur Caire, memorandum, ca. 1931 (based on earlier notes), 2, Caire Family Papers and Diaries, in the possession of Justinian Caire III.

[11] Justinian Caire Company records show that Arthur Caire received almost $20,000 [$530,000] in dividends between 1882 and 1908 while he was actively managing the companies; his sister Amelie and her husband, PC Rossi, though not actively involved, received more than $10,000 in dividends [$265,000] in the same period; Fred Caire received approximately the same amount as Amelie between 1887 and 1908, when he was active in island management; and his sister Aglaë received almost $7,000 in dividends [$177,000] in the five years after she left the family home following her marriage in 1903. It is worth pointing out that in 1900 the annual per capita income was $262 and there was no income tax.

Justinian Caire Co., April 28, 1906.

CHAPTER 13

The 1906 Earthquake, the Fire, and the Fate of Santa Cruz Island

On April 18, 1906, after about two minutes of realignment of the Pacific and the North American tectonic plates, the lives of San Franciscans had changed forever. Many buildings in the city and throughout the region suffered a prodigious amount of damage from the earthquake. The inhabitants staggered out of their badly shaken dwellings into a world that would never be the same. But much worse was to come. As fires from overturned lanterns, ruptured gas pipes, and broken chimneys took hold in the freshening April morning breeze, the real injury was about to be inflicted. When it was over, most of the San Francisco business and commercial district lay in smoking ruins, and some would say that the cheerful confidence and leading position of California's first city disappeared, never to return. The history of the great earthquake and fire of 1906 has been told many times in broad brushstrokes, with the statistics of thousands of lives lost, buildings destroyed, and tens of thousands left homeless. There are stories of heroism and cowardice and the tragedies and curiosities that are always a part of a great cataclysm. But at the same time the great sweeping story of the earthquake and fire is the accumulation of millions of little stories, where the trajectory of individual lives was inexorably altered. Thus it was with the extended Caire family.

The first challenge that confronted Arthur and Fred Caire on that April morning when their world changed was the difficulty of even going across the bay to inspect the damage to their building. It is unlikely that they were able to get into the city early on that day, and within twelve hours it was clear that their building, damaged but still standing, was likely to be gutted in the rapidly spreading fires. The official Santa Cruz Island Company journal entry for April 18 read, "All papers having been charred beyond recognition, and there remaining no trace of letters, documents, statistics, reports, certificates, titles, deeds, patent, vouchers or any other instrument, we are compelled to make all our entries from memory and from such papers as may be on record in the various counties of the State."[1]

Four days later, April 22, 1906, a letter to the superintendent laid out the scope of the problems that they were facing as a result of the San Francisco disaster.

> This mail will probably bring you notice of the dreadful earthquake followed by fire that has destroyed the greater part of San Francisco. Our building is entirely destroyed and we have no means of reaching the city for some days. While this state of affairs continues, we will be obliged to seek for provisions elsewhere and to order from Los Angeles instead of from San Francisco such things as flour etc. . . . As we need all the wool we can get this year, you will have to repeat all the *corridas* [large ones] . . . ; shipments of sheep can be continued regularly. Just now we do not know what we are going to do and we will instruct the bank to honor your drafts anyhow until further orders. Address all your mail to Oakland until further orders. Send mail to FF Caire, 114-11th St Oakland California.[2]

The letter to the Santa Barbara County National Bank, which handled the local financial affairs of the Santa Cruz Island Company, was similarly terse.

> Under present conditions, though we have money in bank we will not be able to meet the drafts of our Superintendent, therefore we beg that you pay all the checks he may draw upon you until we can settle the account with you. Please to pay the taxes as usual and keep the receipt until settlement. As

---

[1] "Santa Cruz Island Company Journal, 1906," Caire Family Papers and Diaries, in the author's possession.

[2] Correspondence cited in this section is found in carbon copies of letters dated April 1906–December 1907, Santa Cruz Island Company Records, in the author's possession.

the whole stock and the building of the Justinian Caire company have been destroyed, we are in a pretty bad [way]; still we have roofs over our heads and with money in bank and very few debts we are better off than many a firm which until yesterday was the object of our envy. You will therefore have to carry the Santa Cruz Island Co for a couple of months for $2500–3000 [$62,000–$74,000] in all, perhaps, at the usual rate of interest.

The correspondence over the next few days dealt with the practicalities of provisioning Santa Cruz Island now that San Francisco, normally the major source of supplies, was for all intents and purposes shut down. The natural reluctance of the Caires to make any major purchases at Santa Barbara's inflated prices was overcome as the superintendent was told to buy some small amount of pasta but to compare prices with Los Angeles to make sure that he was getting reasonable value for money. Arthur further noted that "Things will be somewhat unsettled for about ten days because there is no place where business can be transacted. See that *corridas* are done well because we need *all the wool we can get* more than ever before" (italics in the original).

It was clear that the income from the island was going to have to carry the family finances until Justinian Caire Company could get back up and running. In reply to the superintendent's request for sulphur for the vineyard, Arthur responded that he would have to wait some days because the sulphur works had been destroyed by the fire, and furthermore it was likely to be more than a month before regular shipments of supplies from San Francisco were resumed.

> You will have to be patient for a short while, except in cases where absolute necessity requires the immediate purchase of the articles; in such a case you may order them in S. Barbara even though they cost more. . . . As the fire has destroyed all our records and accounts, we must request that you send us the following by first opportunity. Copy of Monthly Cash Accounts since Jan. 1, 06; copy of Segregation of Accounts since Jan. 1, 06.

He ended by asking that all correspondence be sent to the temporary business address of 908 Harrison Street, Oakland. It would be two years before they would move back to their premises on Market Street.

In spite of the gloomy prediction that it would be more than a month before shipments of supplies could be resumed, it was only a little over three weeks before he was telling the superintendent that a shipment of rice, sugar, and flour was on its way, though he noted that they would have to continue buying pasta in Santa Barbara as there was none to be had in San Francisco. However, aside from the practicalities of supplying the island, there were the other aspects of the business to consider that would have ramifications far beyond the island.

As it had always been in the days of Justinian Caire, but especially in this emergency, the Caire brothers' management focus was on detail and profitability. Ironically, one of the earthquake's potentially positive effects on the Caire fortunes was to create a wine shortage, as much of the wine stored in the city itself was destroyed, creating a temporary opportunity to break the near-monopoly position of the CWA.[3] Captain James Prescott of the *Santa Cruz*, who handled the local wine sales, was now instructed not to accept any new wine orders without first checking the new prices that reflected the shortages, said to be up about 30 percent, to 35¢ [$9] a gallon wholesale. With the destruction of the physical structure of the Justinian Caire Company, the profitability of the island was the major focus of the Caire brothers, but they had other concerns as well.

---

[3] The CWA, formed in 1900, had an 80 percent share of the California wine market, though in the earthquake and fire they lost all of the wine that they had stored in their facility south of Market St., which briefly opened the door for independent producers like the Santa Cruz Island Company.

CHAPTER 14

The Stolen Will

Acquiring essential supplies and generating income were not the only problems that were troubling Arthur and Fred in the spring and summer of 1906. Their mother was nearing the end of a long visit to Italy. She had departed in May 1905 with her daughter Hélène to visit her family in Genoa and her daughter Aglaë and family in nearby La Spezia. Albina's will had been destroyed along with all the other papers and stock certificates in the company safe on Market Street. The will detailed the disposition of her estate, essentially all of the holdings of the Justinian Caire Company and the Santa Cruz Island Company left to her by her husband. Albina left an equal number of shares to each of her children (ten shares each in Justinian Caire Company and seven shares each in the Santa Cruz Island Company), but they were endorsed back to her and she retained ownership of all but four shares of each company. These were the two shares she had given her sons before she left for Italy in 1905, in recognition of the amount of their salaries that they had contributed to her upkeep since Justinian's death.[1]

In those days, intercontinental travel was considered significantly more hazardous than today, and if something were to befall her and she died intestate, the family would have to apply to the courts for an executor rather than having one who had knowledge of the family background and of Justinian's and Albina's intentions. A court-appointed executor would likely divide the estate equally among the six children. The oft-voiced

---

[1] Arthur Caire, memorandum on ownership of stock, ca. 1931, pp. 2–3, Caire Family Papers, in the possession of Justinian Caire III. The share certificates later bore the date of the earthquake, 18 April 1906, to signify that the originals had been destroyed.

contentions of the two sons-in-law—PC Rossi and Goffredo Capuccio, particularly after the earthquake—was that the best course of action would be to liquidate the Caire family assets, including Santa Cruz Island, and share out the cash. This was a situation Arthur and Fred knew that Albina wished to avoid at all costs. After correspondence with her, they determined that a new will should be drawn up and sent to Italy for her signature—a task that was duly done. They sent the new will to her on June 24 by registered express mail in care of the office of Goffredo Capuccio at the shipyard in La Spezia. The expectation was that it would arrive in the usual eighteen to thirty days.

For reasons never fully explained, at the time or afterward, the envelope was opened at the shipyard and its contents read by Capuccio, who was enraged to find that his wife and her sister Amelie were to receive their one-sixth share of their mother's estate as a life estate with their brothers as trustees. This situation would thwart the financial ambitions of both himself and PC Rossi to realize the cash associated with their wives' share of Justinian Caire's legacy.

The exact details of what followed are ambiguous, though one thing is certain. Albina never saw the envelope containing the will, though she did not depart from Italy for San Francisco, via Paris and Le Havre, until August 2, almost six weeks after it was mailed. What is also beyond dispute is that Capuccio made copies of the will and sent the original chasing after Albina in her European travels, which had taken her first to France before she headed back to California. At the same time, one of the copies was quietly sent to PC Rossi, who had been advocating the sale of the island for years. Just after the earthquake he advised putting the island on the market as a remedy for the recent economic problems of the Justinian Caire Company. When he saw the will, Rossi was predictably infuriated that he and his wife, Amelie, would have their share of her mother's estate administered by her brothers. Rossi wrote back to Capuccio immediately, "I cannot do without remarking the insult that such a document hurls at Amelie as well as me, just as against Aglaë and you. . . . For the time being I would advise you not to even mention it to Aglaë, because it would cause her too much sorrow . . . but *when the opportune moment comes we will see what we will have to do*" (italics added).[2]

---

[2] Rossi to Capuccio, 30 August 1906, written on Italian Swiss Colony stationery, cited by John Gherini, *Santa Cruz Island*, 123.

The repercussions of stealing, copying, and inspecting Albina's will would harden her two sons-in laws' attitudes and influence their ambitions in ways that no one could predict, but now that Rossi and Capuccio knew about the trust limitations on their spouses' inheritance, their interest in Santa Cruz Island as a going concern ended. Their logical aim would be to force a breakup of the company and a sale of its assets. Like the unseen pressures that had built up under San Francisco before 1906, this personal correspondence between Rossi and Capuccio would create the tensions that would split the family.

Following the theft and circulation of the will, the stage was set for resentment on all sides, particularly after Aglaë Caire Capuccio and her husband moved from Italy to San Francisco in 1910. The situation was exacerbated by intemperate remarks made by Capuccio as he worked alongside the Caire brothers on Market Street and while his family was ensconced in Albina's home in Oakland. After arriving in California, Capuccio talked about how he and Aglaë had come to California hoping to influence Albina into giving Aglaë's share of her estate to them immediately. He and his wife also complained about the low income they were getting from their nominal 7 percent share of the Santa Cruz Island Company. It later emerged that Capuccio had confided to friends in Italy that he anticipated an early return to his native country with a fortune of $400,000 [almost $5 million].[3] Capuccio was also overheard by his brother-in-law speculating about actuarial tables relating to his mother-in-law's long-term survival prospects. The frictions frequently manifested themselves around the offices of the Justinian Caire Company, where Fred and Arthur were regularly forced to listen to their brother-in-law's opinions.[4] There were habitual disagreements, but for the time being they all managed to rub along. Although the stage was set for a major explosion within the Caire family, there was as yet no spark to set it off.

---

[3] Giustiniano Molfino to Delphine Caire, April 1917, Caire Family Papers, "Letters," in the author's possession.
[4] Arthur Caire diary, entries of 28 July 1911 and 12 December 1911.

CHAPTER 15

The Struggle for Profitability

A s the summer came on, there were signs that business conditions in San Francisco were returning to something approaching normality. In early August, Justinian Caire Company took a temporary lease on a property on Mission Street near their ruined Market Street premises. There was constant attention paid to increasing the profitability of Santa Cruz Island. The same week that the office was moved from Oakland to San Francisco, a deal was struck with local fisherman Ira Eaton. For the rate of $10 [$238] per month, Eaton was granted the "sole right of camping on Santa Cruz Island for the purpose of fishing etc. until April 30, 1907." He was also given full authority to eject any other fishermen and prevent them from establishing themselves on the island. It was at this time that Eaton's new bride encountered the rough-and-tumble fraternity of island fishermen who recognized no one's authority.[1] It seems evident that Fred and Arthur had a new regime in mind, though two months later they were trying to collect both rent payment and confirmation that Eaton was keeping other fishermen and poachers away from the island's shores.

As the Caire brothers struggled to try and recover from the financial repercussions of the earthquake, it was business as usual with the local Santa Barbara meat packing company. The Justinian Caire Company negotiated a sale price of $3.25 for ewes, $2.50 for lambs, and $3.50 for wethers, based on the purchase of at least 4,500 sheep. The Caire brothers advised the island superintendent about this price but cautioned him that it was

---

[1] Eaton, *Diary of a Sea Captain's Wife.*

based on the Ealand Packing Company taking all the sheep in Potrero Norte, not picking and choosing among the flock for the best.

The financial stringency imposed by business conditions in San Francisco continued to plague the Caires, and they instructed the superintendent regularly about shipping as much wine and wool as soon as possible. There were also instructions about sending that year's walnut crop—from the grove of almost 500 trees planted several years before at the Main Ranch—and directions about planting more pine trees at Scorpion Ranch. On November 1, 1906, the superintendent was instructed,

> In regard the walnuts, they will be more secure if placed in double sacks, as they will stand the trip better. Send them up as soon as you can so that we can have the benefit of an early market; . . . There are some pines that must be sent to Scorpion: now is the time to bring them down to the harbor in order to have them ready at any time. Do not neglect this matter.[2]

This attention to detail makes it evident that Justinian Caire's sons were carrying on the tradition of land husbandry begun by their father. Another tradition being continued was to purchase as few provisions as possible in Santa Barbara, keeping their distance from the Santa Barbara merchant class. This lack of patronage even extended to excluding Santa Barbara fishermen, who would have provided a convenient bush telegraph. As Arthur explained to the superintendent on November 19,

> We place ourselves under obligations to them and as is usual with Santa Barbara people they will exact ten times as much from us as we have received from them. . . . Noticing the charge made by Capt. Koch for one trip to the Island we must warn you that whenever you ask these fishermen to take over a message or package they must be given to understand that no compensation is due them. Since they are using our Island as a station without paying rent and the least they could do is render any little service we require. In this connection we will tell you that, so far, Santa Cruz Island has been considered by the people of Santa Barbara as a treasure where everything could be bought that was needed by outsiders, [but] as you notice the people there are careful to charge us the very highest rates and refuse to pay us [anything but] the very lowest rates. You must in all your relations with these unwelcome

---

[2] All quotations in this chapter, unless otherwise noted, are from Correspondence, 1906–1924, Santa Cruz Island Co.

visitors give them to understand that if they do not render us small services we will exact rent from them at a pretty high rate.

By late November 1906, the fall corridas were concluded, with a total of 24,000 sheep rounded up. The 1906 wool clip was sacked and weighed. An agreement was concluded with Thomas Denigan Sons, wool merchants of San Francisco, to buy it for 16.5¢ a pound—totaling just under $20,000 [$455,000]. In spite of the setbacks of the months since the earthquake and fire, 1906 was turning out to be a reasonably good year, with income of approximately $30,000 [$682,000] from sheep, wool, and wine. The company secretary's report for 1906 noted the failed corridas, the sufferings of the cattle the year before, and the small grape crop. But at the same time wine sales were booming, "to such an extent that we may be obliged to refuse orders from anybody except our Santa Barbara customers, [and as a result of favorable weather conditions] we will be able to produce all the hay necessary for the Main Ranch without being obliged to carry it from Scorpion as is done at present." The report further noted that the island had struggled to find management stability, with three different superintendents serving over the course of the year. These were the Revel brothers: first was Ulrico, who quit because of ill health; followed by Ottavio, who was fired after four months for incompetence; and third was Ugo, who was judged to be satisfactory and maintained his position for nine years. Still, even with all the trials and tribulations, the gross earnings for the year were more than $25,000 [$595,000]. These earnings did not include the almost $20,000 for the wool clip that had been sold but not yet delivered. Expenses totaled $27,494 [$654,000], the majority of which were salaries and taxes.[3] The year ended with a relatively modest loss of $4,538 [$112,000], which, given the tumultuous events that had been survived, was better than expected.

Arthur finally was able to visit the island in early December, where he found that the superintendent, Ottavio Revel, was not up to the demands of the job but urged the hiring of his brother Ugo. As mentioned in the secretary's report, this was duly done, and the new superintendent took charge in late December. But if Ugo had any illusions about operating on

---

[3] "Santa Cruz Island Co. Secretary's Report, 1906," Santa Cruz Island Co. Records, in the author's possession.

the island with any autonomy, he was brought up short by the first letter from his new employers on December 28:

> We shall begin our official correspondence with you by calling your attention to several inaccuracies that have entered the cash account and which were not corrected by your predecessor as instructed by us . . . We mention to you several small articles [screwdrivers, glass cutter, etc.] which should be kept in the office and not given out except with a proper memorandum so that they may not be lost.

The wine business seemed set to carry on uninterrupted when another catastrophe struck in the form of a storm that blew into Santa Barbara from the southwest on January 9, 1907. Captain Prescott of the *Santa Cruz*, which was tied up to the wharf in Santa Barbara, disregarded the advice of the locals to ride the storm out in the channel and instead left the schooner in port. Normally the port provided safe anchorage; however, the direction of the winds and waves smashed the schooner against the wharf and did severe damage to the hull. This damage put the boat out of commission for more than three months while $1,600 [$36,000] worth of repairs took place in San Pedro, forcing the company to make excuses about delayed deliveries to both wine and livestock customers. On top of these trials, although the total rainfall of twenty-five inches received by the island that year was slightly above average, almost twenty of those inches fell in the months of January and March, with attendant flooding and damage to roads and fields. Reviewing the blows received by the company over the months following the earthquake, Arthur noted despairingly that they seemed to be assuming biblical proportions: "Earthquake and fire at San Francisco; damage by rain on Island; Schooner rammed at wharf in Santa Barbara: what next?"[4]

The answer seemed to be to press on with one of Arthur's enduring concerns: cutting costs. His detailed instructions to the superintendent included the charge to grow more vegetables so that the island men would consume less meat, to try making cheese and butter, and to attempt redomesticating some of the wild hogs for the local meat market. "Should we hire a man especially to look after this business?" Arthur asked. In 1907 there was even thought given to raising pigeons: "We have noticed that in

---

[4] 23 January 1907 margin note.

several places a good deal of money has been made from the sale of squabs and even full grown pigeons, and as we have ample opportunity to feed these animals without great expense we thought that we should study the matter and choose a proper location for a pigeon house."[5]

As mentioned, the daily portion of meat consumed by the island men was one issue raised with the superintendent. The amount was prodigious, though it varied from ranch to ranch. From statistics supplied by the superintendent, it ranged from one pound per day per man at the Main Ranch to two pounds four ounces per day per man at Scorpion and Christy ranches. On March 25 Arthur noted,

> We must absolutely provide some method of reducing the consumption. To think that every year from 850 to 900 sheep [representing approximately $2,500 ($60,000) in costs] are slaughtered for the employees is rather annoying. . . . We insist that the gardener raise more vegetables and of more varied kinds, both for immediate consumption and for processing fruit of all kinds that should be preserved so that during the winter we may . . . reduce the amount of meat.

In the meantime there was the necessity to charter another boat while the *Santa Cruz* was in the San Pedro dry dock, and a deal was struck with a local captain for $20 per trip to the island. Also included in the correspondence with the superintendent was the usual string of detailed instructions, including notes about refurbishing the saddles during the winter months, putting mares into the fields with the stallions, coming up with a new design for hay sheds, and finding a mason among the workforce who could help build walls for shops and stables. The Caires were also flirting with the idea of retailing their better wines in bottle, thus wringing greater profitability out of one of their more reliable income streams, though Arthur lamented the lack of a trained cellar man.

It was well into April 1907 before the schooner was once again back in service making wine deliveries to San Pedro and Santa Barbara. Meanwhile, on Santa Cruz Island the spring corrida season began with shearing at Christy Ranch. The fact that money continued to be extremely tight compounded the accustomed complexities of running an island ranch. Because of communications and weather difficulties, the steamer meant to pick up the 1906

---

[5] 28 October 1907.

wool clip for delivery to wool merchants in San Francisco was unable to do so, necessitating a three-week delay. Arthur noted on April 19, "Add to this the annoyance of Mr. Ealands's [the Santa Barbara meat packer's] persistent calls for sheep which we cannot very well refuse for fear he may go else-where and you will see how very much worried we are."

Then there was the added irritation of fisherman Ira Eaton and his cav-alier attitude to paying his bills, which were outstanding from the previ-ous September. By July 22, the gentle reminders had turned into threats: "Unless by the end of this week we receive a remittance of the $65 which you owe us, we will consider other propositions in regard to the rent, besides holding you liable for the said $65 at all times. We have given you sufficient time to answer all our different letters and we think you should attend to business a little more promptly."

At the end of the month, the superintendent was told to break up Eaton's camp at Pelican Bay and transport the lumber to Prisoners' Harbor and to allow a Mr. Lewis on to the island to assess ways that he would run a fishing operation. On November 20, Arthur told the superintendent,

> None of the fishermen around the Island has paid rent and no contract is in
> existence with any of them; when you see them exact rent and listen to what
> they have to answer, because while things have gone contrary to our wishes
> this year and we have no time to lose in litigations of any kind, we intend in
> the future to have matters so fixed that any time we can seize the implements
> of the fishermen in case they refuse to pay rent. We will act under legal advice
> and with officers of the law.

In the cases where the company was in a position to do a favor for one of the fishermen, Arthur had another strategy: "When you render a favor to such a man, give him a receipt and mark it for rent because we have a right to exact rent from him and it also ... serves as a lever for the future when we will oblige all the fishermen to pay rent."[6]

Then there was the perennial problem of the island workforce. Not only were costs going up, with the mayordomo now receiving $2.25 [$53] per day, and the squad members getting an increase of $5 [$118] a week, but finding and keeping good reliable labor was difficult. Correspondence with one for-mer employee in Italy seeking to come back to the island inquires of him, "If

---

[6] 20 November 1907.

you know two or three lads, sober and honest, who would like the kind of work we are offering, bring them along with you so that you will have friends who are known and trustworthy in whom we can have confidence as well."[7]

Another potential employee was offered a $60 bonus if he would sign a contract to work for a year. Another two were sent bonuses for the months of June and July to keep them happy.

At the autumn corridas and grape harvest, on September 18, Arthur queried the superintendent with a view to using fewer casual laborers from Santa Barbara and making more of the full-time employees, most of whom were Italian:

> You have made the *corridas* under the direction of Ramon Vasquez ... what do you think of him? Also tell us of how the Italians seem to have acted while working as *vaqueros* in districts that were almost entirely unknown land to them. We are very particular about knowing this, as we must know what reliance we can place upon our regular employees when necessity compels to take them out of the ordinary rut and place them where they are not in their ordinary sphere of work. ... In other words we wish to know whether Mexican blood is absolutely necessary to enable a man to bring the sheep out of their hiding places ... [and] if our Italians can bring the sheep over from Scorpion to the Potrero Norte it is surely a sign that they would learn to bring them over the hills from Pinos Grandes or elsewhere.

At the same time, there was an awareness that overreliance of the permanent workforce on the island would alienate the skilled and experienced vaqueros from Santa Barbara,

> If we employ Italians to make runs for the purpose of gathering sheep during the shearing season, there would be danger of some trouble caused by the regular vaqueros who would work badly and throw the blame upon the Italians. ... When the time comes around to engage them, you should notify them that you intend employing a few Italians, warning them at the same time that all the operations of gathering the sheep will be watched closely and that blame will be placed where it belongs.[8]

Week after week, the flow of detailed instructions continued. The superintendent wanted to get some pipe to supply water to Campo Chino on

---

[7] 2 August 1907.
[8] 20 October 1907.

the coast east of Prisoners' Harbor, and Arthur reminded him that there had been a shipment of pipe from Los Angeles ten years before[!]: "Take enough men there to take apart and clean the sections of pipe, and while they're there, build a corral for sheep." There were also instructions about preparation for the coming vintage and the temperature in the cellar:

> Remember in regard to the vintage that you must not wait until the grapes reach 24 degrees [of sugar content] to begin pressing them. There is great danger that the sugar may run to 26 degrees and above when you wait until the normal strength is reached so that as soon as you notice an average of 22 degrees you may begin the crushing provided this strength is uniform throughout the vineyard and not confined to any patch in particular. As a general rule the Muscat is the first to ripen and therefore should receive your early attention.[9]

Even the garden fence at the main ranch did not escape Arthur's meticulous instructions. On October 19, he wrote:

> We hope that you used something better than ordinary fence posts. . . . When they are in the ground you could paint them green and then use the wires as we told you. This fence should be built so that the west side meets an angle made by the fence that goes from the bridge towards the locust trees of the vegetable garden. [As for making fences around the family residence] You are not to build fences around the residence without first obtaining our consent so that we will be sure to approve what you have done and not have any regrets.

The Santa Cruz Island Company management had its fingers on every detail, down to notes on preserving string beans with salt, then directions for cooking them afterwards. The Caire brothers once again pressed the superintendent to encourage the cook to use more vegetables and to get the men to account for the number of meals supplied for each animal killed. Then there is the suggestion that perhaps eggs could provide a substitute for meat at the morning meal. The variety would also improve the men's general health, noted Arthur. Several weeks later, he acknowledged receipt of the photograph of the garden fence taken by the superintendent and complimented him on its appearance; however, he then asked for changes that would not have been required if he had been consulted: "This is why we

---

[9] 3 September 1907.

tell you to always wait for our decisions before you start any such work."[10] Fencing to protect the barnyard and the flower and the vegetable gardens against cattle evoked a discussion about what type of barbed wire to use, with a note that if it was going to be seen, the superintendent should opt for the more aesthetically pleasing ribbon barbed wire or buckthorn wire rather than the common barbed wire.

The long-term commitment to land husbandry carried on, with lists of trees to plant at all the ranches, starting at the Main Ranch, with elms, ash, acacias, and oaks mentioned among the instructions of October 28:

> For Scorpion, plant deeply with the roots well covered in earth . . . at Prisoners' Harbor, the same following the contours of the beach. Behind the big wooden wall put big rocks to protect it from the sea. . . . One precaution to be taken however is to avoid the planting of the trees in regular rows because we do not care to have an orchard effect where a forest effect should be obtained . . . This system should be followed where we do not raise trees for economical purposes, where we do not expect to make a profit.

Relief at having escaped the worst of the damage to the business in 1906 was tempered by troubles with the crew of the schooner *Santa Cruz*. Conflict had been brewing for a long time between the long-serving Captain James Prescott and his employers. It would seem that the damage the schooner sustained as a result of Prescott's refusal to leave port in the face of the storm in January 1907 set the scene for a rancorous parting of the ways over the summer. From Prescott's perspective, the central issue in the breakdown of working relations was due to the Caires' promise of a pay increase that never materialized. According to an account in the *Santa Barbara Morning Press*, he was being significantly underpaid and unjustly accused of disobeying the orders of the superintendent.[11] There may be some foundation to these charges, as the Caires were noted for their determination to minimize the wages of their employees and had very little tolerance for human error, particularly when it hit their pocketbook.

There followed the difficult task of recruiting a replacement, complicated by the fact that American citizenship was a state requirement for

---

[10] 31 August 1907.

[11] "Prescott Leaves Santa Cruz," *Santa Barbara (Calif.) Morning Press*, 17 August 1907, Santa Cruz Island Foundation archives.

command of a motor-powered vessel registered in American waters. The appointment of George Nidever, who was about sixty-two years old and one of the grand old master mariners of the South Coast and the Channel Islands, was finally concluded by the autumn.[12] Though the Caires would have preferred someone younger, with "business at a standstill and hundreds of head of mutton and thousands of gallons of wine undelivered,"[13] they opted for experience and availability rather than wait for the perfect candidate.

The Santa Cruz Island Company seemed to be recovering strongly. The 1907 company report showed that revenue had doubled to more than $50,000 [more than $1.1 million] but noted that expenses had also risen to almost $35,000 [$797,000]. The blame for the increased expenses was placed on rising taxes, the bill for the repairs to the schooner, and a labor shortage in the area, which had led to an increase in labor costs "due to the passing away of the competent old-time *vaqueros* . . . the younger element is composed of careless and lazy men who have no love for their work." Here again Arthur showed the family disdain for the locals. "If we could manage to retain a few Europeans on the Island for a few years, we would be free in a certain measure from the tyranny of the dishonest *Barbarenos*." The secretary went on to note the increase in number of animals on the island, which was causing "a gradual degradation of the soil . . . with the resulting diminution of pasturage. We are forced to increase our productive area by

---

[12] This George Nidever who the Caires hired was the well-known son of a famous father who shared his name. The father, George Nidever (December 20, 1802–March 24, 1883), was a mountain man, explorer, fur trapper, memoirist, and sailor of German descent born in Tennessee. His autobiographical *Life and Adventures of George Nidever* was popular at the end of the nineteenth century. At twenty-eight he joined a hunting and trapping party that left Fort Smith, Arkansas, in 1830; after a year spent adventuring from Missouri to Texas, the core of the party reached Taos, New Mexico, in 1831. That fall they set out for the headwaters of the Arkansas River. Nidever took part in the battle of Pierre's Hole, and in July 1832 he accompanied Joseph Reddford Walker to California, arriving in 1833. He remained there and joined George C. Yount in a sea otter hunt that had some success. From Santa Barbara he renewed sea otter hunting, pursuing that profession, along with farming and Pacific piloting, for the remainder of his life. He married California native Sinforosa Sánchez at Mission Santa Barbara in 1841. At the end of the Mexican–American War, Nidever joined John C. Frémont at Santa Barbara in 1846 and accompanied him as interpreter to Campo de Cahuenga, where the Treaty of Cahuenga was signed, ending the war. Nidever tried the gold fields briefly but without much success, and he ranched for a time on San Miguel Island. He was buried at Calvary Catholic Cemetery in Santa Barbara, California, in 1883. The only mention of his sons in his memoirs is on p. 87.

[13] "Prescott Leaves Santa Cruz," *Santa Barbara (Calif.) Morning Press*, 17 August 1907, Santa Cruz Island Foundation archives.

enclosing new fields and introducing forage plants which can be irrigated
... it is imperative we have a reserve of hay to get us through the dry years
... [at the same time planning for] flood control." He concluded with a note
on, "the challenges of the terrain ... and the need for crop rotation."[14]

In the following year, more than 84 percent of the island income was
based on the combined wool sales of 1907 and 1908, and total revenue was
down from the previous year to just under $44,000 [$1 million]. The 1908
secretary's report ominously noted that "sales of wine have been somewhat
affected by the prohibition movement in southern California and were
smaller than during 1907." This harbinger of what was to become a nation-
wide trend illuminated the changing character of the Southern California
population as it was influenced by waves of immigration from the conservative teetotal Midwestern heartland. In addition, although overall rainfall figures for the year were above average, "the water fell so irregularly
and in such great quantities at one time that our crops did not receive any
benefit from the downpour. The result was that our fields did not receive
any moisture towards the end of the season and our hay crops were not
satisfactory—in fact we can say that a good deal of our work went for nothing." But in spite of these gloomy notes and the overall reduction in revenue, expenses were still well below this figure, though a paper loss was
shown because of the disbursement of $25,000 [$581,000] in dividends to
Albina and all her children, based on their putative shareholdings, which
she held in trust for them.[15]

In 1909, net revenues increased to a healthy $16,000 [$376,000], based
on wool and livestock sales, with a small contribution from the winery. On
the expense side, Arthur noted the presence of a bill for $3,150 [$75,000] for
the repair of the schooner. He further noted, "our stock needs an infusion
of new blood, that means care must be taken to get rid of all the *coludos*
[wild males] and scrub sheep that roam over the Island and greater attention paid to the preparation of stock for the market."[16] A heavy sum was
credited to the cattle account for that year—the result of selling 299 head,

---

[14] "Santa Cruz Island Co. Secretary's Report, 1907," Santa Cruz Island Co. Records, in the author's
possession.

[15] "Santa Cruz Island Co. Secretary's Report, 1908," Santa Cruz Island Co. Records, in the author's
possession. For example, Amelie Rossi and Aglaë Capuccio each received dividends of $1,750
[$42,000].

[16] "Santa Cruz Island Co. Secretary's Report, 1909," Santa Cruz Island Co. Records, in the author's
possession.

"the first large sale of these animals we have ever made ... [and] we are confident that we are in the right path so far as the development of the cattle industry is concerned."[17] He also noted the need for new residences at Scorpion Ranch and the Main Ranch.

> At Scorpion the present residence is liable to fall to the ground at any time, being undermined by the winter floods. At the main ranch the present residence is not only too small but it is lacking in toilet (it had one) and other conveniences besides being so constructed that an earthquake might cause great damage: a new building would be of immense advantage. The total expense that we mention as required for the improvements of our herd and flock, of the schooner and for the new buildings would amount to about $9750 [$238,000] at the utmost, as far as we can calculate.[18]

He noted that costs for these structures would be easily defrayed by income.

Arthur, as good as his word, and helped by Fred, began seeking advice and plans from a variety of architects, including the renowned Greene Brothers of Pasadena. They also contacted the popular architect Henry Wilson, who published a catalogue of floor plans and photographs of more than 100 bungalows. Given the choice between the Greenes, who would only begin a design upon payment of 7.5 percent of the estimated cost, and Henry Wilson, who promised to furnish three sets of plans for $50, the Caires opted for the more economical option; construction began the following year. It is likely that the brothers' concurrent plans for the building of their own town residences in Oakland on the north side of Lake Merritt influenced this decision.

The financial results of the year 1910 showed a paper loss of approximately $3,000 [$71,000], with revenues of almost $50,000 [$1.17 million] and expenses of almost $53,000 [$1.24 million]. Arthur noted in his report to the shareholders that, "Either because of low prices or severe competition we sold practically no wine during the year and the trouble we had in effecting a settlement with the Santa Barbara butchers delayed the sale of cattle until too late in the season." Included in the outgoings were several extraordinary expenses, notably a small dividend for all family members, a re-fit for the schooner, new tanks for the winery, and the building of the

---

[17] Ibid.
[18] Ibid.

new family house at the Main Ranch. The approximately 3,000-square-foot residence, with ten rooms and several bathrooms as well as a 500-square-foot living room, cost $6,290 [$147,000] and was enthusiastically described in the local press as one of the finest summer homes on the coast.

Commenting on the general problems with the local labor force, Arthur informed the shareholders,

> We find that the difficulty in obtaining capable *vaqueros* for the gathering of the sheep during the shearing season will oblige us to have recourse to some measures that will enable us to overcome the trouble due to the incapacity and the ill will of the *Barbarenos* who are now employed at the *corridas*. For this reason during the past year we have laid out lines of fences that will separate the various districts and enable us to gather the sheep and cattle a little more easily. Several of these fences have already been built and we expect that it will soon be possible for us to keep certain districts entirely free for a time and thus allow the pasture to be renewed ... thus creating a reserve for the feeding of our animals.[19]

This report outlined what was becoming a general trend: both rising prosperity and increasing competition for their skills were making the traditional Santa Barbara casual labor force more reluctant to accept the terms and conditions laid down by the Caires. Whereas their fathers had been happy for the work, the sons did not necessarily accept the enforced solitude and discipline inherent in the Caire management and island life.

All in all, the years up to 1911 were not atypical on the island. The levels of the sheep herd remained at or above their 25,000 head average for this period, with the herd numbers in 1911 rising to the highest level they would achieve in the twentieth century: a little over 35,000.[20] The 1910 and 1911 corridas were especially successful, with between 22,000 and 24,000 sheep shorn.[21] With a good price for wool in San Francisco, these corridas would have represented a substantial income stream for the company, in excess of $20,000 [$468,000]. The cattle herd had also been growing steadily, from 841 head in 1906 to 1,409 head in 1911. So in spite of the downturn in demand for wine, 1911 was one in which a small profit was

---

[19] "Santa Cruz Island Co. Secretary's Report, 1910," Santa Cruz Island Co. Records, in the author's possession.

[20] Symmes & Associates, *Report on Santa Cruz Island*, Section 2, Inventory, Sheet 1.

[21] Ibid., Sheet 2.

eked out, approximating the annual average of $50,000 [$1.2 million] for revenue and expenses. With the winters of 1909, 1910, and 1911 averaging a substantial twenty-eight inches of rain, feed for the large herd was plentiful.[22] The vineyard was producing well. Because of the low demand for its output, in 1911 the winery had almost 230,000 gallons of saleable wine on hand and about another 20,000 gallons maturing.[23] This quantity of wine would have represented more than $25,000 [$600,000] in potential income for the Santa Cruz Island Company as the island maintained its place as the jewel in the crown of the Justinian Caire family's holdings.

The financial records painted a rosy picture, but far from the island in 1910 and 1911 three somber occurrences took place that would have a dramatic impact on Justinian Caire's legacy and lasting repercussions for all his heirs.

---

[22] Ibid., p. 16.

[23] Transcript of appeal in *Rossi v. Caire*, SF 7101 (174 Cal. 74), pp. 110–112, cited in John Gherini, 238.

CHAPTER 16

Death and Disappearance

It was at Christmastime 1910 that Justinian Caire's wife, Albina, made a gift to her children of shares in the Santa Cruz Island Company. Each child received full possession of the seven shares left to him or her by Justinian Caire that he had endorsed back to his wife. For each child, including the two married daughters, it represented a 7 percent ownership interest. As Justinian Caire said to his son when he signed all the shares over to his wife not long before his death, all the shares were Albina's to do with as she wished, and the reason why this gift should have happened at this time is unknown, but it was certainly her right to do it.

Albina was almost eighty years old and had been a widow for thirteen years. She knew that the ownership of shares and the payments from them were causing tensions in the family, and quite possibly she hoped that giving actual ownership to her two married daughters would keep the peace. There might well have been subsidiary reasons, too. There was the planned construction of the new family house at the Main Ranch, with its many bedrooms that would better accommodate the large and growing extended Caire family. It might even have been the emergent specter of income tax that would come into effect in 1912. Arthur and Fred had urged their mother to give their sisters direct ownership, and Arthur volunteered to hand over the stock certificates to his sister Amelie, whose shares had previously been in the name of her husband. On December 21, he asked Amelie to come down to the company offices on Market Street, where he gave her the certificates and explained what they were. She examined them, asking him in the French that was often used within the family, "What are you saying?" Arthur responded in kind, "Mother wants her children to enjoy some of the revenues from the Island even while she is still alive. These shares are for you." Amelie left shortly thereafter, without uttering a word of thanks, noted Arthur.[1]

A few days later the Santa Cruz Island Company declared a dividend, and, like her siblings, Amelie received a check for $350 [approximately $17,500]. But curiously, when her mother called at her home in San Francisco a few days later, rather than a word of gratitude, the mercurial Amelie voiced a series of reproaches and recriminations to the effect that her mother had not done anything for her in thirty years. The company records paint a somewhat different picture. They show that over the years she and her husband had received distributions totaling almost $10,000 [approx. $268,000], including a payment two years before of $1,750 [$43,000].[2]

It was perhaps because she was troubled by Amelie's outburst that Albina distributed five additional shares in the company in June 1911 to Arthur, Fred, and Delphine, giving the sons a total of fourteen shares each and Delphine twelve shares. The discrepancy between their holdings dated from 1905: before leaving for Europe, Albina had given both of her sons two shares each of Santa Cruz Island Company in compensation for the amount of their salaries that they had contributed to her upkeep since Justinian's death. Amelie, Aglaë, and Hélène retained their original seven shares. Soon after the 1911 gifts, Albina sold three shares each to her sons and to Delphine. Each son now had seventeen shares, and Delphine had fifteen, a total 49 percent holding. After the various distributions, Albina retained thirty shares for herself.

The original distribution to the children was spelled out in her famous intercepted will of 1906, in which she left equal shares of her personal estate to each child, but the two one-sixth shares for Amelie and Aglaë would be in the form of a life trust, with their brothers as trustees.[3] As noted earlier, by following the example spelled out in her husband's will, Albina had enraged her sons-in-law.

The year 1911 was marked by two other events, one dramatic and shocking and the other virtually unnoticed. The first of these was the sudden

---

[1] Arthur Caire diary, p. 91 ("ownership of stock").

[2] To put $1,750 into the context of 1911, it was approximately six times the annual per capita income in the United States.

[3] Arthur Caire, memorandum, ca. 1932, p. 92 ("ownership of stock"), Caire Family Papers, in possession of Justinian Caire III.

death of Amelie's husband PC Rossi in Asti. One Sunday morning in early October at the Rossi estate, he took out a light gig with a new, somewhat skittish horse that he wanted to try out. When the horse bolted, Rossi attempted to jump from the gig. In a freakishly similar repetition of the incident with his wife years before, he fell and hit his head, dying from the injuries he sustained.[4]

The whole family was in shock as the body was returned from Sonoma County to the Rossi house in Pacific Heights. It was from here on Vallejo Street that the funeral cortege set out for the requiem mass at the big Italian church of Saints Peter and Paul on Washington Square in North Beach. From the church, the body of PC Rossi was taken to its final destination in Holy Cross Cemetery, on the western edge of the city. Testimonials and praise flowed in the local press for the man who had become a fixture in the business and financial world of San Francisco. Although their feelings for PC Rossi were complicated by his self-assured and unsolicited personal opinions about the family assets, the Caires rallied around to pledge to Amelie that she could rely on their support as she had always done over the years.

The second occurrence of 1911 remains a central mystery in the destruction of Justinian Caire's legacy. In the same month as Rossi's death, the annual notification for the payment of the state corporation license tax was received at the office of the Santa Cruz Island Company at 573 Market Street. As usual, the form required the signature of Arthur Caire and a payment of $5 by November 30. It was placed on the desk of company cashier and secretary Goffredo Capuccio, the man who had played a central role in surreptitiously copying and distributing Albina's will and whose position in the offices of Justinian Caire Company had been engineered by PC Rossi the year before.[5] From there the form disappeared, as did a second reminder, and their absence went unnoticed by the Caire brothers until two days after Christmas, when they were notified that they had failed to pay the tax and had consequently forfeited the corporate charter of the

---

[4] Edmund Rossi, "Italian Swiss Colony" (interview), 66. This version was contradicted by Edmund's younger brother, Fr. Carlo Rossi, SJ, who maintained that PC Rossi was killed in a fall from a wagon that had been sent to pick him up at the Asti railroad station (Carlo Rossi, transcript of interview, 25 July 1977, California Historical Society, San Francisco, Calif.; hereafter cited as Carlo Rossi interview).

[5] Arthur Caire, memorandum, ca. 1931, p. 19, Caire Family Papers, notebook in possession of Justinian Caire III.

Santa Cruz Island Company. The corporation was technically in liquidation and required the unanimous agreement and consent of all stockholders to reinstate its charter. Amelie's son-in-law, Ambrose Gherini, was said to have exclaimed, "[This is] the first ray of light that we have been waiting for."[6] The majority stockholder trustees—Albina, Fred, Arthur, Delphine, and Hélène, with 86 percent of the stock—were now suddenly and fatally exposed to the whims of the two married daughters with their minority 14 percent shareholding.

---

[6] Ibid., p. 27.

CHAPTER 17

Daughters against Mother

On January 2, 1912, the first business day of the new year, Fred and Arthur began their efforts to reorganize the company. All the stockholders—that is to say, all the members of the Caire family, with the exception of newly widowed Amelie—signed to reinstate the corporation. Perplexed, Albina and Delphine went over to San Francisco the next day to seek an explanation from the recalcitrant daughter, but before Albina could say why she had come, Amelie launched into such a violently abusive tirade that her mother and sister felt "obliged to retire." Later that day, Ambrose Gherini, who had been in the house with Amelie when she threw out her mother and sister, sent word to the Caire's attorney, Joseph Bluxome, that neither his mother-in-law nor her sister Aglaë would ever sign articles of reincorporation. In point of fact, Aglaë had signed the articles on January 2, though she would later renege on this promise, claiming that she had signed under duress. In the same conversation Gherini revealed that he, too, had a copy of Albina's will with its trust clause. When and how he came into possession of the will was never made known, but Gherini had married PC and Amelie's daughter Maria just two months after its theft, when it would have been much on their minds.

Reeling from this communication, and having failed to make any headway with Amelie, Albina sent her youngest daughter Hélène over to San Francisco on January 5 to act as intermediary and ascertain her older sister's intentions. Amelie told her sister that she had possessed a copy of her mother's will for six years, showing that the shares of the island given to her and Aglaë were to be unfairly controlled by their brothers. Later that week, Amelie's twenty-four-year-old son Robert called on his grandmother to inform her that he had gone to the Alameda County Courthouse to get a copy of his grandfather's will. He "had the effrontery" (said Arthur in his diary) to tell his grandmother that she was not carrying out the intentions of her late husband. For this he was taken to task by Hélène, who told him that the Caires knew that someone had stolen their mother's will in Italy and that the suspicion fell upon his father. Robert was shocked that anyone would accuse his recently deceased father of dishonesty. Hélène urged him to clear up the matter by airing the exact circumstances of how the will came into his mother's possession. Rather than explain, he responded, "When this affair blows over, you will be surprised to find out how the thing started and when you know how the will was obtained you will find the matter laughable."[1]

But clearly it was no laughing matter for the Caires. Early in the afternoon on January 8, Goffredo Capuccio, Aglaë's husband, handed Arthur a written request for the stock certificates of both Santa Cruz Island Company and Justinian Caire Company that were on the books in his wife's name. Later that day, there was a new twist to the tale in a letter from Ambrose Gherini. The letter, delivered by hand to the Market Street offices, explained that its bearer was an expert accountant who had been selected by Gherini's *clients*, Amelie and Aglaë, to inspect the books of the Santa Cruz Island Company. In a moment of high drama, Fred and Arthur immediately called Capuccio into their private office. Enraged at this "slap in the face to our mother," they told him he was fired on the spot, effective immediately, as they considered him a spy. With Capuccio expelled from the company, the campaign by Gherini continued later that week with a phone call to the Caires' attorney demanding to know why Aglaë had not received her distribution for her nominal shares in 1908, even though he knew that she was not the actual owner of the shares until 1910 and that none of the children had received a distribution that year.[2]

In spite of being on the receiving end of these aggressive tactics, the Caires still refused to believe that they could not restore some civility to the developing war of words. Seeing that the unequal distribution of the shares was such a bone of contention for their sisters, Fred, Delphine, and Arthur offered to return the three shares each they had bought in 1911, hoping that the other side would accept this olive branch. Their hopes were

---

[1] Arthur Caire diary, 6 January 1912.
[2] Arthur Caire diary, 12 January 1912.

immediately dashed. Gherini's response was that his clients were not content with this peace offering, insisting that Arthur and Fred were "morally and legally" bound to return the four shares that they had received in 1905 in compensation for supporting their mother. What is more, he continued, "Mrs. Albina Caire should bind herself to divide her estate equally among her children, and that the children sign an agreement accepting such action on her part!" This declaration was followed by threats of suit and scandal and having Albina declared incompetent.[3] With this uncompromising stance, the battle lines between the majority and minority shareholders in the Santa Cruz Island Company were drawn.

A week later came the first inkling of the strategy being directed by Gherini. In a proposal for a settlement, Gherini told Bluxome that his clients would be "making an offer in regard to the selling of their eventual interest in their mother's estate." The Caires' scorn for this proposal was countered the next week by an order from Aglaë to Arthur, instructing him to transfer one of her seven shares of stock to Ambrose Gherini and another to a Mr. George Steiger, a legal associate of Gherini's. The once tightly held family company was now truly split open. Gherini kept up the pressure a couple of days later, telling Bluxome that unless some action on a financial settlement for his clients was taken by the majority trustees he would advertise the island for sale in San Francisco, Los Angeles, and Santa Barbara. The same day Gherini sent a notice of a meeting of the trustees to be held on January 26 in his office. If it was part of the brash strategy to hurry them into a cash settlement, then the Caire trustees made it clear that they would not attend any meeting called by the minority with their 14 percent holding. But to be on the safe side, they sent Joseph Bluxome to Gherini's office, where he saw that the Capuccios were in attendance.

The next day, January 27, the battle shifted to the office of the Caires' attorney, where the regular meeting of the trustees was scheduled to take place. Thanks to Aglaë's stock transfer, this group now included Gherini and Steiger. From the start of the meeting, Gherini assumed his habitual aggressive stance by insisting that Aglaë's name should appear on all company checks. He followed up with some remarks about the sale of the island, reported Arthur, "in the presence of Mrs. Albina Caire to whom the subject was most disagreeable and without any protest from Mrs. Capuccio."

[3] Arthur Caire, memorandum, ca. 1931, pp. 98–99 ("Ambrose Gherini–lawyer"), Caire Family Papers, in the possession of Justinian Caire III (punctuation in the original).

In the same office on the last day of January, at Gherini's request for a meeting to discuss the Rossi–Capuccio settlement proposal, the Caire brothers met with the architect of their married sisters' legal strategy. Gherini began by asking whether, "the women [his mother-in-law and his aunt by marriage] could not be eliminated in the matter so as to expedite the transacting of the business at hand."[4]

Not for the first time in these early days of confrontation, Fred and Arthur Caire were completely dumfounded. How was it possible, the mystified Fred asked Gherini, not to make any reference to his sisters given that they were the parties at interest? This exchange encapsulated the conflicting approaches of the two sides. As far as Gherini was concerned, he was engaged in a negotiation to achieve the highest possible return for his clients. For the Caires, it was a family dispute that could be put right with the same good will that had always characterized their dealings with each other. Perhaps regretting this revelation of his attitude toward "the women," which Arthur interpreted as disappointed self-interest, Gherini hurried on to describe his clients' position. He noted that about seven or eight years earlier there had been an offer to purchase Santa Cruz Island for a million dollars. Assuming the sale and realization of the million dollars, adding on interest at 6 percent per year would make the current value of the Island $1.48 million [$34 million].

Then he dropped the bombshell. His clients, Mrs. Amelie Rossi and Mrs. Aglaë Capuccio, would sell out their interest in the island valued at this level for $240,000 [almost $5.5 million] each, or about 35 percent of the total alleged value of the island. Recovering his composure, Fred Caire asked Gherini if this $240,000 was sought by each of his clients for the seven percent of the shares she held. Gherini explained that the price was based on their seven shares plus the expectancy—that is, the price that they set on a one-sixth share of their father's ownership of the Santa Cruz Island Company, and their intention was to take up their one-sixth interest in the Justinian Caire Company at some later date. This six-way division of Caire's entire estate remained a fixation of the Rossis and Capuccios throughout the twenty years of litigation, in spite of the fact that it was only ever mentioned in the codicil and, given the longevity of Albina, had no basis in reality.

"Where do Amelie and Aglaë expect that we will find such a sum?" Fred asked.

---

[4] Arthur Caire diary, 31 January 1912.

Gherini explained that at a meeting of the Rossi family, it had been decided, against his advice, that if their mother did not have the money to buy them out, Mrs. Rossi (whose husband had sold his interest in Italian Swiss Colony some ten years earlier at a considerable profit) would not insist upon payment of interest while Mrs. Caire paid off the debt. However, Mrs. Capuccio, whose financial circumstances were not as robust as her sister's, would have to insist on the payment of interest on the unpaid amount.

Here Arthur Caire broke in, "And in case this is not done, it will be a suit of daughters against their mother."

"Well, yes," replied Gherini, matter-of-factly.

"That's a pretty cold-blooded proposition," responded Arthur.

"All my clients want is justice, and they expect one-sixth of their father's estate," Gherini replied, adding ominously, "I have three potential purchasers for the Island."[5]

Within a month, the Caires had gone from an ostensibly close-knit family sharing valuable but not easily saleable property and business assets, to the very real threat of litigation and the forced sale of property that had been accumulated and husbanded for more than half a century.

On the first Monday in February, Mr. Steiger, the new holder of one share given to him by Aglaë, called at the store on Market Street. He had been sent by Mr. Gherini, he said, to look at the minutes of the shareholders meetings of the Santa Cruz Island Company. Coming from a stockholder, this request had to be honored. Arthur and Fred gritted their teeth and complied with his request. Gherini kept up the pressure later that week by issuing a second notice to the bank not to honor any company checks unless signed by Aglaë. With relations between the two sides at a standoff, Gherini sent his colleague David Freidenrich to confer with Joseph Bluxome "on behalf of Mrs. Amelie Rossi" to see if something could be done to reopen negotiations.

If the Gherini strategy was to keep the lawyers talking, the Caires attempted to re-establish the traditional family communications that had served them so well over the decades. When Freidenrich called on Bluxome again three days later, on Friday, February 23, to ask for more information about Santa Cruz Island, he was told that Fred Caire intended to call on his sister Amelie the next day. Fred went up to her house in Pacific Heights only to be told that she and Aglaë had gone to Oakland to speak with their mother. Annoyed, he called on her again the following Tuesday. This time

<hr>

[5] Arthur Caire diary, 31 January 1912.

he was rebuffed for the reason that she was afraid of him and feared he would become violent. The following day Freidenrich told Bluxome that his client, Mrs. Rossi, had been assured by her mother that she intended to divide her estate equally among her six children, and that Freidenrich wanted a meeting with Fred Caire to move things on. Bluxome quickly passed on this information to Fred and Arthur, who were concerned enough to visit their mother that evening. Albina emphatically denied having said anything about the division of her estate and went to the Market Street offices the next day to meet with Bluxome and to clear the air. She confirmed that during the conversation with Aglaë and Amelie she had assured them that she loved all her children equally but what was done was done, and she regretted having given them shares in the island which they were now using against her. She had also told her two married daughters that she intended to keep the disposition of her estate unchanged and hoped "from the bottom of her heart" that their children would not turn on them as they had on her. Fred told Bluxome that he would meet with Freidenrich the following week.

A week went by with no meeting as Fred was awaiting the return home of his sister Hélène, who had gone into Merritt Hospital in Oakland for an operation. He hoped she would be able to act as intermediary and bring some courtesy back into the conversation between Amelie and the rest of her family. On Friday, March 8, Freidenrich called Bluxome to say that Fred was deliberately stalling, and that unless some progress was made on a settlement, his client, Mrs. Rossi, would bring suit for the dissolution of the Santa Cruz Island Company because she wanted what was coming to her, and Mrs. Caire was morally bound to distribute her estate according to the wishes of her daughters. He hinted, but produced no proof, that there had been a conspiracy within the family, pre-dating the death of Justinian Caire to prevent Amelie from exercising her rights. Later that day, Freidenrich called at Bluxome's office to ask for the Caires' response to the demand that they guarantee his client's interests. Upon receiving the predictable answer, he said that Mrs. Rossi would "force the Trustees to do their duty" and that she wanted as much or as little as was coming to her. Furthermore, echoing Gherini's demand from the previous month, she insisted that all Albina's children sign an agreement on the distribution of her estate.

The strong-willed Albina's response was unequivocal. She made clear to Bluxome her response to this threat to influence her decisions about her estate. "I do not recognize the right of any of my children to tell me what use I should make of what legally and morally belongs to me, and I feel still capable of judging things for myself without anyone having to dictate the law to me."[6]

For several weeks, Freidenrich pressed Bluxome for a meeting with Albina. On the 18th of April, she agreed to meet him at the company offices on Market Street. When Freidenrich arrived, he was ushered into an office where Albina waited, flanked by Bluxome, Hélène, and Arthur. Freidenrich opened by acknowledging that a suit brought by a daughter against her mother was unusual, but knowing the intentions of Justinian Caire it was certain that his objective was to have an equal division of his property among all his children. Arthur responded heatedly that the testament of his father spoke for itself when he left everything to his wife and that she probably knew his intentions better than strangers. Here Albina spoke up, methodically taking Freidenrich through the chain of ownership of island shares, including her ownership and control of all but four shares up to the time, sixteen months previously, when she made voluntary gifts to all her children. She added that she had informed her married daughters when she had seen them the previous month that she never would have given them the shares if she had known that the gift would be used against her, and that they knew full well that the gift was made by their mother with the understanding that the island remain in the family.

Freidenrich countered by asking Albina if she knew all aspects of the business of the Santa Cruz Island and Justinian Caire companies. Albina responded that in the management of the businesses, her two sons had her complete confidence and consent, just as they had had the confidence of their father, and that they advised her of everything to do with the companies. Freidenrich responded that although he did not represent Mrs. Capuccio, he knew that she was in difficult financial circumstances and went on to remark that the two married sisters had derived no material benefit from Santa Cruz Island. Here Arthur broke in to say that his married sisters' experience was no different from the other children of Albina and Justinian; that is, they had received periodic distributions based on shares held for them by Albina. He added, "Until my mother made her children a gift of certain shares, the property was practically all her own [with the exception of the four shares she had given her sons in 1905], and in my management

---

[6] Albina Caire to JF Bluxome, 14 March 1912, Caire Family Papers, "Letters," in the author's possession.

of [it], I considered her the owner to such an extent that I would have set fire to it had she so ordered me to do."[7] While this hung in the air, Freidenrich asked if Albina would see her daughter Amelie. When she indicated the affirmative, he added "or her sons," referring to Amelie's oldest sons, the twins Edmund and Robert. This question provoked an angry outcry against dragging the grandchildren into the matter. Arthur remarked that his father had often complained about having to listen to PC Rossi go on about selling the island, and that Justinian Caire had clearly demonstrated how much he loved the island. As he was leaving, Freidenrich remarked that his client wished to avoid litigation as there was litigation enough already, a remark that seemed calculated to raise a glimmer of hope for a resolution.

Several weeks went by with no communication between the two parties. Then on May 7, Albina received a peremptory demand from Amelie for a division of the property based on her ownership of shares in the Santa Cruz Island Company. A couple of days later, Gherini called Bluxome and in the course of the conversation told him, "Your clients intend to drag out this affair until they can get the Legislature to enable them to reorganize,[8] but we will block their game."[9] Almost two months later, in an apparent last-ditch attempt to achieve a settlement, Freidenrich sent a letter to Bluxome telling him that in spite of the lack of fair play on the part of Mrs. Caire and her children, the differences between the two sides could be removed if they would negotiate to divide some of Albina's estate. To what they perceived as this additional insult to their principles, the Caires made no response. A week later, Arthur was served with a "summons and complaint" in the suit of his nephew Edmund Rossi against the trustees of the Santa Cruz Island Company. Suffering from ill health, Amelie had transferred her seven shares to her son, who now assumed the role of lead plaintiff. The same papers were served in the following weeks on Amelie's brother, Fred, her sisters Delphine and Hélène, and her mother. Albina received her summons on June 13, 1912. It was her eighty-first birthday.

The Rossi suit endeavored "to enjoin the directors from carrying on the business of the corporation and to compel them as trustees to wind up its affairs, pay its debts and distribute its assets to its stockholders according

---

[7] Arthur Caire diary, 18 April 1912.

[8] There was a measure pending before the California legislature that would enable corporations such as the Santa Cruz Island Company to reincorporate themselves after a technical lapse of their charter.

[9] Arthur Caire diary, 9 May 1912.

to their interests, and specifically to distribute to Edmund A. Rossi, as plaintiff, seven one-hundredths of said assets."[10]

On the first of November 1912, Arthur met Mr. Steiger at 573 Market Street and took him into the office. Steiger told Arthur that he was there to look at the minutes and the books of the Santa Cruz Island Company. When Arthur asked to see in writing on whose authority he was working, Steiger said that he had been sent by Mr. Freidenrich and Mr. Gherini as the attorneys for Amelie and Aglaë. Arthur told him that he was aware that Mr. Freidenrich was acting for Amelie, but that technically Aglaë, because she had originally signed the reorganization papers to reinstitute the corporate charter, was his codefendant in the Rossi suit. After a heated discussion about who best understood the law, Arthur asked him for proof that he represented his sisters. Steiger answered that he only had his word that he had come from the office of Freidenrich and Gherini. When he was told that this was not enough, he asked if Arthur also refused to show the books to Amelie and Aglaë. Arthur responded that his sisters could come at any time and would be shown any paper or accounts they asked to see and he would make it a point to give them any explanation they required, but he would not show the accounts to anyone unless duly authorized in writing by his sisters.

The following Monday, Arthur was subpoenaed to produce the books of the company and make a deposition at the office of David Freidenrich, which he duly did, though he refused to answer some of Freidenrich's questions. Ten days later he found himself in the chambers of San Francisco Superior Court judge Sturtevant to justify his refusal to answer. After Arthur explained himself to the judge, he and Joseph Bluxome were leaving the judge's chambers when a fuming Gherini confronted them, angrily reproaching Bluxome and Arthur for having done nothing about selling the island.[11]

At the end of November, Gherini called Bluxome to say that Aglaë, now living in Asti, where her husband had been given a job with Italian Swiss Colony, intended to change her position on reorganizing the corporation. She would start a new suit in her own name. She was taking this action because, among other reasons, "Mrs. Amelie Rossi thought that she should not bear the whole burden of the actions against the Trustees and that Mrs.

---

[10] Ellison, "History of the Santa Cruz Island Grant," 279, cited in Livingston, "Study," 633. A memorandum by Arthur Caire, "As to Undue Influence," notes the summons on Albina's eighty-first birthday (Caire Family Papers, notebook, p. 24, in the possession of Justinian Caire III).

[11] Arthur Caire diary, 19 November 1912.

Capuccio should bear her share." "*And also run the risk of disinheritance,*" Arthur noted in pencil next to this entry in his diary.[12]

At the Caire family home in Oakland, Christmas 1912 came and went, marked by the arrival of a box of flowers for Albina that contained the unsigned calling card of Mrs. Amelie Rossi but no message of any kind. The details about how the Rossis and Capuccios had learned of Albina's will began to trickle out the following March. On the fifth of March 1913, Gherini gave Bluxome the Rossi–Capuccio account of how the will arrived after Albina's departure, was mistakenly opened by a clerk in the shipyard where Capuccio worked, and was turned over to Capuccio, who read it, made a copy for himself, sent another copy to Rossi, and returned the original to the Caires. As mentioned previously, this story would appear to be highly economical with the truth. Arthur noted that the document was sent from San Francisco on June 24, 1906. At that time, mail usually took eighteen days to reach La Spezia, so even allowing for a full thirty days, the document would have reached Italy more than a week before Albina left for home via France on August 2. In addition, Arthur noted that opening letters addressed to someone else was a felony, as was copying their contents, not that the effort of mounting an international prosecution years after the event would be likely to yield much success.

With the explanations put forward by the Rossis and Capuccios in mind, Albina wrote to her daughters, asking for clarification. Less than a week later, on March 20, 1913, the answer came back in the form of a notice of a second lawsuit, instituted by Aglaë in which she asked that a receiver be appointed to oversee the dissolution of the corporation, a case that the court postponed pending the outcome of the first suit. Much to the Caires' embarrassment, news of the litigation began to percolate through the San Francisco business community. Near the end of March, Arthur had a call from a property group asking if the family was ready to sell the Santa Cruz Island, to which he answered that the holders of 86 percent of the island stock had no interest in selling, particularly in view of the continuing litigation. The caller asked if they had any objection to a meeting with Mrs. Rossi and Mrs. Capuccio. In spite of his annoyance, Arthur had to admit that he could not prevent them discussing the matter with anyone, but his frustration and embarrassment had only just begun.

---

[12] Arthur Caire diary, 14 December 1912.

CHAPTER 18

First Defeat in the Courts

On June 9, 1913, Judge Sturtevant of the San Francisco Superior Court ruled in favor of the plaintiff, Edmund Rossi, acting on behalf of his mother.[1] Albina, Delphine, Arthur, and Fred, as controlling trustees, were directed to wind up the affairs of the corporation because it had forfeited its charter. The court's opinion stated that all shareholders were entitled to an accounting of the corporation's assets, which should be distributed according to their respective shares as of 1911 when the charter was forfeited. This was a major blow to the Caires in their attempt to keep the legacy of Justinian Caire intact. They announced that they would appeal the decision. Gherini countered by urging Edmund to hire the celebrated lawyer Orrin Kip McMurray to act as co-counsel with him on appeal. This was done, and McMurray, well known and influential throughout the California legal establishment as professor of jurisprudence at the University of California, became attorney of record through all ensuing legal actions.[2] Four days after the adverse ruling, a disconsolate Albina signed a codicil to her will revoking the gift of Santa Cruz Island Company shares to the two daughters who had dragged her into court. She transferred those shares to her other four children and gave the family house in Oakland to her daughters Hélène and Delphine.

"The Lawsuit," as it became known in the family, rumbled on in the background as the Caires attempted to keep both the Santa Cruz Island Company and the Justinian Caire Company operational and profitable.

---

[1] *Edmund A. Rossi v. Arthur Caire, et al.*, San Francisco Superior Court, No.43295.
[2] John Gherini, *Santa Cruz Island*, 131.

Unfortunately, the climate weighed in to add to their troubles. The winters of 1911–12 and 1912–13 were two of the driest and coldest on Santa Cruz Island in the early years of the twentieth century. The Caires were forced to sell the entire livestock herd in 1913, taking it to its lowest total in the history of ranching on the island. It took seven years for the sheep population to recover, and the Santa Cruz Island Company never regained its former levels of meat or wool sales. Not only that, almost all the 1912 rainfall came in the single month of March, and most of the rain in 1913 fell in February, with subsequent damage and loss to crops and island infrastructure. With sheep and cattle dying from exposure and the threat of more litigation hanging over them, the Caires hurried their livestock to market. Predictably, this forced sale in 1912 meant accepting rock-bottom prices, 25 to 50 percent under what they might have expected in normal years. The books for the year 1912 made dismal reading, with a loss of $24,000 [$550,000].[3]

The litigation wore on, and because its primary aim was to force an inventory and accounting—and ultimately a sale—the Caires were constrained, Arthur noted,

> [from taking] the measures that would be necessary for the development of the property. We have not ventured to act decisively, even when we obtained a reviver of our Corporation through the passage of a Rehabilitation Act [1913]. . . . We thought it prudent to proceed very slowly as our affairs were still in litigation pending an appeal to the Supreme Court of the state [*Rossi v. Caire*, 1916]. Had the decision of the Supreme Court sustained the findings of the lower court, what would have been our position? Would we not have incurred the censure of the court . . . and been adjudged as having carried on business in defiance of the law, though the Corporation was in liquidation?[4]

The following year, 1913, also showed a loss, which was not surprising given the previous year's scarcity of rainfall and the forced sale of most of the livestock. The superintendent also reported rumblings of discontent from the men over wages. Arthur and Fred, because of the lawsuit and reverses caused by natural forces, felt unable to countenance any increases.

---

[3] Symmes & Associates, "Report on Santa Cruz Island," Section 2, Inventory, Santa Barbara, 1922, sheet 1; and "Secretary's Report, 1912," Santa Cruz Island Co. Records, collection in the author's possession. (Unless otherwise noted, all documents from Santa Cruz Island Co. Records are in the author's possession.)

[4] Arthur Caire diary, 118.

Albina with Caire grandchildren in the garden at the Main Ranch, ca. 1912.
Left to right: Albina, Lucille, Justinian II, Jeanne, Marie,
Delphine, Helen, Vivienne.

Caire family members, ca.1914, under the Italian Stone Pine planted by
Albina by the side of the family house. *Back row, right*, Albina;
back row, second and third from left, Fred and Lillian Caire.

Delphine and Albina on the wharf
at Prisoners' Harbor, ca. 1918.

To make matters worse, in September the schooner lost her bearings in the fog on her way back from a re-fit in San Pedro. Captain Nidever's compass was later found to be affected by dampness, and the *Santa Cruz* went onto the rocks at Rincon, south of Santa Barbara, where it remained trapped for almost two months before being pulled free by tugs. Necessary repairs cost almost $7,500 [$168,000].

Over the next two years, the rates for saleable cattle responded to wartime demand by almost doubling, but the company had reduced its livestock to such low numbers that there was no basis left for growth of the herds and therefore nothing to sell. The lawsuit was beginning to dominate company strategy. In 1917, Arthur noted with bitter prescience that his married sisters and in-laws "are people who absolutely refused to help to conserve their own interests, who absolutely did their level best to jeopardize said interests and who forced these interests into a position where a loss was bound to be sustained, clamoring for the condemnation, under a charge of mismanagement, of those who were trying to obtain good results!"[5]

In San Francisco, Judge Sturtevant followed up his initial 1913 ruling in April 1914 with an order to the Caires to distribute $35,000 [$778,000] derived from the sale of the corporation's property. He further ordered them to sell all the company's real and personal property—all the assets that made the island a going concern.[6] Faced with this eventuality, the Caires filed an objection and moved for a new trial, only to have the motion denied. Later that month, with the legal tide running strongly in their favor, Gherini and Freidenrich called for a meeting to see if the Caires were ready to settle. Bluxome took their proposal to the ever-defiant Albina, whose response was blunt and to the point. The only basis on which she would consider a settlement would be "filial submission without conditions."[7] When Freidenrich was apprised of her answer, he answered that if that was the case, the affair would be carried out to the bitter end—a fight to the finish. After many more months of legal maneuvering, the California Supreme Court agreed to hear the case.

In the meantime, on July 2, 1915, the Caires received the news of the sudden death of their brother-in-law Goffredo Capuccio at Asti. After his

---

[5] Ibid., 119.

[6] *Edmund A. Rossi v. Arthur Caire, et al.*, San Francisco Superior Court, No.43295.

[7] Arthur Caire diary, 22 April 1914, p. 44.

summary dismissal from the Justinian Caire Company, he had been given a job at the Italian Swiss Colony winery and was living with his family on the Rossi estate near the winery when he suffered a fatal stroke.[8] Arthur hurried up to Sonoma County to reassure Aglaë that, as always, she could count on her family in her time of need. This seeming restoration of family harmony was marred by what Arthur described as a "very disagreeable scene" with his other sister Amelie, which concluded with her boasting that she had some documents in her possession that would embarrass the family. If they existed, she went to her grave without revealing them.

Two days later, Goffredo Capuccio—aged forty-nine; twice employed and twice dismissed by the Justinian Caire Company and Santa Cruz Island Company; confidante of PC Rossi and his son-in-law Ambrose Gherini; husband of Aglaë; and father of Goffredo, Jr., aged eight, and Aglaë ("Cita"), aged five—was laid to rest near PC Rossi in Holy Cross cemetery in San Francisco. At the funeral Arthur renewed his pledge of family protection to Aglaë, a promise reiterated by Albina in correspondence with her. At the end of July 1915, Gherini's colleague George Steiger, to whom Aglaë had given one of her shares as a way of furthering the aims of her legal team, appeared at the store on Market Street to say that Aglaë needed help. When asked about Capuccio's estate and will, Steiger admitted that there was neither an estate nor a will. Albina responded that she wanted to hear directly from her daughter about her situation, not through intermediaries.

They finally met in mid-September, along with Arthur and Delphine, at Albina's house in Oakland. The two older siblings made it clear to Aglaë that they were very anxious to help her as they always had in the days before the troubles, but that she would have to drop her lawsuit and dismiss her lawyers as a first sign of good will. Aglaë began to waver under the pressure, and Albina asked that she be left alone with her daughter so that they could speak with less hesitation and greater freedom. Aglaë's remarks to her mother revealed a mirror image of the Caires' perspective about the rights and wrongs of the case. She questioned her mother's right to dispose of her stock as she pleased and claimed that the will intercepted in Italy in 1906 had in some way hastened her husband's death. Never the strongest of characters, she went on, "My husband made me promise that I would not

---

[8] Edmund Rossi was superintendent of the Italian Swiss Colony Asti winery at the time (Edmund Rossi, "Italian Swiss Colony" [interview], 67).

be dependent on anybody . . . but he has left [me] absolutely nothing. When I signed the reorganization papers [in January 1912], I did so under duress. I was afraid of my brothers, I don't know why; I do not know how to express it, but I was afraid."

On her way out, Aglaë was treated to a diatribe from Arthur about PC Rossi, Amelie, and Gherini. She defended Rossi, saying, "If Papa helped Pietro, you must not forget that Pietro paid interest on the money loaned to him. . . . Amelie and I were always treated differently from the others."

"Yes, you got more," Arthur thought to himself. Then he told her to always remember that if she trusted him, she would find him her best friend, but she would have to stop all proceedings in the lawsuit; they would have to be active steps, and she must not allow matters to rest because her family could hardly be expected to help her carry on her litigation against them. "Yes, I will think it over," she responded.[9]

Then everything went quiet for more than four months. At the end of January 1916, Arthur, perhaps alarmed at Aglaë's silence regarding the family's proposals, wrote her to ask what measures she planned to take. Shortly afterward, he received her response. The Caires' lawyer, Joseph Bluxome, was notified by Gherini's office that in the matter of the suit against her family, Aglaë had taken responsibility away from Mr. Steiger and placed matters directly in the hands of Ambrose Gherini. "This is her answer to our offers of September 1915!" remarked Arthur in his diary.[10] The news of Aglaë's decision meant that Gherini's hold on the litigation was relatively complete. His mother-in-law, Amelie, was in failing health, and she had appointed her eldest son Edmund, who relied heavily on Gherini, as her representative.

But things seemed to be more positive for the Caires in terms of the lawsuit. A new law had been passed by the California legislature in 1913 decreeing that after a corporation lost its charter, it could be reinstated by the payment of the taxes due and appropriate penalties. This was done, and the Caires held a shareholders' meeting at the end of January 1915 and elected Fred, Arthur, and Delphine directors of the revived corporation. The assets of the old corporation were then voted to be transferred to the revived entity. Later that year, the California Supreme Court handed down

---

[9] Arthur Caire diary, 14 September 1915.
[10] Arthur Caire diary, 31 January 1916.

its ruling that seemed to offer another ray of hope to the Caires.[11] In their decision, the court reversed Judge Sturtevant's ruling that the trustees must sell all the corporate property and distribute all the cash. If the corporation had sufficient money to pay off the corporate debts, they could distribute the assets to the shareholders, including land in kind, rather than force a sale of the assets.

This was a procedural victory for the Caires, but the court noted that it did not affect the fact that the corporation had terminated, an "absolute death," and was to be wound up for the benefit of the stockholders. The California Supreme Court had ruled that upon forfeiture of the corporation's charter, through the nonpayment of the tax, the corporation's property belonged to the shareholders at the time of the termination of the existence of the corporation, subject to the administration of the former directors (the Caires) now acting as trustees. The Rossi and Capuccio shareholders were entitled to distribution of the assets in excess of the debts and obligations of the defunct corporation but only in the course of winding up the corporation. In addition, they further ruled that there was no duty to sell the remaining assets, which could be distributed in kind to the shareholders as tenants in common.

Essentially, with this ruling of 1916 both parties were in the same position that they had been when the litigation began in 1912. And as Gherini noted with satisfaction some time later, this ruling "settled all of the law involved."[12] Based on their mother's gift of Santa Cruz Island Company shares in 1910 and their brothers' inadvertent nonpayment of the corporation tax in 1911, Amelie and Aglaë's legal team had achieved their goal and pried open the Santa Cruz Island Company forever.

---

[11] *Rossi v. Caire*, 174 Cal. 74, 161 Pac. 1161 (1916) (action begun 1912).

[12] John Gherini, *Santa Cruz Island*, 133.

CHAPTER 19

A Fight to the Finish

W as this the moment for both sides to have called a truce and found a
way to negotiate, probably by a division of Santa Cruz Island? Many
of the principals in the original litigation were now dead. PC Rossi had died
in 1911, Goffredo Capuccio in 1915, and after years of poor health Amelie
Caire Rossi died in 1917, resolutely refusing to the last to reconcile with her
mother, who was now in her eighties. It was left to the younger generations
to make approaches at negotiation. In August 1919, Edmund Rossi visited
Arthur to seek a way to end "this costly litigation." But by now both sides
were well entrenched, and the issue of legal fees began to come to the fore.
At their meeting Arthur forced Edmund to admit that his legal team was
working on a fee basis that was contingent on their winning. Arthur told
his nephew that he would consider negotiating a settlement only if Edmund
dropped all of the lawsuits. A cessation of the lawsuits clearly would have
been unacceptable to Gherini and Freidenrich, the lawyers of Rossi and
Capuccio. They had undertaken many thousands of billable hours of work
on behalf of their clients, in addition to the cost of Orrin McMurray's fees.
Given that McMurray was one of the top legal professionals in the state, his
fees alone would have been considerable.

As the legal expenses mounted it was natural that the principals on both
sides should seek a solution that did not involve lawyers, but from the start
it had all been too personal. The innuendos that continued to be spread
by the Rossi camp inferring Albina's incompetence and Fred and Arthur's
mismanagement and dishonesty rankled the Caires immensely, as was
doubtless the intent. Beyond this, the Caires were fixated on the island as

the legacy of their father, who had specifically requested that the business of the Santa Cruz Island Company be carried on by his children. He had made his two sons the trustees for their sisters. The stated opinion of his son-in-law PC Rossi that the island should be viewed as just another asset in the Caire holdings to be eventually sold and the proceeds distributed had been unthinkable for Justinian Caire. All but two of his heirs were of the same mind. Led by their stern mother, they viewed any talk of selling the island as treacherous betrayal, which is exactly how they saw the actions of their married sisters and their in-laws. The Caire brothers saw their married sisters as pawns in the hands of in-laws who had no feeling for the uniqueness of the island and no recognition of the time, effort, and expense that had been dedicated to the development and husbandry of this very special environment. Arthur noted in his diary, "[Edmund Rossi] was told plainly that our side accepted no conditions and we would not give up anything we had as we were determined not to allow any slur on our mother's actions and to fight for our rights to the bitter end."[1]

Though the Rossi, Capuccio, and Gherini families had legal right for the forced breakup of the Santa Cruz Island Company and the family fortune on their side, the moral justification that guided their actions was deeply flawed. They based it on the codicil to Justinian Caire's will, in which Caire divided his estate equally among his children. But of course this was only to occur in the event that his wife predeceased him. She outlived him for almost three decades. The plaintiffs also nursed their sense of injustice that they should be treated as wards of their brothers despite the fact that it was Justinian Caire's expressed desire, stated in his will and its codicil, that the family businesses be "continued by my two sons ... with as little change and alteration as possible."[2]

When it came to motives, for the Caires it was simply a question of their father and mother's legacy; of family loyalty respected and family values betrayed. For the Rossis and Capuccios, Ambrose Gherini masterminded a legal strategy of minority shareholder rights, with an overarching sense of injustice legitimized by the codicil. Arthur Caire speculated that at the outset, Gherini and Capuccio had assumed that the threat to break up the family holdings and public scandal of a lawsuit between family members

---

[1] Arthur Caire diary, 22 August 1919.

[2] Justinian Caire, will dated 24 January 1889 and codicil dated 28 January 1889, Probate Alameda County Superior Court, Case 5540.

would be enough to persuade the Caires to part with a large sum of cash. When they were rebuffed, they resorted to litigation in an effort to save face, and then the legal strategy took on a life of its own, incurring costs that only a victory would satisfy.[3]

This would be a fight to the finish, with no quarter given or taken. As one of the Caire attorneys, Frank Deering, told Gherini, "They [the Caires] would rather pay their attorneys than their sisters and in-laws."[4] The Caires felt that they had natural justice on their side, but Ambrose Gherini had a more pragmatic view of what really mattered before the law.

The next move was from the Rossi camp. They filed an action in San Francisco for an accounting to force the trustees to wind up the affairs of the corporation, to account for the proceeds, and to distribute the assets, though the action did not demand a sale of the property as the California Supreme Court had determined such a forced sale was too invasive. The Caires based their defense on the grounds that the corporation had been revived and should carry on business as before, with majority and minority interests. Early in 1917, Judge Sturtevant signaled his agreement with the Caires' argument and dismissed the accounting action. Any elation they might have felt was subdued by Rossi's legal team, now joined by Aglaë, appealing this decision. In February 1919 the California Appellate Court reversed the decision of Judge Sturtevant and maintained that Rossi was entitled to an accounting. After a further appeal by the Caires, the California State Supreme Court concurred, holding that when the corporation had died, the rights of the shareholders to receive the corporate assets became "vested." They became an ownership interest that could not be taken away afterward, because at the time that the corporation lapsed there was no statute that allowed for its revival.[5] This judgment drove a spike into the heart of the Caire strategy to force their sisters back into the revived corporation. It set the stage for the other theater where the Caires' downfall would be acted out: the courtrooms of Santa Barbara, within sight of the island that lay at the heart of the controversy.

For this next aspect of his legal strategy, Gherini had Edmund Rossi (acting for his deceased mother) and Aglaë Capuccio launch another suit to force the partition of the island into separate parcels that would be

---

[3] Arthur Caire diary, 99–100, 115–16.

[4] Unpublished memo of Ambrose Gherini, 1937, 3–4, cited in John Gherini, *Santa Cruz Island*, 133.

[5] *Rossi v. Caire*, 174 Cal. 74, p. 83 (1916).

assigned and distributed to the various shareholders, in kind. The lawsuit was filed in Santa Barbara because of the requirement that it be brought in the county where the property was located.

As well as being fought in the courts, the battle over Santa Cruz Island was also being fought in the local press, something that the publicity-shy Caires found particularly difficult. Stung by allegations in court from the Gherini–Rossi side that she had tried to "defraud" her daughters, Albina felt compelled to publish a statement in the local newspapers on June 23, 1918. In it, she took readers of the Santa Barbara and Oxnard papers through the transfer of ownership of shares from her husband to herself and from her to her daughters, "a gift made by me unto them . . . for love and affection." She reaffirmed her faith in her sons and her own participation in all the proceedings that flowed from the forfeit of the charter of the Santa Cruz Island Company and her willingness to accept the consequences of her actions. For a family that had maintained a certain financial and social aloofness from the local community, this situation was a very public comedown.[6] Albina was eighty-eight years old at the time, and this was her last-ditch attempt to set the record straight and make an appeal to her daughters' families over the heads of their lawyers. It was no more success-ful than any of the other efforts. Her older married daughter, Amelie, had died the year before, never having reconciled with her mother, and Aglaë and Albina remained estranged up to the time of Albina's death in 1924.

In the Santa Barbara court battle the two sides divided along predict-able lines, with the plaintiffs arguing that they were entitled to a share of the island assets of the dissolved corporation and the trustees arguing that the reinstated corporation owned the assets rather than the individual shareholders. The case was heard in Santa Barbara Superior Court. In Sep-tember 1920 the court found for the plaintiffs, a judgment that predictably wound its way up to the California Supreme Court, where it was upheld in 1922.[7] This ruling meant the Rossis and Capuccios were legally entitled to a distribution of the corporate property.

Given the likelihood of a costly survey and partition of the island, the expense of which would have to be borne by all parties, approaches regard-ing negotiation were made once again. Gherini met with Frank Deering

[6] Albina Caire, "Legal and Official," *Santa Barbara (Calif.) Morning News*, 23 June 1918; and Albina Caire, "Legal and Official," *Oxnard (Calif.) Daily News*, 23 June 1918.

[7] *Capuccio v. Caire* 189 Cal. 514 at 524–525 (1922).

sometime in 1922 and presented an offer to sell his clients' interest in the island for $500,000 [$6.4 million], or slightly more than 18 percent of the most recent valuation obtained by Arthur. Given that the year before Gherini and his law partner, David Freidenrich, had negotiated with their clients for a near one-third interest of their island shares in lieu of fees, this would have meant a half share of a $165,000 [$2.1 million] windfall for Gherini, plus any further legal fees. In any case, the Caires rejected this offer out of hand. The bemused Gherini later recalled his surprise that they had not responded with a counter offer.[8] His surprise revealed that he continued to misread the Caires' motives. The aged yet still imperious and unbending ninety-one-year-old Albina refused to countenance any dealings with her treacherous offspring who had betrayed the memory and expressed intentions of her husband, and her sons acceded to her wishes.

With only a few months to live (Albina died in 1924), incensed by the knowledge that her private letters to her daughter Aglaë were being passed on to Gherini, she sent three letters—one to Gherini, one to Edmund Rossi, and one to Aglaë. In this correspondence Albina stated her case, analyzing the way the lawsuits had developed, assessing motives, and allocating blame where she believed it was deserved. To Gherini she wrote, in part,

> A man who would have had his honor at heart, and had not been so avid to acquire wealth by any means possible would not have taken upon himself to assist the rebellion of two daughters against their mother. . . . You on the other hand, seeking to profit from the mental state of your mother-in-law (Amelie Caire Rossi) after the tragic death of her husband, set her on that evil road while thinking only of your own interests. . . . Do you think I have forgotten that at the beginning of this dirty blackmail suit [1912], you made the proposal to "eliminate the women" from the negotiation.[9]

Albina and her family clearly believed that Gherini's motives had been financial from the very beginning of the rift within the family.

To her grandson Edmund Rossi, Albina wrote the following:

> If I have waited until this day to express to you all the indignation that I have felt about your behavior, it is because I still had hope that you would ultimately open your eyes and would understand the odious nature of your

---

[8] Memorandum by Frank Deering, 1922, quoted in John Gherini, *Santa Cruz Island*, 146.
[9] Albina Caire to Ambrose Gherini, 19 March 1923, Caire Family Papers, "Letters" (original in Italian, translated by Carla Zoso), in the author's possession.

actions ... it was your duty to calm my unfortunate daughter, instead of assisting her in listening to the advice of your attorney and the husband of your aunt Aglaë, both of them blinded by their cupidity. ... It is not a secret for anyone that, for many years, your mother's unhealthy state affected her judgment and made her see things in a false light, leading her to exaggeration, as you have often witnessed yourselves, and even driving her to alter the truth (how many times has your aunt Aglaë expressed that opinion!).[10]

Finally, Albina wrote to her daughter Aglaë a letter that detailed the ways in which she felt Aglaë had betrayed her. Albina talked about her husband's will, which left his entire estate to her, not, as Aglaë had claimed, to his children. She spoke of the low regard in which she and her husband held Capuccio and of her own generosity to them, with gifts sent from San Francisco and others given when she was staying with them in Italy in 1906. Then she moved on to her major theme:

Don't these various gifts prove persuasively that I was well-disposed towards you as I believed you a submissive daughter? How could I imagine that I had to do with two traitors who, in accepting all my kindnesses, were only looking for an opportunity to do me harm? ... Someone [in Italy] broke into the envelope [containing my will], someone studied/examined the contents, someone made a copy and the Capuccios sent the copy to the Rossis. What a beautiful example to leave to your children and what should they think of their parents when they come to know about all your intrigues! In the meantime [1910] you arrived from Italy and installed yourself at my home with your children, your maids ... I was feeble minded enough to consent to your husband becoming my bookkeeper, I let you stay under my roof for five months and this is how I have been rewarded. Your husband had hardly been admitted to the store when he commenced a ... system of espionage ... in an effort to discover some hidden deceptions that only existed in his perverse imagination. Finally, when your brother [Arthur] ... had to expel him from the store, he departed leaving behind him a debt of $2,000 [$46,000] that he had written on the books. ... The only thing that remains to be said is to repeat to you ... if you resolve to change your conduct and to ask my pardon ... I will welcome you with joy ... [but] if you have the intention of coming to me with any other goal, I forbid you to present yourself to me.[11]

---

[10] Albina Caire to Edmund Rossi, 19 March 1923, Caire Family Papers, "Letters," in the author's possession.
[11] Albina Caire to Aglaë Capuccio, 19 March 1923, Caire Family Papers, "Letters," in the author's possession.

To Albina, and the sons and daughters who stood by her side, negotiation with the two rebellious and unstable daughters, or those who encouraged them, was tantamount to surrender to blackmail. Resistance was a defense of basic principles and values, even if it meant that the Caires lost everything in the process. For Gherini and his clients, on the other hand, it was a simple matter of negotiation to find the right amount that would satisfy them. Referees were appointed by the Santa Barbara court to make a survey of Santa Cruz Island, a prerequisite for the partition. Those referees prepared to go to work in spite of various appeals and motions by the trustees.

The Caires might have been brought low, but for the other side in the litigation there was also a price to be paid. Ownership of the inheritance for which they were ostensibly fighting began to slip from the hands of the Rossis and Capuccios. From the outset, they had been unable to pay anything toward the substantial fees that accumulated year by year in pursuing the legal actions masterminded by Gherini. In 1921, with the endgame in sight and no possibility of paying off their legal bills, negotiations took place between Edmund Rossi (negotiating for both the Rossis and the Capuccios) and the legal team of Ambrose Gherini and his colleague David Freidenrich. In a consequence that will hold no surprise for those familiar with the perils of protracted litigation, the two lawyers emerged as owners of almost a third (four and one-half) of the fourteen shares given by Albina to her two married daughters in 1910.[12] This ownership share would expand over the next eleven years of continued litigation and negotiation until the entire portion of Santa Cruz Island for which the Rossis and Capuccios had fought for two decades was in the hands of the Gherini family.

---

[12] Memorandum of Agreements, 28 January 1921, quoted in John Gherini, *Santa Cruz Island*, 157.

Family portrait at the Main Ranch in front of the house and dining room, ca. 1928. *Standing from left*: Jeanne Caire, Helen Caire, Fred Caire, Lillian Caire, Mary Caire, friend, Miriam Caire. *Seated*: George Olson, Didi Caire, Marie Caire, Vivienne Caire, friend.

CHAPTER 20

Distant Thunder

While there was hope of success in the courts, the Caires kept the Santa Cruz Island enterprise going as best they could. In fact, during the second and third decades of the century, the legal rumbling of the San Francisco and Santa Barbara courts was like distant thunder on a summer day. The island remained a world unto itself.[1] For the large Caire family, along with friends and cousins, the days of summer would slip by in an idyllic haze of trips to Prisoners' Harbor and other charming destinations. With its sweeping arc of beach bisected by the wharf, which extended out into deep water, at Prisoners' the picnickers could paddle in the shallows while the older children taught the younger ones to swim in the protected harbor. The pet dogs were often included in the party, enthusiastically joining in the swimming. On public holidays, they shared the harbor with a flotilla that sailed its way over from the mainland. Other summer family expeditions involved the charabanc, which could accommodate nine or more adults and children—the men in their stiff collars, and everyone anticipating a picnic lunch prepared by the Chinese cook, with cuts of meat (principally lamb) to be spit-roasted on long sharpened sticks over an open fire in imitation of the traditional corrida barbecue method of the vaqueros.

On riding parties to picnic somewhere in the central valley, one might have encountered the bespectacled Fred Caire, his white shirt carefully buttoned up, hair and moustache well-trimmed, sitting comfortably astride his spirited horse Pueblo. Usually riding alongside would be his tall wife, Lillian, sitting side-saddle and upright on her horse, Pato, her face partially hidden by a straw hat of generous proportions and her voluminous dress

---

[1] Caire family unpublished memoranda and picture archives, Helen Caire, *Santa Cruz Island*, 1993.

swaying with the slow canter. They were surrounded by teenage girls who sat daringly astride ("western style") their horses sporting modish hats, jeans, or heavy riding skirts and cowboy-style shirts. At the Main Ranch the younger Caire children frolicked in the kitchen garden amidst the corn that had grown to twice their height or played in the two-wheeled wicker dog cart drawn by two ponies.

On more formal outings to Prisoners' Harbor, the entire Caire family turned out dressed in white: Fred Caire in his collar, tie, and straw hat; Lily Caire and the older girls in full-skirted white dresses and straw bonnets. The youngest children were still in knickerbocker trousers and shirts with ankle boots as they posed for a photographer in front of the house at Prisoners' Harbor in about 1915. The images of an outing to the Sur in 1917, with the subjects formally dressed and posed on a rocky shelf above the pounding surf, are reminiscent of contemporary Impressionist paintings of the French Riviera.

Days at the Main Ranch were a virtual wonderland for children, with pet lambs, calves, ponies, horses, and dogs. The gracious family house, built a year before the litigation began, was nearly 3,000 square feet. It was a U-shaped structure surrounding a courtyard, with a wide veranda curving around the facade facing the entrance to the Main Ranch from Prisoners' Harbor. It contained eight bedrooms, two maids' rooms, and a 500-square-foot living room. This focus of family life had a large fireplace, hardwood floors, and a beamed ceiling. The dining room and kitchen were separate structures, probably to reduce the risk of fire. The Caire house was capable of entertaining on an impressive scale. It gave a real sense of permanence and stability to the island ownership, even as it was being eroded in the San Francisco and Santa Barbara courts.

Far from the troubles of the mainland, the Main Ranch retained its air of immutability. Looking westward from the Sur road, the track parted the acres of vines that swept up the hills on either side. A mantle of fog might sit beyond the upper portion of the valley at Portezuela, as the family compound lay concealed within its grove of trees and flower-filled garden planted decades before. In the other direction, the road leading eastward out of the Main Ranch was lined with the windbreak eucalyptus trees planted in the days of Justinian Caire, with a California rail fence keeping the cattle out of the vines and hay crops. On the road to La Playa, one could see the tracks made by the narrow wheels of one of the horse-drawn carts or carriages mixing with the tire tracks of the truck and Model T, criss-crossing the stream that flowed toward the harbor. In the nearby fields, two tractors were used for plowing and reaping, but much of this work was still done with horse-drawn implements. In the vineyard, the workers in their shirts and hats moved slowly along the rows, tending the vines.

There was often abundant entertainment as the Caires welcomed friends from San Francisco and southern California, who arrived on the schooner *Santa Cruz* or on their own yachts. Ira and Margaret Eaton had managed to patch up their relationship with the Caires and establish a resort at Peli-can Bay on the island coast facing Santa Barbara. Their daughter described an elaborate lunch in 1919 for the guest of honor, John Barrymore. Served with no small ceremony by two maids, it was one of several occasions that the Caires entertained the most famous actor of his generation.[2] The summer of 1919 was also enlivened by a visit from the U.S. Navy destroyer *Hart*. After a formal lunch at the Main Ranch, Lily, in a full-skirted dress, white shoes, fancy straw hat, and parasol and Fred, in riding boots, trou-sers, jacket and shirt, and fedora hat, were welcomed on board by Captain Jones, who showed them around the vessel. It was this vision of Fred Caire as the old-fashioned California grandee that moved Barrymore to tell the local paper that Caire was one of the men whose lifestyle he most admired.

Throughout the 1920s the Caires continued the policy of welcoming researchers from Stanford, the California Academy of Sciences, Mills Col-lege, the Santa Barbara Botanic Garden, and the Santa Barbara Museum of Natural History. They specialized in various fields—notably geology, biology, and archaeology—and were often guests at the Main Ranch for weeks at a time. Fred Caire also carefully collected some specimens him-self, which were proudly displayed in the family house.

The Caires felt constrained by the lawsuits from extensively investing in or upgrading their operation, lest in the continuing legal actions the courts were to rule that these expenditures were an improper exercise of their authority as trustees. Despite this constraint, the years 1917, 1918, and 1919 all showed a substantial profit, and while there was hope for a posi-tive outcome in the courts, the Caires continued to plow resources into the various ranches, including Scorpion Ranch. They had a new frame house built there in 1914 at about same time as the new family house at the Main Ranch. The Scorpion Ranch house was constructed on the exact location

---

[2] Eaton, *Diary of a Sea Captain's Wife*, 222–23.

as the old, the builders placing the concrete piers for the foundation in line with the older foundation. The simple board-and-batten house had six bed-rooms and a small common room, with an entry room on the north side and a covered porch on the south side facing the creek and hills. In 1915 the Caires had two substantial new hay storage barns built at the east end at Campo Grande at a cost of $1,092 [$24,000].[3]

Yet with the prohibition amendment working its way through the U.S. Congress and then the state legislatures, the Caires were looking at a bleak future for one of their main income streams. For the moment, things were on an even keel, and they even experienced a spike in income when they liqui-dated their wine inventory as buyers sought to stock up on supplies in antic-ipation of the demand that would arise after the Volstead Act took effect. Wool sales, too, were especially strong in these years, as adequate rainfall in the winters of 1916–1917 and 1917–1918 coincided with wartime demand to help raise income. But in 1920, when scant rainfall combined with the first full year of Prohibition, the Santa Cruz Island Company plunged into loss for the first time in many years. The Caires watched their vineyard income fall by almost 90 percent, from $37,000 to $4,000 [$398,000 to $43,000], as they struggled to sell their grapes on the local market.[4]

As if to underscore the anxiety that they were feeling, Fred gave up his management role in Justinian Caire Company to focus full-time on the Santa Cruz Island Company. When the superintendent was dismissed in 1924, Fred took direct control of the day-to-day ranching operations. The decline of the ranching business brought on by the constraints of the law-suits was accentuated by labor shortages following the war, the changing nature of the California economy, and the lack of capital for investment. The Caire livestock also began to feel the effects of regular illegal visits by fishermen who supplemented their diet and income by shooting sheep and cattle in remote canyons and bootlegging the carcasses in ports like San Pedro. There were occasional exchanges of gunfire with island employees, but because of the rugged island topography, positive identification was extremely difficult, and few prosecutions resulted.[5]

The cumulative effect of these pressures began to be noticeable in the

---

[3] Santa Cruz Island Co. Records; and Superintendent's Reports, quoted by Livingston, "Study," 542–43.

[4] "Secretary's Report, 1915," Santa Cruz Island Co. Records.

[5] Fred Caire to Col. Edward Wentworth, Armour Livestock Bureau, 13 March 1940, Caire Family Papers, "Letters"; and McElrath, On Santa Cruz Island, 33–48.

daily life of the ranch. There was little Fred or Arthur could do to arrest the decline except to try and eke out a profit wherever they could and cooperate with the court-appointed surveyors and agricultural consultants.

As the years had passed after the death of Justinian, his sons continued the management of the businesses he founded "with as little change and alteration as possible," but therein laid the seeds of their downfall. Inevitably, the economy of California grew and developed in ways completely unforeseen by Justinian and his pioneer colleagues. The main market of the Justinian Caire Company—the mining industry—was in inevitable decline, and the wine business went through cycles of consolidation, boom, and bust. There were new industries on the rise—oil, transport, diversified agriculture, timber, and services for a growing population—and what had been a profitable combination of imported products and local expertise in the nineteenth century became more and more out of step with the twentieth, particularly with the distraction of the legal actions to which the Caire brothers were subjected.

As it was with the Justinian Caire Company, so it was with the Santa Cruz Island Company. By the early twentieth century, on the California mainland, the days of the open range were long gone, the wine industry was almost completely consolidated by the CWA, and the balance of transport swung more and more toward land-based modes of shipping. Yet the Caire operation, largely because of geography but also because of the limitations imposed by the lawsuits, continued for the most part as it had in the days of Justinian Caire. Though partly successful attempts were made to use fencing to limit the spread of the sheep, the vertiginous canyons with which Santa Cruz Island is scored were perfect hiding places for the increasingly wild herd, undisturbed by the annual corridas. And although there was diversification into wine and walnuts, those ventures would never provide the economic salvation of the island enterprise, which was more and more deprived of capital investment, especially in the 1920s with the loss of income attributable to Prohibition and the costs of the partition. On the mainland the large land holdings of families in a similar situation as the Caires at the turn of the century found profitability through mixed agriculture, ready access to markets using rail and road, and land sales to an urbanizing California population. The Santa Cruz Island Company, perched beyond the continent's edge, remained wedded to the old ways of open range livestock management and sea transportation that had prevailed in the previous century.

The younger generation off to the harbor
with a load of wool sacks, ca. 1928.

CHAPTER 21

Partition and Downfall

The trustees submitted the inventory ordered by the court, and in early 1922 an agricultural engineering firm, Symmes & Associates, was appointed to confirm the inventory and make an evaluation of the ranch. They sent their representatives Leslie W. Symmes and Clifford McElrath to Santa Cruz Island, and they produced their report in May 1922. McElrath, who had worked on the island as cattle foreman in 1919 and was promoted shortly thereafter to superintendent until 1921, was critical of the Caire style of management. In McElrath's view, "It was probably 40 or more years behind the mainland in its methods of farming and livestock management. It was in fact a piece of California from the 1870s and 80's. Spanish and Italian were the accepted languages unless one considered the dialect used by the Italian vineyard and farm hands when talking to me. This was a mixture of Spanish and Italian with a little English thrown in."[1]

Another employee, Red Craine, reminiscing sixty years later, spoke of the island the way it was in the 1920s:

> They had a cook over there who had been with them for 16 years, a guy by the name of Hercules Pico. You knew what you were going to eat every meal that you sat down at the table, 365 days a year, with him. He baked wonderful sourdough bread.... You got in the morning mutton chops and boiled beans and that bread and coffee. At noon you got roast mutton and beans and bread and coffee. At night you got stew and beans and bread and coffee. Other than once in a while on a Sunday morning ... he would make hotcakes.[2]

---

[1] McElrath, *On Santa Cruz Island*, 51.
[2] Red Craine, interview by John Gherini, 13 September 1983, quoted in Livingston, "Study," 624.

The family house at the Main Ranch, 1920s.

At the end of 1924, the court-ordered surveyors delivered their findings in the partition suit. Combined with Symmes's report of 1922, the surveyors and referees recommended the division of the island into seven tracts, one tract per shareholder in the Santa Cruz Island Company at the time of the lapse of the corporate charter in 1911. In essence, the Caires retained the western 90 percent of the island, including the Main Ranch, central valley, Prisoners' Harbor, and all the land west of a line running roughly from China Harbor on the north coast to Sandstone Point on the south coast. The surveyors wisely took advantage of the natural physical barrier of the transverse range, the Montañon, to separate the two factions.

The Capuccio, Rossi, and Gherini interests were allotted the eastern 10 percent of the island, including the ranches at Scorpion Harbor and Smugglers Cove. The bill for the surveyors' work, which had taken the better part of a year, was $54,000 [$680,000], including fees, expenses, and interest. The Caires were liable for 86 percent of the total [$585,000]. There were various appeals by the Rossi/Capuccio/Gherini interests, supported by the testimony of McElrath, that objected to the findings of the referees as inequitable. Gherini was particularly aggrieved about access to the mainland

Loading wine at Prisoners' Harbor, ca. 1917.

Justinian Caire II at the Cascade, ca. 1930.

Loading wool, early twentieth century.

from his and his clients' parcels.[3] The referees responded robustly in court. Survey team leader Frank Flournoy said, "We took into consideration the water supply, the actual value such as pleasure resorts, hotel sites, harbors and landings . . . and the purposes of the land in Tracts 6 and 7 are about the same as of the rest of the Island. I could not see any particular difference." Referee Doulton, an expert in local real estate, commented, "They [the Rossis, Capuccios, and Gherinis] are getting the cream of the whole thing . . . 'a principality,' . . . and don't know it."[4] Arthur Caire noted that they were getting "450 acres or 31 percent of Class A land [excellent for any use] and 650 acres or 25.4 percent of Class B land [good for most uses] and still they are not satisfied even though the balance of their land is the best grazing land on the Island—easiest to run, giving the best mutton and best wool. On the assessors list they get the equivalent of 21% of the [top value] real estate."[5]

[3] *Cappucio v. Caire,* 207 Cal.200, 211, 277 p. 475 (1929).

[4] L.A. No. 9165. In the Supreme Court of the State of California, *Aglaë S. Capuccio, Plaintiff and Appellant vs. Arthur J. Caire, et al., Defendant and Respondents, Edmund A. Rossi, Defendant and Appellant,* 1928, pp. 26–27.

[5] Arthur Caire, Santa Cruz Island Company Records, 1931 Accounts, Caire Family Papers and Diaries.

The referees' recommendations were upheld, and the island was now effectively two properties. The Caires ran the western 90 percent, and Ambrose Gherini took on the mantle of owner and operator of the eastern 10 percent of the island. In the spring of 1927, the opposing parties divided up the livestock of the island. Gherini kept all of the sheep located on the east end, but prior to the division Fred Caire supervised the final shearing of all island sheep in May. The clip, now fallen to 234 sacks weighing a total of 82,000 pounds, was packed and stored in the warehouse at Prisoners' Harbor and divided with 14/100ths allocated to Gherini and his clients.[6] The story of Santa Cruz Island would now effectively become two stories.

The idyllic summers continued for the younger generation. But as the decade of the 1920s began, the island grazing lands suffered from two of the driest winters in living memory and their winery was sealed by order of the Volstead Act, drastically cutting the vineyard income. Hence, the elder Caires faced the grim reality of their financial situation and began to explore other possible sources of income. For about $100 per week, the island became a favored location for the Los Angeles-based producers of the burgeoning movie industry, who saw the advantages of creating exotic locations near their base in Los Angeles. The Eatons, with their concession at Pelican Bay, just to the west of Prisoners' Harbor, provided readily accessible dormitory and catering facilities for the movie crews working on films such as *Pearls of Paradise* (1916), *Diamond in the Sky* (1917), *Male and Female* (1919), *Peter Pan* (1924), and *The Rescue* (1928).[7] The producer Henry Otto made a series of films on the island, usually with a nautical theme, featuring as many as fifty diving girls.

Additional income was secured from selling rock to the city of Santa Barbara for its new breakwater: almost a quarter of a million tons was blasted from the cliffs above Fry's Harbor. This sparked an idea for building two breakwaters to enclose the entrance to Fry's, presumably to make it into a completely secure yacht harbor. Preliminary drawings were commissioned, but the scheme never matured.

The Santa Barbara population was encouraged to view Santa Cruz Island as an attractive camping destination, with the Eatons hosting large groups of visitors most weekends of the holiday season.[8] Hunters for the

---

[6] Company records show that the clip in the 1880s averaged 800 sacks.

[7] Eaton, *Diary of a Sea Captain's Wife*, 212–18, 233–34.

[8] Ibid., 203–204

wild boar also provided a small income, buying permits to pit their hunting skills against these ferocious adversaries in the remote canyons of the island.[9] There was also an exploration deal struck with Standard Oil for $5,000 [$63,000] and "one-sixth of all oil, asphaltum and other hydrocarbons extracted and saved there from." Although the $5,000 was welcome, there was no oil windfall resulting from the test drilling.[10] Nothing short of a major oil strike could make up for the income lost because of Prohibition and a national recession in agriculture that was hitting California and other parts of the country.

As the litigation wore on, the Caires also looked for financial salvation from outside investors who would follow the lead of the Eatons and lease part of Santa Cruz Island for recreational purposes or possibly buy the entire part of the property under their control. These negotiations were always complicated by the continuing lawsuits and the different requirements demanded of potential buyers by each side. In the end they came to nothing. There were also reports throughout the 1920s of a high level of interest by the state of California or the federal government in acquiring the island. In 1926, the *Santa Barbara Daily News* quoted Steven Mather, first director of the newly established National Park Service, saying, "Santa Cruz will become as popular as Catalina under development for park and resort purposes . . . eventually motor roads will lead to all parts of the island. Hotels will be available, and attractive lodges will be a feature, while free campgrounds will always be available to the public."[11] The state acquisition story rumbled on through the decade, but with the stock market crash of 1929 and the ensuing Great Depression, the state and federal governments turned their attention away from recreation land purchase and on to more pressing problems.[12]

The Caires' financial situation was becoming increasingly untenable. Ultimately they were humbled by the legal triumphs of Ambrose Gherini.

---

[9] "Island Wild Boar Hunting Lures 39 Visitors in One Day," *Santa Barbara (Calif.) Morning Press*, 2 July 1932.

[10] Lease details in a letter from Standard Oil Company, 13 December 1929, Santa Cruz Island Company Records, "Letters."

[11] *Santa Barbara (Calif.) Daily News*, 1926.

[12] A report commissioned for the National Park Service in 1933 stated, "The owners of Santa Cruz Island place a valuation [$4m] far in excess of its assessed valuation. The island does not produce a very substantial revenue and in some years it is said to show a loss, but taxes are low and the owners have been able to hold it for a possible future sale." The author suggested an offer of $1.5–$2 million, or a sale of parts of the island with scenic values but no value for agriculture. This report was not acted on. Quoted in Livingston, "Study," 645.

His relentless tenacity and greater grasp of what was essential under the law had brought victory to him and the descendants of Justinian Caire that he represented. Gherini left no legal avenue unexplored in his pursuit of Justinian Caire's legacy. When Hélène Caire died without a will in 1929, the minuscule allocations due to her Rossi and Capuccio relatives from Hélène's one-sixth share of the inheritance from Albina were pursued with all the energy devoted to the larger sums from the previous decades.

The Caire majority had defended their principles and their holdings for as long as was possible through the courts, at immense financial and emotional cost. They could do no more. Their situation was made worse by their struggle to keep the island operating as a going concern through the progressively worsening agricultural conditions that prevailed throughout the decade of the 1920s. Hampered by a lack of investment capital, court-enforced prohibitions against capital improvements and investments through the years of litigation, and livestock that were declining in terms of the quality of meat and wool and prevented from realizing any income from their winery because of Prohibition, they found themselves in the traditional position of the agriculturalist in hard times. They had a property that was potentially worth a large sum of money, but they were strapped for cash to pay the operating costs month by month, let alone consider investing in the desperately needed tractors, livestock, upgrading of the schooner, and a host of other suggestions made in the agricultural survey-ors report of 1922. Their losses mounted, from $5,600 [$70,000] in 1929 to $6,800 [$88,000] in 1930. Gherini knew that he had the Caires on the ropes, taunting them with offers to sell his clients' tiny interests in the Justinian Caire Company for $700 a share and in the Santa Cruz Island Company for $10,000 a share [$1.8 million total].[13] This interference highlighted the fact that Arthur and Fred were trying to satisfy their creditors by entertaining potential purchasers' interest in both these entities in hugely adverse macroeconomic circumstances, all the while encumbered by the completely unrealistic demands of minority shareholders.

But the Caires' tribulations were about to significantly worsen. The Capuccio and Rossi families had paid the fees of Gherini and his partner David Freidenrich for the San Francisco-based litigation with more than a third of their patrimony. Now it was time to pay for the legal fees associated

---

[13] Arthur Caire to Fred Caire, 21 February 1930, Santa Cruz Island Company Records, "Letters."

with the partition suit. The Caires fought this action on the grounds that they should not be liable for fees in a partition that was not for the common benefit. This argument was accepted by the trial judge in Santa Barbara, who coincidentally had been a member of a camping party on Santa Cruz Island years before. Gherini appealed, and the California Supreme Court reversed the trial court's decision.[14] In the meantime, Gherini himself was being sued for the fees due his co-counsel, a matter that was settled with the payment of $25,000 [$314,000] to the son of now-deceased David Freidenrich. In exchange for this compensation, Freidenrich, Jr., relinquished his claim to any part ownership of the 34 percent of the Rossi–Capuccio tracts on the island that had been negotiated in 1921 with Edmund Rossi.

On Gherini's appeal for fees in the partition suit, the California Supreme Court upheld the view that fees should be paid by all parties in the suit, but it sent the case back to the trial court to decide the level of the award. Unfortunately for the Caires, the matter was not returned to the Santa Barbara court of Judge Crow, who had first ruled in the case. He was forced to excuse himself on grounds of serious illness, and the matter was turned over to his colleague Judge Collier in Los Angeles, who was much more sympathetic on the question of legal fees. Judge Collier set the fees awarded to Gherini at $75,000 [approximately $1.2 million]. The sum was contested and upheld by the California Supreme Court as reasonable, given the nature and amount of work involved, the protracted character of the litigation, and the great value of the property.[15] The Caires were liable for 86 percent of the fees, plus interest on the time taken for the appeal, a total of $69,700 [$1.1 million].

It was 1932 and the vortex of the Great Depression, now in its third year and showing no signs of bottoming out, began sucking down the strong along with the weak. Wine-making had resumed on Santa Cruz Island after the repeal of Prohibition, but as one agricultural analyst wrote, "With strong outside competition and apathy on the part of the owners . . . wine inferior in quality to that previously produced was turned out and the industry failed to fully revive."[16] A wine historian noted, "The habit of drinking wine, never very firmly established in America, had been quite

---

[14] *Cappucio v. Caire*, 207 Cal 200, 277 p. 475 (1929).

[15] *Cappucio v. Caire*, 215 Cal. 518, 529, 11p.2d 1097 (1932).

[16] Warren, Earl, "Agriculture of Santa Cruz Island," 34, quoted in Livingston, "Study," 644.

lost in the fourteen years of Prohibition. . . . On Santa Cruz Island the feeling may have been that winemaking was now more trouble than it was worth."[17] Given this background and Fred and Arthur's focus on trying to sell the property to any serious buyer, it is unlikely that they had the inclination, energy, or resources to invest in wine production. The sheep business continued as it had, but as the number of wild sheep grew in proportion to the tame flocks, the island began to appear overgrazed. The family returned to the island for the corridas and shearing, which now took place only in the spring, and marketed the sheep and wool at prevailing dismal Depression prices.

Coming out of the adverse agricultural conditions of the previous decade, the Caires had borrowed to pay the fees in the San Francisco accounting action, and they had borrowed to keep the island going. When the court ruled that the Caires were liable for $69,700 [$1.1 million] in legal fees to Gherini, it was the final straw in this twenty-year legal, ethical, and emotional saga. Conceivably, in more temperate circumstances, there might have been some negotiation about financing the fee payable to Ambrose Gherini over a period of time, thus allowing the Caires to find a way out of their financial morass. But such negotiations were not an option—the gloves had long since come off in this fight to the finish. Gherini insisted that the Caires would have to find the entire sum immediately, and if that meant they had to borrow it at 6 percent in the depths of the Depression, then so be it. Adding to the Caires' financial woes, in 1932 the Justinian Caire Company showed a loss of $16,500 [$260,000].

It was the end of the road. To pay Gherini, the Caire brothers took out a mortgage on Santa Cruz Island for the first time in the history of the Caire ownership. Although they toyed with the idea of negotiating a $250,000 [$3.75 million] loan to pay off their obligations and seek investment capital for restocking and renewing the vineyard, the appetite for risk-taking in such an adverse economic climate by the seventy-three-year-old Arthur and the sixty-seven-year-old Fred was gone. Ambrose Gherini settled into his role as master of the east end of the island, and the Caires began the long search for a private buyer of this trophy property that had been the cherished possession of their family for more than half a century.

---

[17] Pinney, *Wine of Santa Cruz Island*, 92–93.

CHAPTER 22

The Gherini Era Begins at the East End

In the survey completed in 1924, chief surveyor Flournoy and his team partitioned Santa Cruz Island into seven parcels of varying sizes to each of the seven shareholders. The court-appointed referees allocated the parcels based on the percentage interest of the individual shareholder at the time of the forfeiture of the corporate charter in 1911. In their allocation of the tracts, the surveyors tried to be as equitable as possible. They judged the value of the land as an agricultural resource as well as its potential for recreational or residential use. The surveyors also considered access to the parcels from the mainland and tried to maintain the integrity of the land use patterns that had prevailed since the 1880s. In retrospect, there seems no alternative to the solution proposed: tracts 6 and 7, the eastern 10 percent of the island, including the Scorpion and Smugglers ranches, went to the Capuccio–Rossi–Gherini interests. Tracts 1–5, the western 90 percent, including the Main Ranch, Christy Ranch, and Prisoners' Harbor, were allocated to the Caire family. The smaller share to the plaintiffs was justified by "the rich fertile land in the canyons and mesa with additional good grazing" as features of the east end adding to its value as property.[1] Ambrose Gherini filed protests that he and the interests he represented deserved more acreage and perhaps access to Prisoners' Harbor, with its deep water wharf, but his arguments were to no avail with Judge Crow and the referees.

---

[1] Quoted in Livingstone, "Study," 643.

With the conclusion of the partition suit in the mid-1920s Gherini's victory was in sight, although he had to wait until 1932 for his final triumph over the Caires. The Capuccio and Rossi families had already begun to cede ownership of their shares of the island in lieu of payment to their legal team in 1921, and in October 1926, Aglaë Capuccio sold the remainder of her island holding to the Gherini interests, which included those of Ambrose's wife, Maria Rossi Gherini. In the same month that he finalized his acquisition of the Capuccio interest, Ambrose Gherini began managing the two parcels as one ranch, operating through a shell company called the National Trading Company, a fact that he had trumpeted in the local press the year before.[2] As of December 31, 1927, Gherini and his wife together controlled just short of 40 percent of the company, while eight of Maria's siblings owned the remainder.[3]

Gherini's first strategy was to form a partnership with resort developers as a way of cashing in on his newly acquired property, "to make it the show place of southern California . . . a resort that will rival Catalina."[4] The realities, including a lack of water and no direct access to or from the mainland, rendered this ambition impossible, particularly after the courts rejected his petitions to grant him or his clients the use of the wharf at Prisoners' Harbor. At the same time, Gherini was beginning to experience some of the challenges of running an agricultural enterprise separated from its market by twenty-five miles of open sea. The first year of operation, however, brought an income of $4,992 [$62,000] to Gherini and $1,171 [$14,500] to each of the other shareholders, for a total profit of more than $14,000 [$174,000]. Gherini also received $2,584 [$32,000] in commission for his management services.[5]

But in the years that followed, he lamented the underutilization of the east end, noting that, "the number of sheep with relation to the size of the range shows clearly that far from the maximum return is being obtained. It is much like operating a factory far short of its capacity. The building up of

---

[2] *Santa Barbara (Calif.) Press*, 28 July 1925.

[3] John Gherini, *Santa Cruz Island*, 182–83; and National Trading Company, "Financial Report of Scorpion Ranch Operations, 1926–1927," quoted by Livingston, "Study," 674. Aimee Rossi's interest had already been purchased by her sister Maria when Aimee entered the Sacred Heart Order.

[4] *Santa Barbara (Calif.) Press*, 28 July 1925.

[5] John Gherini, *Santa Cruz Island*, 182–83; and National Trading Company, "Financial Report of Scorpion Ranch Operations, 1926–1927," quoted by Livingston, "Study," 674.

a worthwhile flock upon the present unsatisfactory basis is a very difficult task." He also reported on "the meager means available and all of the difficulties inherent in the property." In closing the report for 1929, Gherini complained that his "assumption of responsibility of management" had resulted in his being paid "absolutely nothing ... it is now two and a half years that this work has been carried on by the writer with absolutely no cooperation or assistance from the co-owners of the property. Such a situation is too unjust to need further comment."[6]

Yet these setbacks and difficulties did not deter his ambition to be the owner of the entire east end, and by June 1932 Ambrose Gherini and his wife Maria Rossi Gherini owned all of the shares of the eastern end of the island, having bought out the interests of all her siblings. Maria owned two-thirds of parcels 6 and 7, and her husband owned the remaining third, making the east end of the island officially the Gherini ranch.[7] They had fought for twenty years for this outcome, but the reality turned out to be somewhat less profitable and enjoyable than they had hoped. Scorpion Ranch was the headquarters of the eastern end of the island and had substantial buildings and facilities dating back to the 1880s, but in the early 1920s, with the writing on the wall, the Caire family had scaled back on investment and maintenance of the Scorpion and Smugglers ranches. More important, there were no all-weather loading facilities for animals or cargo at either ranch. During the Caire era, cargo for the east end of the island had been lightered to and from the schooner anchored in Scorpion Harbor, and livestock were driven overland to Potrero Norte and Prisoners' Harbor for shipment to the mainland. These transportation options were not available to the Gherinis, given that their ownership of the island was confined to the east end. In addition to experiencing transportation difficulties, the Gherinis also faced the continuing challenge of sea communications, which existed during their entire tenure at the east end.

---

[6] National Trading Company, "President's Reports of Scorpion Ranch Operations for the Year 1928, 1929" quoted by Livingston, "Study," 675, 677.

[7] John Gherini, *Santa Cruz Island*, 184.

CHAPTER 23

The Gherinis Search
for Profitability

A fter their initial resort development plans came to nothing, the Gherinis had to face the same constraints that had confronted ranchers
and agriculturalists over the previous seventy years. The inexperienced
Gherini found that he had taken on an undercapitalized, somewhat dilapidated ranch, with a flock that was too small to generate enough income to
cover costs, let alone return a profit. With the country nose-diving into
the Great Depression, he tried running the ranch at minimal cost, with his
sons Pier and Francis providing much of the labor and his wife doing the
books.[1] Although at one point in 1931 the sheep headcount spiked at 5,182,
the average count hovered around 2,500. Sales of sheep and lambs ranged
from 500 to 1,400 annually. The Gherinis sheared the sheep in the spring
only, the best time being April and early May before the still-green grasses
seeded.[2]

They had no boat to provide dependable transportation and had to rely
on a patchwork of arrangements with local fishermen and even, from time
to time, the Caires. The Gherinis struggled to build a wharf themselves at
Scorpion, only to see it destroyed repeatedly in winter storms. Their transportation problems were underlined when family tragedy struck in July
1933. Ambrose Gherini's youngest sister, Carolyn Gherini Imboden, committed suicide by hanging while on a summer visit to Santa Cruz Island

---

[1] John Gherini, *Santa Cruz Island*, 185.
[2] Balance Sheets, Scorpion Ranch, 1927–1944, quoted in Livingston, "Study," 677.

with her young daughter. Maria Gherini was forced to go cap in hand to her cousins for transportation of her sister-in-law's body to the mainland on the *Santa Cruz*.[3] Small wonder that shortly thereafter Gherini told his son Pier that he was "fed up" with the island. In 1936, the fifty-eight-year-old attorney suffered a severe stroke that left him partly paralyzed, and active management of the east end of the island passed to his wife and children, in particular his sons Pier and Francis.[4]

The Gherini family soldiered on, selling 1,000 to 1,400 sheep a year, eventually transporting them in their own boat, a former Alaska fishing vessel that they christened the *Natco*. There would usually be two or three permanent employees on the island, supplemented by casual labor to help out with corridas and by family members in the summer holidays. The dream of cashing in on Santa Cruz Island by developing their holdings as a resort remained tantalizingly out of reach. The challenges of the Depression were followed by those presented by World War II. With Francis, who usually piloted the *Natco*, away in the Navy and Pier in the Air Force and with travel to and from the island restricted by the wartime regulations, the family struggled to keep the operation going with whatever local labor they could find. Ambrose Gherini thought he saw a ray of hope when wartime exigencies resulted in the government takeover of Edwin Stanton's factories, forcing Stanton, the new owner of the Caire holdings, to re-negotiate his loan with the Caires. In a meeting with the Caires in 1943, Gherini suggested that if Stanton could not fulfill his financial obligations the Caires should foreclose, join forces with the Gherinis, and offer the island for sale as one entity, "to see us all wealthy [because] the Island was worth millions. If we held it, then we should all sell together."[5] The Caires treated this proposal with their habitual disdain for his schemes and carried Ed Stanton through his period of financial difficulties.

Through the postwar period, the overall impression of the Gherini ranch was that of a shoestring operation with an emphasis on making do with minimal investment and maximum ingenuity. A regional drought in 1948 forced the Gherinis to remove and sell 2,240 head of their herd, which

---

[3] *San Francisco Examiner*, 20 July 1933; and Maria Gherini to F. F. Caire, 18 July 1933, Santa Cruz Island Foundation archives.

[4] John Gherini, *Santa Cruz Island*, 185–86.

[5] Meeting with Ambrose Gherini, 4 June 1943; and Jeanne Caire, memorandum and transcript, 4 June 1943, San Francisco, Caire Family Papers, in the author's possession.

resulted in both decreased stock levels for a number of years and financial setbacks. The balance sheet for 1948 saw the year ending with only 450 sheep, and fewer the following two years. The ranch saw little or no profit during the early 1950s. The year before he died, Ambrose Gherini wrote to his son Pier of his dissatisfaction with "the situation" on the Island. "As it is, all we are doing is to load expenses upon ourselves and operate the place for the benefit of the hands. That simply does not make sense." In 1952, only 150 sheep were counted on the Gherini property, and the numbers only gradually increased to their former levels by 1956.[6]

Like almost everyone who spent time on Santa Cruz Island, the Gherini descendants developed a deep appreciation of the island's rugged charm that went hand in hand with its isolation and physical challenges even as they struggled to keep it economically viable.[7] One suggested reason for the Gherini family's persistence with sheep ranching in these conditions is that it was perhaps encouraged by the widowed Maria Rossi Gherini after her husband died in 1952. Profits, if existing at all, never reached great amounts, and labor expenses grew. The grandchildren of Ambrose and Maria Gherini continued to work on the ranch through the 1970s. The National Park Service Study summarized this period thus: "In essence the Gherinis did not live on the island but made occasional income from its operation; they kept the structures in fair condition although they rarely spent much time and money on building projects. . . . One could surmise that the sheep ranching operation, never a big profit-maker, was not seen as a long term use of the land and so the existing buildings were kept only in a state of preservation for day-to-day utilitarian uses." [8]

As the years passed and the family continued to run their small sheep operation to cover costs, the dreams of turning the east end of the island into a resort never completely went away. But Southern California attitudes to land ownership and conservation were evolving. By the 1960s there was a groundswell of public support for the purchase and preservation of the Channel Islands in as pristine a state as possible, anticipating the argument between private property rights and environmental protection that would dominate the final years of private island ownership.

[6] Ambrose Gherini to Pier Gherini, 13 June 1951, and Pier Gherini to Ambrose Gherini, 22 June 1951, quoted in Livingston, "Study," 679–81; and Warren, "Agriculture of Santa Cruz Island."

[7] John Gherini, Santa Cruz Island, 193–200.

[8] Livingston, "Study," 681–83.

It had long been known that there were significant amounts of oil under the seabed in the Santa Barbara Channel. In the 1920s there had been several exploratory leases granted on Santa Cruz Island to oil companies such as Standard Oil and Richfield. Like the Caires and the Stantons, the Gherinis entertained hopes of oil income from their holdings. Various companies were involved in drilling on the east end in the mid-1960s, and Richfield sank a well to a depth of almost 5,000 feet. They found no oil or gas but a plentiful supply of water near the old trail over the Montañon that had connected Scorpion with the Main Ranch in earlier times. The efforts of the Union Oil Company in drilling down more than 7,000 feet near Cavern Point, just north of Scorpion Harbor, did not yield significant returns.[9]

In 1963 the Gherini family took another tack. They hired architect George V. Russell to develop a conceptual plan to combine residential, commercial, and recreational development, with a marina for 150 boats, 500 residential lots, hunting lodges, horse trails, and a predicted population of 3,000 people.[10] The public hearings on the plan, conducted by the Santa Barbara County Planning Commission, brought out advocates both for the private development of Santa Cruz Island and for the preservation of public access to open space within the county. The planning commissioners reflected the prevailing conservative property rights ethos and gave a generally positive response to the Gherini proposal. This response was countered by conservation groups, notably the Sierra Club, who saw the scheme as a threat to preservation of the unique island ecosystems. In the background was the National Park Service, which had been flirting with the idea of incorporating Santa Cruz Island into a Channel Islands National Park since the 1920s.

The Gherini position was that the federal government could step in at any time and make a bid for their holdings, but in the interim the National Park Service could not prevent the family from pursuing their own commercial interests. Opponents of the development scheme charged that the Gherinis were merely talking up the asking price that they would eventually have to accept from the government when the inevitable park was authorized. In 1966 the Santa Barbara County Planning Commission approved the Gherini development plan in the face of vigorous local protests.

This decision was upheld by the board of supervisors, but times were

[9] Livingston, "Study," 705.
[10] John Gherini, *Santa Cruz Island*, 202–203.

changing, and one of the long-lasting outcomes from the tumultuous decade of the 1960s was a heightened environmental awareness. This new attitude put the autocratic tradition of island land management on a collision course with both public sentiment and the state and federal governments. The general concern for the fragility of the local marine environment was thrown into sharp relief in the aftermath of a major oil spill in the Santa Barbara Channel in January 1969. The spill coated the coastline with thick tar and wreaked a great deal of damage to wildlife and the recreational tourism assets of the Santa Barbara area. The oil spill, emanating from a platform operated by Union Oil, became a potent catalyst for the tide of public opinion that would strongly influence legislative action regarding the Channel Islands in the coming years.

Not long after the 1969 spill, when it became public knowledge that the Gherinis had applied for drilling permits with Union Oil, there was again public outcry. Once more the family locked horns with the Sierra Club. The Gherinis prevailed in their efforts to sell permits for drilling on Santa Cruz Island, but an era of environmental challenges had begun, spurred on by the oil spill and the passage the following year of the California Environmental Quality Act. The future of the island was sealed in the 1972 general election, when the voters of California passed a popular initiative establishing the California Coastal Zone Conservation Act and creating the California Coastal Commission. This body had jurisdiction over land use planning for sensitive environments, such as Santa Cruz Island, making "any development on it difficult if not impossible."[11] In addition to the immense investment needed to overcome the inherent shortcomings in water resources and infrastructure that had doomed earlier schemes, the new legislative environment meant that the Gherini family's development dreams finally faded and disappeared.

---

[11] John Gherini, *Santa Cruz Island*, 213.

CHAPTER 24

The Last Days of Ranching on Santa Cruz Island

Once again the Gherini family turned their attention to the subsistence sheep ranching operation that had prevailed since the 1930s, but Pier and Francis Gherini, whose father had died in 1952, were also getting on in years; hence, they examined ways they could extricate themselves from the burdens of active involvement in running a sheep ranch that was barely profitable and was onerous in its responsibilities. Like their father before them, they were fed up with the difficulties of running a ranch "in the sea," and it would appear that the constant aggravations gradually outweighed the affection they felt for Santa Cruz Island.

A solution seemed to present itself in the late 1970s in the person of William "Pete" Petersen, who had worked on the island in the previous decade, both on the Gherinis' ranch and on a wildcat drilling operation prospecting for oil on the east end. Endlessly resourceful and inventive, Petersen fit the operational pattern that dominated during the Gherini era: improvise and make do. With the help of a young English woman, whom he later married, and a small group of ranch hands, in five years he succeeded in building up the herd on the east end of the island to approximately 5,000 sheep. Just about the time when Petersen was convinced that he had turned the corner to financial stability, a double tragedy struck.[1]

The first was the crash of the light plane in which he was traveling back to the island; the accident left him badly injured and in need of months

---

[1] John Gherini, *Santa Cruz Island*, 206–210; and Petersen, *Once Upon an Island*.

of hospitalization. The second was the decision by the Gherinis that they would reap a much greater and reliable profit from their island holding if they copied the success of their neighbor Carey Stanton. Stanton was operating a hunting venture on what had been the Caire holdings of the western 90 percent of the island. His business catered to the passion for extreme sport shooting within the hunting population of southern California. As the Gherinis knew from Stanton's enterprise, these hunters would happily pay hundreds of dollars a day for the opportunity to stalk wild sheep and hogs with their crossbows and high-powered rifles. It was a potent financial incentive for the Gherinis, and within days of Petersen's near-fatal injury, an agreement was reached with local hunter, guide, and entrepreneur Jaret Owens to start a hunt club.[2]

In late April 1984, the Petersens were served a thirty-day eviction notice. This eviction was a bitter pill for Pete and Michel Petersen, who had struggled mightily against very tall odds to build a viable ranching operation on Santa Cruz Island. However, given that they were $14,000 in arrears with rental payments, they were not in a strong bargaining position once the Gherinis had decided that hunting and other income from recreation was the way forward on the east end of the island. The Petersens rounded up as much of their herd as they could and departed, leaving the wild sheep to Jaret Owens and his hunting customers.

On the mainland, like all the coastal counties, Santa Barbara had to draw up a local coastal plan for the approval of the coastal commission. Over the protests of the Gherinis, the plan substantially increased the zoning of the minimum parcel size on Santa Cruz Island from 10 acres to 320 acres. When applied to their holdings, this meant that no more than twenty-one dwelling units would be allowed, instead of the five hundred units that had been approved in the previous decade. The commission also forbade any oil development on Santa Cruz Island, which initiated years of litigation between the owners and the commission, but public sympathy was on the side of conservation and against the supremacy of private property rights. With legislation introduced in Congress to establish a Channel Islands National Park, the trend was clear. The higher courts upheld the

---

[2] Owens had previously worked for the Santa Cruz Island Hunt Club on the Stanton side of the Island. He paid 25 percent of gross proceeds to the Gherini family for exclusive use of their island property. Livingston, "Study," 710.

actions of the Coastal Commission, noting the biological significance and ecological sensitivity of the area.[3]

This was the end of the road for the Gherinis. The era in which the public accepted the preference of private property rights over protection of special environments was finished, and a new era was about to begin. It would look forward to preservation and restoration of ecologies affected by over a century of land and animal husbandry. The seventy-six-year-old Pier Gherini, who was in failing health, and his brother Francis, two years his junior, now embarked on a long negotiation to achieve the highest possible return on their family's seventy-one-year investment.

It had taken three generations, but Ambrose Gherini's grandchildren would finally achieve his great ambition of making a fortune out of his holdings on Santa Cruz Island. Public Law 96-199 in 1980 authorized the federal purchase of the east end of the island, but negotiations dragged on through the decade, with the Gherini family offering to sell about 700 acres of the hilly sections of their property along with a trail easement from Smugglers and a half-acre site at the cove for a ranger station. A visiting research scientist inspected the property and pronounced it "thoroughly trashed" by human influences. Family disagreements and lack of government appropriations delayed progress, but the death of Pier Gherini in 1989 refocused minds as his heirs asked to sell his interest to enable them to pay estate taxes. The federal government purchased Pier Gherini's quarter interest from his heirs in December 1989 for almost $4 million. The next two quarter interests, belonging to Pier Gherini's sisters, were purchased in 1992 for $4 million each. The remaining quarter interest was owned by Pier's brother, Francis, who felt that the purchase price received by his siblings was not enough, even though appraisals of his quarter interest in the property dipped as low as $2.9 million in the following years.[4]

An impasse ensued, which raised public concern and pressure for a settlement between Francis Gherini and the National Park Service that would finally open the east end to the public as a national park. Legal and legislative maneuverings from both sides rumbled on through 1996 and 1997, including a "legislative taking," or federal seizure, of the property

---

[3] *Pier Gherini et al. v. California Coastal Commission,* 204 Cal.App.3d 699 (1988), quoted in John Gherini, *Santa Cruz Island,* 213–14.

[4] Livingston, "Study," 713–14.

signed by President Clinton and a federal lawsuit launched by Gherini on grounds that he had been denied his rights under the Fourteenth Amendment, equal protection under the law.[5] Finally, on February 10, 1997, after seventeen years of negotiation and litigation, the National Park Service owned the east end of Santa Cruz Island in full. Another two years passed before a court awarded Francis $12.9 million, plus interest, for his share of the east end, but his triumph was short-lived. Francis Gherini died on April 28, 1999, at age eighty-four, just days after the verdict was announced; less than a month later his wife died.

The National Park Service faced additional costs in removing the Gherinis' semi-wild horse herd and almost 10,000 sheep. Animal rights concerns ruled out shooting them on the island, and their capture and transfer to the mainland took almost two years and more than $2 million. The last sheep on the island, perhaps descendants of the first flocks taken out there by Dr. Shaw in 1852, were finally gone by the end of 1999. This removal broke the final link with the agricultural legacy of Justinian Caire, but in its buildings, design, and layout, the Scorpion and Smugglers ranches still give ample testimony to his vision of nineteenth-century land husbandry.[6]

---

[5] *Francis Gherini v. United States of America et al.*, No. CV 97-0819, U.S. District Court, Central District of California.

[6] Cited in Livingston, "Study," 716.

CHAPTER 25

The Stanton Era of 1937–1986: Changing the Guard

In early May 1937, one of the most painful meetings of Fred Caire's long life took place in the family house at the Main Ranch. Fred had crossed the Santa Barbara Channel on the *Santa Cruz* with the new owners of Santa Cruz Island, Edwin and Evelyn Stanton, to complete the handover of the property that had meant so much to his family since he was a child. The disparity of generations and styles could not have been more apparent. Trying to run the complex ranching operation during the years of bitter intrafamily litigation had taken their toll on the seventy-two-year-old Caire. He chatted with the Stantons on the veranda of the eight-bedroom family home that he and his brother, Arthur, had commissioned twenty-seven years earlier to accommodate their mother, their eight children, and their many cousins. In his stiff collar and tie, with his formal manners, the gentlemanly Fred embodied the traditional nineteenth-century Californian, one who had been heavily influenced by San Francisco's culture, with its European immigrant communities and its links to the early years of statehood and the Gold Rush.

The new owners were a startling contrast, a southern California success story of the twentieth century. At forty-two, Ed Stanton was a successful businessman with a forceful personality who enjoyed a drink and an amusing anecdote. He had been a track star at the University of California and an Olympic contender whose business success was based on the new southern California industries of oil and manufacturing. A rugged outdoorsman who was born and bred in Southern California, Ed was accompanied by his wife, Evelyn, who was forty. Evelyn Carey Stanton, who had dropped her first name of Gladys after her marriage, was a native of Detroit, Michigan. She had married Ed twenty years before and was the mother of their two sons. Their first child, Edwin L. Stanton, Jr., was born in 1918, followed by Carey Q. Stanton in 1923. The neo-Georgian Stanton family home was in fashionable Hancock Park on the western side of Los Angeles.[1]

In the lingering years of the Great Depression, it had taken from 1932 until 1937 for Santa Barbara real estate broker Nick Liatis to find someone of Stanton's means who was interested in this truly unique piece of real estate. Stanton sold one of his automotive factories to get the cash to buy this outstanding property. He made a down payment of $250,000 and signed a note for the remaining $500,000 of the purchase price of $750,000 [total $11.2 million] to complete the purchase. Wild rumors circulated about the purchase price, and Stanton did not deny to waiting reporters that the deal totaled a million dollars. The mystery and rumor about the purchase price stemmed from the fact that the deed as recorded did not carry any tax stamps. As the biggest real estate deal in the history of the county, Santa Barbara's recording office simply did not have enough stamps on hand to cover the size of the sale. Stanton, who wanted to avoid monetary publicity, heeded legal advice that the stamps might be applied after recording the transaction.

Prior to making the channel crossing with Fred Caire, Ed had made a number of tours of Santa Cruz Island on horseback and had big plans to revitalize the ranching operation on the island. This had gone into a gradual decline in the 1920s and 1930s, as the years of litigation took their emotional and financial toll on the Caires—particularly the necessity of paying the legal fees of their sister's son-in-law, Ambrose Gherini. Stanton clearly took to heart the recommendations of the court-ordered agricultural survey and inventory of the island from fifteen years earlier. It recommended reducing the size of the sheep herd while increasing its quality and expanding the number of cattle as a way of bringing the island back to profitability.

As they chatted in the family residence, Evelyn entertained her host, who would soon be leaving his island forever, with her ideas for decoration in and around the house, such as filling one of the upturned island carts with soil

---

[1] "Island Sold. Million Paid by L.A. Capitalist," *Santa Barbara (Calif.) News Press*, 22 April 1937, Santa Cruz Island Foundation archives; Richard Bergen (Stanton family attorney), interview by Marla Daily, 11 March 1992, transcript, Santa Cruz Island Foundation archives; and Livingston, "Study," 719.

Ed Stanton, 1937, the year of the purchase.
Photograph courtesy of the Santa Cruz Island Foundation.

Carey Stanton at age sixteen and his mother, Evelyn Stanton (*behind gate*), 1939.
Photograph courtesy of the Santa Cruz Island Foundation.

and planting geraniums in it for a visual focus in the formal flower garden created by Fred's mother fifty years before. Evelyn also gave voice to some thoughts about brightening up the house by giving the pieces of dark Victorian furniture left by the Caires a coat of white paint. It had been made for the Caires years before by craftsmen in San Francisco and Italy, and the thought of painting it white would surely have set the brothers' teeth on edge and would have Justinian and Albina Caire turning in their graves. But there was no getting around it. The Caires' time on Santa Cruz Island was over, and a new chapter was beginning. Fred took his leave of the Stantons and rode down to Prisoners' Harbor to board the *Santa Cruz* for the last time.

The deeds had been filed by April 10, and Stanton became official owner of the former Caire family Santa Cruz Island holdings, parcels 1–5 from the partition of 1924: 54,750 acres of the total 62, 250 acres. The remaining two parcels, consisting of 7,500 acres and once owned by the descendants of Justinian Caire's daughters Amelie and Aglaë, were now under the ownership of Ambrose Gherini and his wife, Maria Rossi Gherini, eldest daughter of Amelie Caire Rossi. Ed Stanton, anxious to win over local opinion, called a lunch press conference to announce the completion of the transaction and his intention of "maintaining the island property as a great, typical, old-fashioned California ranch."[2] At the same time he declared his willingness to invest in restocking the island's herds of sheep and cattle, to overhaul the schooner *Santa Cruz*, and to build an airstrip on the island to facilitate a quick commute between his office in Los Angeles and Santa Cruz Island. Also at the press conference was Santa Barbara realtor Nick Liatis, who confirmed that the sale of the island was not only the biggest deal he had ever put together, but also the largest single realty transaction in terms of both acreage and money that had ever occurred in Santa Barbara County.

Stanton was as good as his word. In October the first of 10,000 head of sheep were shipped to the island aboard the schooner *Santa Cruz* and the *Vaquero*, which was hired from the owners of neighboring Santa Rosa Island. The twenty-five carloads of sheep, purchased in Arizona and temporarily corralled on Punta Gorda Street, were herded on to Stearns Wharf by "two expert sheep dogs of the Island, Spot and Shep," to be ferried over to the island as quickly as possible.[3] But before this, Stanton closed a chapter of island history with the cancellation of the Eaton's lease of Pelican Bay. Within weeks of the change of ownership, the Eatons were notified that their lease was terminated and they must remove their belongings. And with their marital relationship similarly ended, Margaret Eaton left Santa Barbara to live with her daughter in Hollywood, closing another chapter in island life.[4]

---

[2] "Island Sold. Million Paid by L.A. Capitalist," *Santa Barbara (Calif.) News Press*, 22 April 1937, Santa Cruz Island Foundation archives.

[3] "First of 10,000 Head of Sheep Shipped to Island," *Santa Barbara (Calif.) News Press*, 13 October 1937, Santa Cruz Island Foundation archives.

[4] Eaton, *Diary of a Sea Captain's Wife*, 250.

The following year Stanton introduced hog cholera as a way of control-ling the wild pig population. He also introduced a program to poison the ravens plaguing the island. The hogs seemed somewhat impervious to the virus, but the ravens were noticeably reduced.[5]

The changes continued. Although Prohibition had ended with the repeal of the Volstead Act in 1933, and the Caires had tried to restart the win-ery business by selling varietal wines in bottle to local customers like the Arlington Hotel, Stanton did not see profitability in this traditional island income stream.[6] When he was advised that the 26,000 gallons stored in the winery were gradually spoiling, he instructed one of his employees to empty the vats, and the thousands of gallons of wine, along with the proud history of winemaking on the island, drained away into the dust of the Camino del'Este. Or, as Justinian Caire II, who had stayed on as superin-tendent to ease the transition between the Caires and the Stantons, put it, they just "pulled the plug and let it go down the road."[7] The grapevines, first planted in the 1880s, were the next to go, torn out to create more grazing land in the central valley for the expanded sheep and cattle herds.

Unfortunately, the plan for making the island herd more docile by the introduction of 10,000 domesticated sheep came to nothing, as the new-comers headed for the hills to join their wild cousins, adding to the deg-radation of the rangeland. In 1939 Stanton ranch hands began to round up sheep for shipping to packing houses on the mainland, collecting about 35,000. In the next decade, professional hunters killed some 20,000 more, but the sheep continued to multiply and populate the island's ranges. According to one of the hands working for Stanton, "They were every-where you looked.... They had multiplied and multiplied—due to the fact that you couldn't catch them very well, and they didn't have fences enough to get them down into small pastures where you could control them. The island was overrun with them. In fact, they were just denuding the island. ... We estimated that there were probably around at least 30,000 head of sheep on the island at one time."[8]

---

[5] Memorandum by Santa Cruz Island Co., 25 November 1944, Caire Family Papers and Diaries; and Edwin L. Stanton to Ambrose Gherini, 5 December 1938, cited in John Gherini, *Santa Cruz Island*, 162.

[6] Memorandum by Jeanne Caire, 6 March 1978, Correspondence, "Letter from Jeanne Caire to Mary B. Brock," Caire Family Papers and Diaries, in the author's possession.

[7] Quoted by Pinney, *Wine of Santa Cruz Island*, 94.

[8] Red Craine, interview by John Gherini, 13 September 1983, quoted by Livingston, "Study," 722.

The Stantons continued to welcome researchers as the Caires had done. With Ed Stanton's permission, M. Woodbridge Williams of Pomona College spent about six weeks on Santa Cruz Island in the summer of 1939 studying the land snails and making botanical and marine biological observations. He was sometimes accompanied on his explorations by Evelyn Stanton and her young son, Carey. That same year, with the Stantons' blessing, the Los Angeles County Museum began a major five-year expedition, spending nine days on the island, based in the central valley, Cañada del Puerto and Prisoners' Harbor. The openness of the Stantons contrasted with an unwelcoming attitude at the eastern end of the island. Williams wrote that Ambrose Gherini was especially harsh on scientists and trespassers, claiming that he once confiscated the results of an archaeological dig by the Santa Barbara Museum of Natural History.[9] On another occasion, when Gherini found out that artifacts had been removed without his permission by researchers from the University of California, he demanded their return. They were duly sent back from Berkeley to the east end of the island.[10]

The Stantons were enjoying the gracious island life, but as a possible ace in the hole, in 1940 Ed Stanton sent a letter to an old friend who had just been appointed as director of the National Park Service making him aware that Santa Cruz Island was available for purchase as a park. Stanton's prescient letter predicted that it was only a matter of time before it would be acquired by the federal government, and that this should take place while it was still in its natural state.[11] The letter went unanswered.

With the onset of World War II, the price for wool skyrocketed, and by 1943 Stanton was getting top dollar for all the wool he could produce. At the same time, because of the war, he was hard-pressed to find the skilled labor he needed to cash in on the inflated market prices. In addition to the manpower famine induced by the war, there were Coast Guard restrictions on travel to and from the island. A year later Stanton announced that he would exterminate the 40,000 sheep on the island and replace them with polled Hereford cattle.[12] The decision in 1944 to focus on less labor-intensive

---

[9] Williams, "Notes on Land Snails"; and M. Woodbridge Williams to Dewey Livingston, 1 June 1999 and 29 July 1999, quoted by Livingston, "Study," 775.

[10] Olson, "On the Island of the Dead" and *Chumash Prehistory*, 1–21.

[11] Edwin Stanton to Newton Drury, 9 September 1940, quoted in Livingston, "Study," 750.

[12] "Santa Cruz Island Sheep Lose Weight—They're Being Sheared," *Santa Barbara (Calif.) News Press*, 9 May 1943, Santa Cruz Island Foundation archives; and "Ventura County Yesterdays, 25 Years Ago, November 1944," *Ventura Free Press*, 1 December 1969, Santa Cruz Island Foundation archives.

cattle might well have been connected with the death of Edwin, Jr., during the Normandy landings in June. The elder Stanton son left behind a wife and a newborn baby boy, Edwin Stanton III. Edwin, Jr., had been the heir designated by his parents to manage the island, a responsibility that would eventually fall to his younger brother, Carey. As with many people, the war played havoc with Stanton's finances, and he entered into extended and ultimately successful discussions with the Caires to renegotiate his mortgage.

The cattle business continued to be the main focus of the Stanton operation in the boom of the postwar period, though the challenges of ranching in southern California hit home in the drought years of 1948 and 1949. Lack of rainfall required the evacuation of the entire herd from the island. The cattle operation was resumed in the latter year, and that winter was notable as one of the few recorded times when the central valley was completely blanketed in snow. The Stantons reorganized the layout of the island operations to accommodate cattle, and although there were complications associated with running a ranch "in the sea," many observers agreed that the advantages of isolation from predators, noxious weeds, and diseases resulted in healthy cattle that commanded a good price at market.

CHAPTER 26

The Caire Legacy Disappears, and the Carey Stanton Era Begins

A long with the transformation of the herd, the physical legacy of the Caires gradually faded as more and more of the structures of Santa Cruz Island changed over the ensuing decade. For domestic lighting the former owners had made do with kerosene lanterns, but the Stantons decided to move with the times by installing generator-powered electricity for lighting and appliances. In 1950 a faulty refrigerator in the wooden family residence caught fire. The blaze quickly spread to the house, burning it to the ground. Sparks borne on a westerly wind ignited the roofs and all the contents of the nearby winery buildings—the huge oak vats, barrels, carts, tools, and winemaking apparatus.[1] There was, of course, no fire department to call for help, and the small number of ranch hands could only look on and try to keep the conflagration from spreading to the superintendent's house, the comedor, and the bunk houses. When the fire at last died down, all that remained of the Main Ranch compound to the east of the superintendent's house were the brick walls of the winery. The rest was a smoking ruin. Across the valley from the much-reduced family compound, Justinian Caire's diminutive brick chapel, which had taken pride of place among the vines at its dedication fifty-nine years before, now stood

---

[1] *Santa Barbara News Press*, 13 June 1950.

forlornly alone, surrounded by a few overgrown Blackwood acacias, vulnerable to earthquake damage and the vagaries of weather.

After the fire, Stanton immediately hired the well-known Los Angeles architect H. Roy Kelley and set about replacing the old family house with a modern two-bedroom ranch style home, appropriately named Phoenix House. At the same time, perhaps disheartened by these setbacks, he listed the island for sale at $50 per acre, or $2.7 million [$33 million]. There were apparently no takers for this "outstanding cattle ranch, lending itself ideally for a large colony or subdivision."[2]

Although Stanton was operating in the tradition of the gentlemen rancher for whom profit was not a necessity, in most years his island operation was in the black. Along with the modest cattle business, there was income to be had from leasing portions of the island. The year before the fire at the Main Ranch, with the Cold War heating up, Stanton leased a hilltop east of Prisoners' Harbor to the federal government for a radar and missile-tracking station, which eventually became home to about thirty Navy and civilian technicians. The lease provided both income and maintenance of some of the island roads as well as the pier at Prisoners' Harbor. It was also a handy and economical means of keeping keep the ranch provisioned, using the Navy supply vessel that called at the island from Port Hueneme.

It may have been useful and financially advantageous to have the Navy on Santa Cruz Island; however, in seeking to redirect the creek bed of the Cañada del Puerto in the 1940s to accommodate their road, employees of the Army Corps of Engineers caused the destruction of the long-disused adobe house that had stood at Prisoners' Harbor for almost a century. The causeway that they constructed across the creek diverted its water into the old house during the flood season. The front and rear walls suffered severe damage. After a number of years in this dilapidated condition, Carey Stanton had the house dismantled for safety reasons in January 1960.[3]

And it was on the rocks at Prisoners' Harbor on December 7, 1960, with a Santa Ana wind blowing out of the northeast, that the schooner *Santa Cruz* was wrecked. After serving the owners of the island faithfully and surviving the waters and hazards of the Santa Barbara Channel for sixty-seven

[2] Coldwell, Banker & Co. listing memo, 6 March 1950; and Edwin L. Stanton to Ambrose Gherini, 26 June 1950, cited in John Gherini, *Santa Cruz Island*, 167.

[3] Daily and Stanton, "Santa Cruz Island," 21, cited by Livingston, "Study," 729.

years, the *Santa Cruz* was a total loss, and another chapter of Santa Cruz Island history disappeared.

The cattle operation continued through the 1950s, more or less breaking even. An oil exploration lease granted to the Richfield Oil Company in 1954 brought in welcome income but no oil revenue. The abandoned sheep became feral, and in 1957, with Ed Stanton in failing health, his surviving son Carey took over the management of the island, charged by his father with the task of keeping it profitable. He had completed his medical education at Stanford just after the war and then had practiced pathology and internal medicine for about ten years. He later characterized his move to the island as his being "overtaken by good sense. . . . It was . . . the wisest decision of my life."[4]

The quiet, intensely private life on the island suited Carey Stanton perfectly. With his scholarly interests, Stanton enjoyed meeting scientists and students who visited the University of California Santa Cruz Island Reserve, which he made possible in the mid-1960s. The University of California, Santa Barbara (UCSB), held a summer geology class on the island in 1963. It was such a success that the next year the quarters were moved from tents to semi-permanent buildings. In 1966 UCSB established the Santa Cruz Island Field Station about one-half mile to the west of the Main Ranch. Stanton encouraged scientific study of the island and allowed his 54,000-acre portion of the island to become part of the Natural Land and Water Reserve System (now the National Research System) of the University of California in 1974.

Philanthropic and civic-minded, Stanton contributed to many organizations and served on a variety of boards, including those of the Santa Barbara Botanic Garden, Santa Barbara Historical Society, Santa Barbara Museum of Natural History, California Historical Society, and Society of Architectural Historians. An avid historian by avocation, a collector by nature, and a "stickler for detail" by his father's description, Carey Stanton developed an unequalled passion for collecting Santa Cruz Island objects: books, maps, photographs, art, and artifacts. In 1958 Stanton commissioned his old friend from Stanford days, the artist Richard Diebenkorn, to design a flag for him that would represent the island. In addition to his simple, abstract, and graceful rendition of the historic image of the cross

---

[4] Stanton, *Island Memoir*, 11.

on a hill, Diebenkorn produced a series of paintings on his many visits to the island.

Carey Stanton took the responsibilities of island land husbandry very literally, striving to maintain the memory of the previous century of human habitation while working with his trusted foreman, Henry Duffield, to keep the cattle operation functioning. Duffield was truly one of a long line of island characters. Hired by Ed Stanton in 1960 to run the island's cattle business, he did so for a quarter of a century. Paralyzed from the waist down by polio contracted in his thirties, Henry was known as "the cowboy in the red jeep with hand controls, never without his rifle in a scabbard, his flask of Ancient Age Bourbon in his glove box, and his several dogs at his side."[5]

As for the character of Carey Stanton, his enduring image from these years was summed up by a visitor from the Santa Barbara Historical Society. After a pleasant day on the island, they were pulling away from Prisoners' Harbor at sunset, and "there stood Dr. Stanton, short of stature and mild-mannered, alone on the pier waving to the group as the huge island loomed behind him."[6] *Los Angeles Times* feature writer Charles Hillinger became friendly with Stanton after writing an article about the island in 1956. Hillinger recalled one visit: "We consumed vodka martinis on a different beach every day, ate a picnic lunch, and then fell asleep for a couple of hours." The writer noted Stanton's punctiliousness, "He had a cook and would always dress formally for dinner in Brooks Brothers suits and black knit ties, even though he usually ate alone." Hillinger claimed that Stanton would listen to traffic reports from the mainland to remind himself of his good fortune to be on a quiet island. But he could still summon up a sense of outrage at thoughtless behavior. On one memorable occasion, incensed by rubbish left on an island beach, Stanton tracked down the offending yachtsman at work on the mainland and deposited the garbage on the perpetrator's desk.[7]

There was still the need for more income than the cattle operation and the Stanton family oil resources could provide. Another small area of the island was leased for research to a subsidiary of General Motors in 1965. Between the two leases, Stanton could eventually count on about $150,000

---

[5] Daily, *Chapel of Holy Cross*, 45.
[6] Recollection of Jane Rich Mueller, quoted in Livingston, "Study," 745.
[7] Hillinger, *Channel Islands*, 123–24, cited in Livingston, "Study," 746.

in yearly income. And with the advent of personal mobile communications, yet more income was accrued by leasing sites to wireless communications companies on the high mountains of the island facing the mainland.

In the 1960s Stanton also saw an opportunity to cater to the hunting fraternity of southern California who wanted more than the usual challenge in terms of rugged terrain and wily and powerful prey. Starting in 1966, for almost twenty years the Ventura-based Santa Cruz Island Hunt Club (Santa Cruz Island Club) operated as a partnership between Carey Stanton and two local entrepreneurs. The club began as a sheep- and pig-hunting enterprise with both a rifle season and an archery season, and in 1981 it expanded to include summer recreational visits. In 1966 a two-day hunt cost $100 [$663]. For this sum, a customer received round-trip airfare, guides, meals, lodging, two trophy animals, and one lamb. By 1985, the cost of a club hunt had increased to $600 [$1,200] per person. The Santa Cruz Island Company received 25 percent of the club's gross receipts. By its last year of operation, the club was netting the Santa Cruz Island Company about $250,000 [almost $500,000] in income. In the end, plagued by insurance problems and by the desire of Carey Stanton's new partners in island ownership, The Nature Conservancy, to eliminate the feral sheep, the Santa Cruz Island Club ceased operating in December 1985.

CHAPTER 27

"It Was 1912 All Over Again": Enter The Nature Conservancy

The Nature Conservancy was established in 1951 and became one of the largest private non-profit conservation organizations in the United States. In 1976 it entered the complex negotiations undertaken by Carey Stanton in circumstances that ironically mirrored the intrafamilial litigation of the Caires. The deaths of Ed Stanton in 1963 and of his wife ten years later had triggered estate duties that were paid out of securities they had set aside for that purpose. Upon Evelyn Stanton's death, the Santa Cruz Island Company was reinstated, with two-thirds of the stock controlled by Carey Stanton and one-third going to his nephew, thirty-two-year-old Edwin Stanton III. Carey was enjoying his modest but pleasant lifestyle on this unique property, conserving it as he saw fit and as his parents intended, but there was little income that could be shared out with the other principal shareholder.

Eddie Stanton saw himself as one-third owner of a potentially very valuable piece of real estate from which he was deriving no income or benefit, but he kept his dissatisfaction to himself until after the death of his grandmother. At the start of 1976, he filed suit against his uncle to dissolve the Santa Cruz Island Company and submit to an accounting. He alleged mismanagement by his uncle and grandmother, the use of the Santa Cruz Island Company for their personal benefit, and the contentious transfer of valuable non-island assets, such as the Stanton Oil Company, to the Santa Cruz Island Company. As Carey was uncomfortably aware, his nephew's goal, like minority shareholders Amelie Caire Rossi and Aglaë Caire Capuccio sixty-four years before, was to dismantle the company and claim his inheritance.[1] The charges of mismanagement and a lavish lifestyle would have been very difficult to prove, given the income of the company and Carey's financially conservative and parsimonious nature, but at its core the suit echoed the same complaint that the two married Caire daughters had made in 1912. They and Eddie Stanton were part owners of a valuable asset from which they were not benefiting to the extent they deemed appropriate.[2]

Carey Stanton's dilemma was similar to the Caires in that he felt he had natural justice on his side, but he knew from the Caire history that protracted litigation would be costly and would threaten his preservation and control of the island he loved. He was desperate for a solution that would allow him to retain control of the island and provide cash to buy out his nephew. Stanton had been approached by both the National Park Service and The Nature Conservancy in the 1970s, but all that the Park Service offered him was the opportunity to donate his interest in the island to them to become part of the Channel Islands National Monument. Deeply skeptical about the way that governments change according to the political party in power, and fearful that there would be no guarantee that his lands would not develop into a gaudy tourist attraction, it was Stanton's absolute conviction that his island holdings should never end up in the hands of the federal or state government. The only other solution on offer was that of The Nature Conservancy.

What emerged from complex negotiations lasting almost two years was a global solution that included a payment of $900,000 to Edwin III for his shares of stock in the Santa Cruz Island Company. There was a similar payment to Carey for half of his stock, though he was given the power to vote the shares formerly belonging to Edwin III. The Nature Conservancy also paid the other Santa Cruz Island Company obligations. For his part, Carey agreed to leave his shares to the conservancy in his will and granted complete ownership of 78 percent of his holdings (42,300 acres) to The Nature Conservancy but reserved the full use, control, income, and possession of this southern portion to the company until 2008. The Nature Conservancy took title of the northerly 12,200 acres and leased it back to the Santa Cruz Island Company.

---

[1] *Edwin L. Stanton III, Plaintiff, v. Santa Cruz Island Company, et al., Defendants*, Los Angeles Superior Court No. C180228, Santa Cruz Island Foundation archives.

[2] Marla Daily as quoted by John Gherini, *Santa Cruz Island*, 168–71.

Finally, Stanton donated a conservation easement over his entire acreage, which promised to achieve the contradictory aims of eliminating the feral sheep that were degrading the flora while continuing the control of feral animals through hunting. It was a minefield of slippery terminology. Yet this pragmatic solution seemed to promise that Stanton would be able to simultaneously preserve the island of which he was passionately fond, retain financial autonomy and stability, maintain the Santa Cruz Island Hunt Club income, and settle his nephew's lawsuit. It cost The Nature Conservancy a little over $2.5 million to complete the transaction, but a number of the terms of the accord with Stanton would ultimately cause friction between the two parties.

The conservation easement put The Nature Conservancy on a collision course with the Santa Cruz Island Company and its lucrative hunt club. It gave the conservancy the right to forbid activities that would degrade the natural flora and fauna and to enforce the restoration of impacted areas. Inexact terms such as "selective reduction of or elimination of feral animals" and "selective control techniques as heretofore conducted" would provide a field day for legal minds on both sides of what would become a very fractious relationship.[3]

The hunt club had become an important revenue stream for the Santa Cruz Island Company. Its continued success depended on a ready supply of the wild sheep that The Nature Conservancy now wanted to eliminate. As the 1980s wore on, the Santa Cruz Island Company found itself in an adverse financial position brought on by the loss of oil and gas income and the drought of 1983–1984, which seriously reduced income from cattle operations. The Nature Conservancy's sheep removal program further eroded the financial viability of the Santa Cruz Island Company. The lawyers were again circling and ready to do battle when Stanton grudgingly agreed to the elimination program being concluded no later than 1987, at which time he hoped The Nature Conservancy's active involvement in the management of the island would end.

Against this backdrop of uncertainty and rising tension, in 1985 Stanton established the Santa Cruz Island Foundation as an organization devoted to preserving the history of the California Channel Islands. He hoped negotiations with The Nature Conservancy would guarantee a physical presence for his foundation on the island but became alarmed and depressed by the

---

[3] Livingston, "Study," 747–48; and John Gherini, *Santa Cruz Island*, 172–77.

maneuverings of their legal team, which indicated no firm undertakings to support the foundation. In early 1986, his great friend and ranch manager Henry Duffield suffered a stroke that paralyzed his upper left side. Disconsolate at the thought of no longer being able to take an active part in the management of the ranch, Henry shot himself on the island on November 23, 1986, and was buried in the island's cemetery.

The loss of his great friend and the continued pressure he felt from The Nature Conservancy was making Stanton's life miserable. Unhappy and alone, he died suddenly on December 8, 1987, at aged sixty-four in the old superintendent's house on the island from complications brought on by his medications. Carey Stanton was buried in the family plot adjacent to the chapel at the Main Ranch. The Stanton portion of Santa Cruz Island land passed to The Nature Conservancy, and his personal estate was left to the Santa Cruz Island Foundation, his two enduring island legacies.

Under the auspices of The Nature Conservancy and, later, the National Park Service, a new and largely untried chapter in the preservation of Santa Cruz Island was about to be written. Within a few weeks, the Stanton ranching operation was closed down and the cattle shipped off the island. Twentieth-century sensibilities regarding ecological systems and habitats now came to the fore. The Caires had tried to "civilize" the island according to their understanding of contemporary agricultural and conservation practices. The Stantons applied their own similar ideas about preservation. For The Nature Conservancy, the island represented a unique opportunity to attempt a comprehensive, science-based plan to restore the island's ecology to its natural state, which had been dramatically changed by more than a century of intensive land husbandry. From the point of view of The Nature Conservancy, the first essential task was eliminating the thousands of feral sheep and pigs. Despite the best efforts of the nineteenth- and twentieth-century owners at controlling these populations, the feral sheep and pigs had caused serious damage to the island flora, and their removal was a top priority, undertaken even before the sudden demise of Carey Stanton. The sheep were removed by the late 1980s, but the pigs were adept at hiding in the steepest, most inaccessible parts of the island. Finally a group of professional hunters from New Zealand destroyed the last of them in 2006.

The programs for the restoration of the island's natural environment have demonstrated the complexity of the task and, more than once, the law of unintended consequences, but the removal of feral pigs and sheep is now allowing native vegetation to reclaim the island. Formerly rare plant species, such as island buckwheat, Santa Cruz Island live-forever, and Santa Cruz Island silver lotus are now almost commonplace. Oak woodlands and bishop pine forests are expanding, and native bunchgrasses are returning. The Nature Conservancy and its partner, the National Park Service, who purchased the final interest in the eastern end of the island from the Gherini family in 1999, are facilitating the return of indigenous flora by eliminating invasive, nonnative weeds, such as the nonindigenous wild fennel that spread vigorously after the disappearance of sheep and pigs. Oak seedlings are flourishing for the first time in 150 years. Seldom-seen endemic plants are now sprouting across the island's hills and valleys. Island foxes—the endangered cat-sized descendants of the mainland gray fox—are back in strong numbers after the removal of the nonindigenous golden eagles. Bald eagles, who had been victims of DDT, have been reintroduced under the auspices of The Nature Conservancy and are once again soaring above the island and successfully hatching young for the first time in half a century.[4]

The tradition of island research continues to flourish under the auspices of the National Park Service, The Nature Conservancy, the University of California, the Santa Barbara Museum of Natural History, the Santa Cruz Island Foundation, and others. Recent activities include studies of vegetation change, native shrub recovery, fennel and feral pig eradication, prescribed burns of exotic plants, as well as specific studies of stream fauna and individual plant and animal species. Both prehistoric and historic archaeology studies continue, and the National Park Service is completing a series of cultural landscape inventories in the east end and isthmus.[5]

And so, after almost 150 years, with the southern California mainland altered beyond all recognition, Santa Cruz Island is a testing ground to see if the clock can be turned back a century and a half. Can it return to an appearance that would ultimately be more familiar to its original inhabitants, the Chumash islanders, than to Justinian Caire or any of his descendants? Perhaps so, but the memory of their contribution is preserved, as Carey Stanton intended, through the work of the Santa Cruz Island Foundation. It acts as the custodian of the era of Euro-American activities on the island, where for a brief moment in California history one man could be master of all he surveyed.

---

[4] Nature Conservancy website, "Santa Cruz Island," www.nature.org/wherewework/northamerica/states/california/preserves/ (accessed 2009).

[5] Livingston, "Study," 777–79.

Chronology, 1910–1932

Following is a chronological list of lawsuits and other significant events that occurred between 1910 and 1932:

Early 1910	G. Capuccio rehired by Justinian Caire Company
Christmas 1910	Stock distribution to all children of Albina Caire
October 1911	PC Rossi dies suddenly
November 1911	Corporate charter tax reminder goes missing; charter expires and corporation "dies"
January 2, 1912	Amelie Caire Rossi announces she will block reorganization of company (she is later joined by Aglaë Caire Capuccio)
January 8, 1912	Capuccio is fired from Justinian Caire Company; moves with family to Rossi house at Asti
January 31, 1912	Gherini's demand for $250,000 [$5.7 million] for each daughter is refused
June 1912	Start of first suit, *Rossi v. Caire*
March 1913	Start of *Capuccio v. Caire*
June 1913	*Rossi v. Caire* (decision in favor of Rossi—no revival of corporation)
July 1915	G. Capuccio dies suddenly at Asti
1916	Appeal on *Rossi v. Caire* (1913 decision upheld)
1921	*Rossi v. Caire* (upheld previous decision)
1922	*Capuccio v. Caire* (action for partition—won by plaintiff)

1922	*Rossi v. Caire* (decision in favor of Rossi)
1929	*Capuccio v. Caire* (decision in favor of Capuccio for fees to be shared by all)
1932	*Rossi v. Trustees of Santa Cruz Island Company* (plaintiff attorney fees set at $75,000 [$1.2 million])

Superintendents, 1875–1937

Following is a list of Santa Cruz Island Company superintendents during the Caire regime, compiled from the company payroll records.

Jean Baptiste Joyaux	1875–October 1884 (dismissed by board of directors)
Charles Dugan	November 1884–March 1885
Jules and Leopold Blanchard	April 1885–October 1886
Leopold Blanchard	November 1886–March 1887 (J. Moullet assistant from September 1886)
J. Moullet	April 1887–October 1892
G. Capuccio	November 1892–June 1894 (dismissed)
J. R. Fiala	July 1894–October 1895 (resigned)
A. Clemént	November 1895–May 1897 (dismissed)
Leon Valadié (vineyardist)	June 1897–April 1898 (acting superintendent; stayed on as vineyardist)
Carlo Erbetti	May 1898–February 1902
Ulrico Revel	March 1902–July 1906 (resigned because of ill health)
Ottavio Revel	August 1906–December 1906
Ugo Revel	January 1907–April 1916 (resigned)
A. Swain	September 1916–July 1919 (resigned)
C. McElrath	August 1919–September 1921 (resigned)
Ugo Revel	October 1921–September 1924
F. F. Caire	October 1924–1932
Justinian Caire II	1932–1937

Selected Bibliography

ARCHIVAL AND MANUSCRIPT COLLECTIONS

Caire Family Papers and Diaries.

    Caire, Arthur. Diaries, 1911–1940. In the possession of Justinian Caire III.

    Caire, Delphine A. Journal, Volumes 1–4. In the author's possession.

    ———. "Memoirs, 1933." Translated by Jeanne Caire. In the author's possession.

    Caire, F. F. Family photograph archive. In the author's possession.

    Caire, L. A. Jeanne. "Memoirs, 1972." In the author's possession.

Justinian Caire Company Journals, 1906–1912. Justinian Caire Company Records. In the author's possession.

Santa Cruz Island Company Records. In the author's possession.

Santa Cruz Island Foundation Archives. Santa Barbara, Calif.

BOOKS, ARTICLES, AND OTHER PUBLISHED WORKS

Armstrong, Le Roy, and J. O. Denny. *Financial California: An Historical Review of the Beginnings and Progress of Banking in the State.* Reprinted. Ayer Publishing, 1980. First published 1916 by Coast Banker, San Francisco, Calif.

Ascension, Antonio de la, Father. "Father Ascension's Account of the Voyage of Sebastian Vizcaino." Translated by Henry R. Wagner. *California Historical Society Quarterly* 7 (1928): 345–46.

———. "Spanish Voyages to the Northwest Coast in the 16th Century." Translated by Henry R. Wagner. *California Historical Society Quarterly* 7, no 4 (1928): 295–394.

Bancroft, Hubert H. *History of California.* 7 vols. Berkeley, Calif.: Bancroft Library, 1886–1890.

———. *The Native Races.* 5 vols. Berkeley, Calif.: Bancroft Library, 1874–1875.

Bell, Katherine M. *Swinging the Censer: Reminiscences of Old Santa Barbara.* Compiled by Katherine Bell Cheney. Hartford, Conn.: Finlay Press, 1931.

Benmelech, Efraim, and Tobias J. Moskowitz. "The Political Economy of Financial Regulation: Evidence from U.S. State Usury Laws in the 19th Century." *Journal of Finance* 65, no. 3 (2010): 1029–1073.

Brandyer, T. S. "Flora of the Santa Barbara Islands." *Proceedings of the California Academy of Sciences* 1, no. 2 (1888).

Bremner, Carl St. John. *Geology of Santa Cruz Island* (Occasional Papers No. 1). Santa Barbara, Calif.: Santa Barbara Museum of Natural History, November 1, 1932.

Browne, J. Ross. *Crusoe's Island, Early Life in California and Along the Coast (1850–1869)*. New York, 1871.

Caire, Helen. "A Brief History of Santa Cruz Island from 1869 to 1937." *Ventura County Historical Society Quarterly* 27, no. 4 (Summer 1982): 3–33.

———. *Santa Cruz Island*. Spokane, Wash.: Arthur H. Clark, 1993.

Caire, L. A. Jeanne. "In Memoriam: Delphine A. Caire." *California Historical Society Quarterly* 24 (1949): 81–83.

Camp, Charles L. "The Chronicles of George C. Yount, California Pioneer 1826." *California Historical Quarterly* 2 (April 1923): 2–3.

———, ed. *George C. Yount and his Chronicles of the West, Early Southwest and California from the 1820's*. Denver, Colo.: Old West Publishing Co., 1966.

Centro per la Cultura dell'Impresa, Milano, Revista No. 4. "Il Cantiere Navale del Muggiano, tra Storia e Futuro." November 2006.

Cleland, Robert Glass. *The Cattle on a Thousand Hills*. San Marino, Calif.: The Huntington Library, 1951.

Costanso, Miguel. "Diary—The Portola Expedition 1769–1770." *Academy of Pacific Coast History* 2, no. 1 (August 1911): 162–327.

Crocker Langley San Francisco Directory, 1904–14. San Francisco, H. S. Crocker Co.

Daily, Marla. *California's Channel Islands*. Santa Barbara, Calif.: Shoreline Press, 1997.

———. "California Channel Islands Encyclopedia." Unpublished manuscript. Santa Barbara, Calif.: Santa Cruz Island Foundation, 2010.

———, ed. *California's Channel Islands, Island Anthology*. Santa Barbara, Calif.: Santa Cruz Island Foundation, 1989.

———. *California's Channel Islands—1001 Questions Answered*. Santa Barbara, Calif.: McNally & Loftin, 1987.

———, ed. *Chapel of the Holy Cross, 1881–1891, Santa Cruz Island* (Occasional Paper No. 5). Santa Barbara, Calif.: Santa Cruz Island Foundation, 1991.

———, ed. *Northern Channel Islands Anthology* (Occasional Paper No. 2). Santa Barbara, Calif.: Santa Cruz Island Foundation, 1989.

———, ed. *Santa Cruz Island Anthology* (Occasional Paper No. 1). Santa Barbara, Calif.: Santa Cruz Island Foundation, 1989.

Daily, Marla, and Carey Stanton. "Historical Highlights of Santa Cruz Island." *La Reata* 5 (Fall 1983): 14–19.

———. "Santa Cruz Island: A Brief History of its Buildings." Unpublished article. Santa Barbara, Calif., 1981.

Davidson, George. *U.S. Coast Survey: Coast Pilot of California, Oregon, and Washington Territory.* Washington, D.C.: U.S. Government Printing Office, 1869.

Duhaut-Cilly, A. "Account of California in the Years 1827–28." Translated by Charles Franklin Carter. *Quarterly of the California Historical Society* 8, nos. 2–4 (June–December 1929): 214–50.

Eaton, Margaret Holden. *Diary of a Sea Captain's Wife.* Santa Barbara, Calif.: McNally and Loftin, 1980.

Ellison, William Henry. "History of the Santa Cruz Island Grant." *Pacific Historical Review* 6, no. 3 (September 1937): 270–83.

Englehardt, Zephyrin, o.f.m. *Santa Barbara Mission.* San Francisco: James H. Barry Company, 1923.

Gherini, John. *Santa Cruz Island.* Spokane, Wash.: Arthur Clark, 1997.

Gherini, Maria Rossi. "Santa Cruz Island." Interview with Edward S. Spalding. *Noticias: Santa Barbara Historical Society* (1959): 1–11.

Gibney, C. A., Benjamin Brooks, and Edwin M. Sheridan. *History of Santa Barbara, San Luis Obispo and Ventura Counties.* Chicago: Lewis Publishing Company, 1917.

Gleason, Duncan. *The Islands and Ports of California.* New York: Devin-Adair Company, 1958.

Hillinger, Charles. *Channel Islands.* Santa Cruz, Calif.: Santa Cruz Island Foundation, 1999.

Hittell, Theodore H. *History of California.* 4 vols. San Francisco: N. J. Stone, 1898.

Holder, Charles F. *The Channel Islands of California.* Chicago: A. C. McClurg & Co., 1910.

———. *Recreations of a Sportsman on the Pacific Coast.* New York: G. P. Putnam's Sons, 1910.

Holdredge, Helen. *Mammy Pleasant's Partner.* New York: G. P. Putnam's Sons, 1954.

Huse, Charles. *A Sketch of the History and Resources of Santa Barbara, City and County.* Santa Barbara, Calif.: Daily Press, 1876.

Kroeber, A. L. *Handbook of the Indians of California.* Berkeley, Calif.: California Book Company, 1953.

Lewis Publishing Company. *The Bay of San Francisco: The Metropolis of the Pacific Coast and Its Suburban Cities.* Vol. 2, *A History.* Chicago: Lewis Publishing Company, 1892.

Livingston, Dewey S. "Draft Historic Resource Study." Unpublished manuscript, National Park Service, Department of the Interior, 2006.

McElrath, Clifford. *On Santa Cruz Island*. Santa Barbara, Calif.: Caractacus Corporation, 1993.

Menzies, Archibald. "Journal of the Vancouver Expedition, Extracts Covering the Visit to California." *Quarterly of the California Historical Society* 2 (1923): 2–265.

National Italian American Federation. "Andrea Sbarboro and the Development of Italian Americans in California's Wine Industry" (biography). Milestones. http://www.niaf.org/milestones/year_1881.

Newmark, Harris. *Sixty Years in Southern California, 1853–1913: Containing the Reminiscences of Harris Newmark*. Edited by Maurice H. Newmark and Marco R. Newmark. New York: Knickerbocker Press, 1916. Scanned and reprinted by Cornell University Press, Ithaca, N.Y.

Nidever, George. *The Life and Adventures of George Nidever*. Edited by William Henry Ellison. Berkeley: University of California Press, 1937.

Officer, Lawrence H., and Samuel H. Williamson. "Purchasing Power of Money in the United States from 1774 to Present." August 2006. http://MeasuringWorth.Com.

Olson, Ronald L. *Chumash Prehistory*. Berkeley: University of California Press, 1930.

———. "On the Island of the Dead." *California Monthly* 21, no. 3 (1927): 166–67.

O'Neill, Owen, ed. *History of Santa Barbara County, State of California, Its People and Its Resources*. Santa Barbara, Calif.: Harold McLean Meier, 1939.

Ord, Augustias de la Guerra. *Occurrences in Hispanic California*. Washington, D.C.: Academy of American Franciscan History, 1956.

Palou, Fr. Francisco. *Historical Memoirs of New California*. Edited by Herbert Eugene Bolton. 4 vols. Berkeley: University of California Press, 1926.

———. *Spanish Exploration in the Southwest, 1542–1706*. Edited by Herbert E. Bolton. New York: Charles Scribner's Sons, 1916.

Perkins, Joseph L. *A Business Man's Estimate of Santa Barbara County*. Santa Barbara, Calif., 1881.

Petersen, Michel. *Once upon an Island* (Occasional Paper No. 9). Santa Barbara, Calif.: Santa Cruz Island Foundation, 1998.

Phillips, Michael James. *History of Santa Barbara County*. 2 vols. Santa Barbara, Calif., 1927.

Pinney, Thomas. *The Wine of Santa Cruz Island*. Santa Barbara, Calif.: Santa Cruz Island Foundation, 1994.

Rockwell, Mabel M. *California's Sea Frontier*. Santa Barbara, Calif.: The Channel Coast, 1962.

Rogers, David Banks. *Prehistoric Man of the Santa Barbara Coast*. Santa Barbara, Calif.: Santa Barbara Museum of Natural History, 1929.

Rossi, Edmund. "Edmund A. Rossi: Italian Swiss Colony and the Wine Industry." Interview by Ruth Teiser. March 1, 1971. Regional Oral History Office 4-86, the Bancroft Library, University of California, Berkeley.

Stanton, Carey. *An Island Memoir.* Los Angeles: Zamorano Club, 1984.

Starr, Kevin. *Inventing the Dream: California through the Progressive Era.* New York: Oxford University Press, 1985.

Storke, Yda Addis. *A Memorial and Biographical History of Santa Barbara, San Luis Obispo and Ventura Counties.* Chicago: Lewis Publishing Company, 1891.

Tapis, Fray Estevan. "Biennial Mission Reports." In *California Mission Documents.* 4 vols. Santa Barbara Mission Archives Library, Santa Barbara, Calif.

Tays, George. "Captain Andres Castillero, Diplomat, An Account from Unpublished Sources of His Services to Mexico in the Alvarado Revolution of 1836–38m." *California Historical Quarterly* 14, no. 3 (September 1935): 230–68.

U.S. Treasury. *U.S. Coast and Geodetic Survey—Annual Report 1886.* 39th Cong., 2nd sess., 1886. Vol. 14, no. 8, serial set vol. 1296.

Wagner, Henry R. "Juan Rodriguez Cabrillo, Discoverer of the Coast of California." *California Historical Society Quarterly* 7 (March 1928): 20–77.

———. "The Voyage to California of Sebastian Rodriguez Cermeño in 1595." *California Historical Society Quarterly* 3, no. 1 (1924): 3–24.

Warren, Earl, Jr. "The Agriculture of Santa Cruz Island with a Survey of California's Other Islands." Thesis, University of California, Davis, 1952.

———. "California's Ranches in the Sea." *National Geographic Magazine* 114, no 2 (August 1958): 256–83.

Weber, Lin. *Old Napa Valley.* St. Helena, Calif.: Wine Ventures Publishing, 1998.

Wentworth, Edward Norris. *America's Sheep Trails.* Ames: Iowa State College Press, 1948.

Wheeler, George M. *Report Upon the United States Geographical Surveys West of the One-Hundredth Meridian, in Charge of Capt. George M. Wheeler, Corps of Engineers, U.S. Army.* Vol. 1, *Geographical Report.* Washington, D.C.: U.S. Government Printing Office, 1889.

Williams, M. W. "California's Offshore Islands." *Pacific Discovery* 7, no. 1 (1954): 16–17.

Williams, M. Woodbridge. "Notes on Land Snails from Santa Cruz Island." *Pomona College Journal of Entomology and Zoology,* March 1940.

Williamson, Samuel H. "Seven Ways to Compute the Relative Value of a U.S. Dollar Amount, 1774 to Present." MeasuringWorth 2010 (April).

Woodward, Arthur. *The Sea Diary of Fr. Juan Vizcaino to Alta California 1769.* Los Angeles: Glen Dawson, 1959.

COURT CASES (IN CHRONOLOGICAL ORDER)

Thomas Wallace Moore v. M.J. Box, Santa Barbara County District Court, 2nd Judicial District (November 9, 1857).

Rossi v. Caire, 174 Cal. 74, 161 Pac. 1161. S.F 7101 (1916) (action begun 1912).

Capuccio v. Caire, action begun in Superior Court San Francisco, March 1913.

Rossi v. Caire, 39 Cal. App 776, 180 Pac. 58 S.F. 2587 (1919).

Capuccio v. Caire, 38 Cal. App Dec. 179 (May 1921).

Rossi v. Caire, 186 Cal. 544, 199 Pac. 1044 S.F. (July 28, 1921).

Rossi v. Caire, 189 Cal. 507, 209 Pac. 374 S.F. 10,233 (Sept. 13, 1922).

Capuccio v. Caire, 189 Cal. 514, 209 Pac. 367 L.A. 6845–Judge Richards, Myers dissenting (Sept. 22, 1922).

Capuccio v. Caire, No written opinion by Supreme Court, Appeal dismissed (July 1923).

The Santa Cruz Island Company v. Rossi, Capuccio, U.S.A. et al. (filed 1923 in U.S. District Court, So. Dist. of California). Dismissed for want of prosecution July 14, 1924.

Capuccio v. Caire, 77 C.D. 571 to same effect as above (April 22, 1929).

Capuccio v. Caire et al., 207 Cal. 200, 277 Pac. 475 L.A. 9165 73 A.L.R. 8 (May 3, 1929).

Capuccio v. Caire, 215 Cal. 518, Pac. L.A. 12,342 (May 23, 1932).

Edwin L. Stanton III v. Santa Cruz Island Company, et al., Los Angeles Superior Court No. C180228 (1976).

Pier Gherini et al. v. California Coastal Commission, 204 Cal.App.3d 699 (1988).

Francis Gherini v. United States of America, No. CV 97-0819 (1997).

Index

References to illustrations are in italic type.